THE MAKING OF NORTHERN NIGERIA

AFRICA.

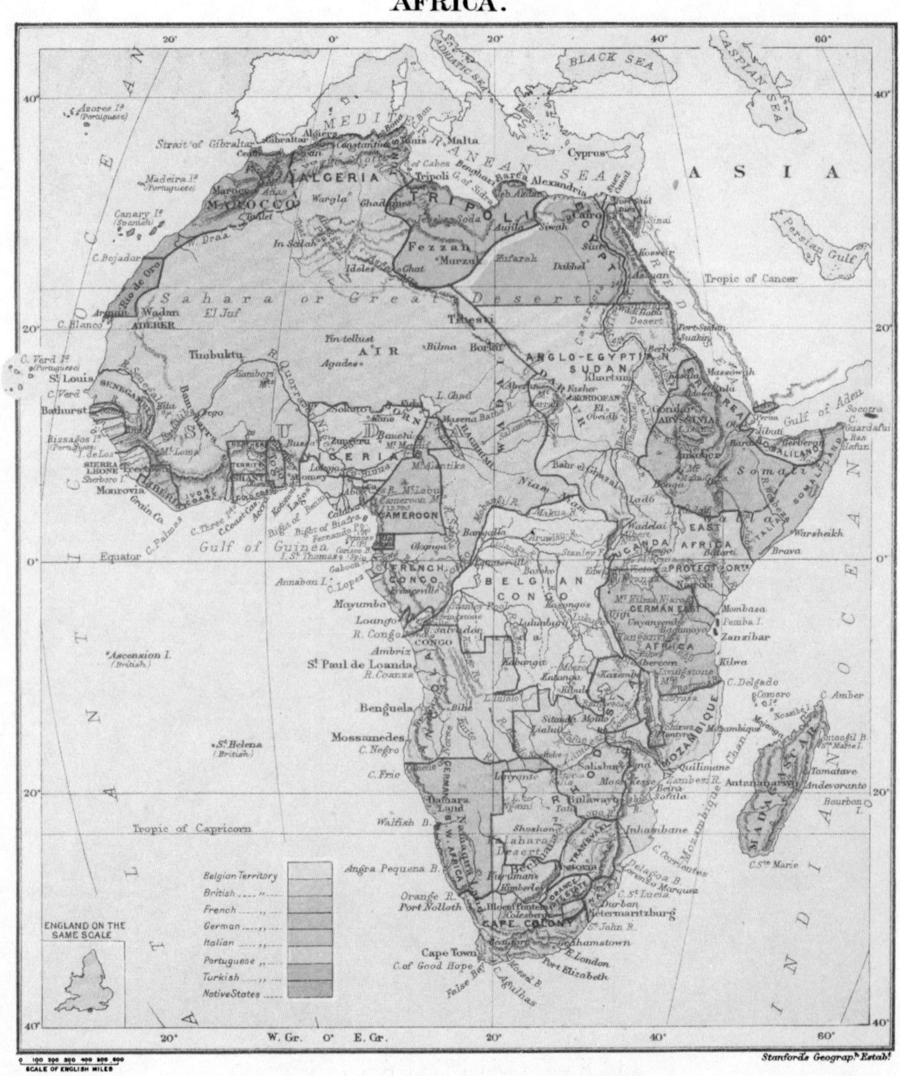

BLACK SEA
CASPIAN SEA
MEDITERRANEAN SEA
A S I A
Strait of Gibraltar
Gibraltar
Malta
Cyprus
Azores Is (Portuguese)
Madeira Is (Portuguese)
Canary Is (Spanish)
ALGERIA
MAROCCO
TRIPOLI
Fezzan
Murzuk
Tripoli
Benghazi
Alexandria
Cairo
EGYPT
Siwah
Kufarah
Dakhel
Persian Gulf
Tropic of Cancer
C. Bojador
Rio de Oro
C. Blanco
ADERER
Sahara or Great Desert
El Juf
Tibesti
AIR
Agades
Bilma
Borku
Timbuktu
ANGLO-EGYPTIAN SUDAN
Khartum
KORDOFAN
El Obeid
Suakin
Port Sudan
Massowah
ERITREA
ABYSSINIA
Gulf of Aden
Socotra
C. Guardafui
SOMALILAND
Somali
Warsheikh
Brava
C. Verd Is (Portuguese)
St. Louis
C. Verd
Bathurst
SENEGAMBIA
SIERRA LEONE
Monrovia
LIBERIA
IVORY COAST
ASHANTI
Lagos
Gulf of Guinea
Bight of Biafra
Bight of Benin
L. Chad
Bauchi
CAMEROON
Equator
I. St Thomas
Annabon I.
C. Lopez
FRENCH CONGO
BELGIAN CONGO
Bahr el Ghazal
Lado
UGANDA
EAST AFRICA
PROTECTORATE
Mombasa
Pemba I.
Zanzibar
GERMAN EAST AFRICA
Kilwa
C. Delgado
Comoro Is
Mayumba
Loango
R. Congo
Ambriz
St Paul de Loanda
R. Coanza
Benguela
Mossamedes
C. Negro
C. Frio
Ascension I. (British)
St Helena (British)
MOZAMBIQUE
Mozambique
Quilimane
Zambesi R.
Sofala
Inhambane
Salisbury
Bulawayo
C. Amber
MADAGASCAR
Tamatave
Andevoranto
Antananarivo
Bourbon I.
Tropic of Capricorn
Walfish B.
Damara Land
Kalahara Desert
Angra Pequena B.
Orange R.
Port Nolloth
Kimberley
Pretoria
ORANGE RIVER STATE
Delagoa B.
Durban
Pietermaritzburg
CAPE COLONY
Cape Town
C. of Good Hope
False Bay
C. Agulhas
Grahamstown
E. London
Port Elizabeth
C. Ste Marie
INDIAN OCEAN
ATLANTIC OCEAN
Belgian Territory
British
French
German
Italian
Portuguese
Turkish
Native States
ENGLAND ON THE SAME SCALE
W. Gr.
E. Gr.
0 100 200 300 400 500 600
SCALE OF ENGLISH MILES
Stanford's Geograph. Estabt.

THE MAKING
OF
NORTHERN NIGERIA

BY

CAPTAIN C. W. J. ORR, R.A.

LATE POLITICAL DEPARTMENT, NORTHERN NIGERIA

WITH MAPS

DARF PUBLISHERS LTD
LONDON
1987

FIRST PUBLISHED 1911
NEW IMPRESSION 1987

ISBN 1 85077 138 3

Printed and bound in Great Britain
by A. Wheaton & Co. Ltd, Exeter, Devon

PREFACE

On the 1st of January 1900 the British nation assumed the responsibility of governing the inhabitants of a vast area in the African continent, and entrusted the task to a handful of British officials. Now that more than ten years have passed, it has seemed to me right that those on whom as administrators this task has been imposed, should render some account of their stewardship. In this book, therefore, I have endeavoured to give a brief history of the manner in which the duty has been performed, and to indicate some of the main problems which have demanded solution. I have spared no pains to set out the facts accurately, and with this object I have confined myself to official records, and have based myself mainly on the Annual Reports submitted by the High Commissioner to the Secretary of State for the Colonies, which are printed and presented each year to the Houses of Parliament. I owe a debt of gratitude to Sir George Goldie and the Earl of Scarbrough for materials with which they have kindly provided me for the chapter on Chartered Company Administration. I am also greatly indebted to Mr. E. J. Arnett, Resident of

Kano, for general assistance, and for the facts relating to Education in Chapter XVI.

In the later chapters, in dealing with the various problems which the Administration is attempting to solve, I have endeavoured merely to state them, and to avoid expressing personal opinions. If in the latter respect I have not always been successful, and if the personal pronoun obtrudes itself too frequently, my excuse must be the extraordinary interest which my seven years' work in Northern Nigeria has aroused in me. Circumstances beyond my control have severed my connection with Nigeria, but its problems and the welfare of its inhabitants will always remain one of the greatest interests of my life.

C. W. J. O.

CYPRUS,
20th September 1911.

CONTENTS

CHAPTER VIII

CHAPTER IX

CHAPTER X

CHAPTER XI

CHAPTER XII

CHAPTER XIII

CHAPTER XIV

CHAPTER XV

CHAPTER XVI

CHAPTER XVII

APPENDICES

MAPS

ERRATA

Page 231, line 1, *for* suspended *read* superseded.

Page 255, line 4 from bottom, *for* novel *read* moral.

"SUCH a work as is being accomplished under our eyes in those lands is no mean corrective to more sordid ideals, to the effect on our national character of commercial or of class greed, of the hot pursuit of trivial pleasures, or of that keen struggle for privilege and social distinction which are so discreditable to much of our community. The officers who risk health and life in the swamps of the White Nile or who are sacrificing their best years to the welfare of fellow-men of humble races in remote and desert solitudes, are illustrating, and, in their several degrees, are adding strength to the qualities which are the best inheritance of our nation. Enterprise such as theirs cannot but excite emulation and brace the national fibre. What the salt seas were to our forefathers in the spacious days of good Queen Bess, the untrodden spaces of new lands are to their descendants. It has been said, or sung, that the East calls us. It is neither East, nor West, nor any one quarter of the world, but the lust of adventure and the love of enterprise that are calling to the men of our race. Every undeveloped people, every unexplored country, is calling. Athens and Rome, long centuries ago, heard that call and followed it. We are treading, not unworthily let us hope, where free and fearless men of old trod before us. Wherever there are to be found great areas peopled by strange tribes, wherever mighty rivers roll from sources little visited by man, wherever seemingly illimitable forests bar the way to human intercourse, wherever the mystery and the fascination of the unknown or the unfamiliar are felt—all such lands are calling to adventurous spirits among us, for whom there is little room in the crowded field at home, or prefer to the well-worn paths of the old world the hazards and the freedom of a world which to them is new. A century ago it was—as it still is—India ; to-day Nigeria, East Africa, Rhodesia, and the Egyptian Soudan are calling. The work which our countrymen are doing there quickens the pulses of their brothers at home : their lives will not wholly be lost sight of in the national roll-call of citizens who have added to the lustre of their country. Politicians—not a few—will decry them : men of the world will make light of them : but the cause of humanity and the hearts of the helpless will gather hope and encouragement from their labours."
—*The Making of Modern Egypt*, p. 415, Sir AUCKLAND COLVIN, K.C.S.I., K.C.M.G., C.I.E.

"It is particularly to be hoped, at a time when public interest has been prominently drawn to the relations and the territories of the European Powers in West Africa, that more attention will be paid in England to the extent and nature of our responsibilities in that region. Nigeria is not merely by far the most considerable of our West African possessions, but the only British Dependency in any part of the world which approaches the Indian Empire in magnitude and variety. Our administrators there, in most inadequate numbers and under very difficult conditions, but with our Indian experiences to help them, are confronting problems almost as large and delicate as those which first inspired the administrative genius of Great Britain in the East. It is time their work were better understood."—*The Times*, August 12, 1911.

CHAPTER I

INTRODUCTION

An ancient map purporting to depict the continent of Africa shows it as a narrow strip depending from Europe by a small isthmus which spans what are now the Straits of Gibraltar. The unknown cartographer of bygone ages represents the southern shores of this narrow strip as washed by the ocean, which is here labelled "Sea of Sahara."

The map represents with sufficient accuracy all that was once known by Europe of Africa. The Sahara, a sea of sand, not of water, cut off from the ancient world all knowledge of the gigantic mass of land stretching far away into the southern hemisphere. It is the stupendous barrier which Nature, for some inscrutable reason, has erected between the Mediterranean littoral and the countries of Equatorial Africa,—a barrier where the bones of a vast multitude have mingled with the wind-swept sand. It extends across the entire continent from west to east, from the Atlantic to the Red Sea: to traverse it from north to south at its narrowest point entails a journey of more than two months. But such travellers as are courageous enough to undertake this journey are rewarded by finding themselves in a land where agriculture flourishes under favourable conditions. The interminable sand gives place to soil watered by innumerable rivers and streams; the burning rays of the sun are tempered by cool breezes and frequent rain; vegetation flourishes, and the earth brings forth plentiful harvests. Nature indeed seems anxious to make amends for the desolation with which she has covered so much of Northern Africa, by pouring out her gifts in the regions which fringe the southern edge of the Sahara Desert. Here lies a high plateau of pasture land, lightly covered with vegetation, needing little more than a scratching of the soil and a scattering of seed to produce crops capable of supporting a large population. Farther south, towards the equator, the plateau shades into broken ranges of rocky hills, and behind them lie dense forests and swamps, matted and choked with tropical vegetation, and sodden with malarial miasma. Bounded thus on the north by the desert, on the south by pathless forests, this narrow strip of favoured earth has attracted from earliest times wandering tribes and immigrants from far-off regions, who have either driven out, or intermarried with, the original inhabitants and settled on their land.

Our earliest account of this region, so remote and so curiously severed from connection with Asiatic and European civilisation, is derived from Herodotus. Writing more than 500 years before the Christian era, he chronicles a story of five Nasamonian youths from the country bordering the Mediterranean, in the hinterland of what is now Tripoli, who started on a voyage of exploration across the desert in a south-westerly direction. Passing, so runs the story, first the region inhabited by man, then through a country infested by wild beasts, they reached the desert, and after many days of travel came to a place where they found trees growing in a plain; while they were gathering the fruit, there appeared a band of "small black men," who seized them and carried them off through swamps and morasses to a city by which flowed a large river from west to east, in which were crocodiles. The story was related to Etearchus, King of the Oasis of Ammon, who repeated it to the Greeks of Cyrene, from whom Herodotus obtained it. The river was apparently believed by Herodotus to have been a tributary of the Nile, and Etearchus seems to have entertained the same idea. Ptolemy, writing in Alexandria more than five centuries later, on the subject of African geography, speaks of two large rivers in the interior of the continent, named respectively the Gir—probably the Congo—and the Ni-geir; and for many centuries it was supposed that the latter flowed eastward across the continent and fell eventually into the Nile, and was the river seen and described by the Nasamonian youths.

The interior of the continent was known as the Soudan, the Land of the Blacks; or Ethiopia, a name vaguely used for the regions lying west of Egypt. To the Egyptians, the Persians, the Greeks, and the Romans, the fact was mainly of interest because Ethiopia provided them with their black slaves, for which purpose they no doubt believed it mainly existed.

It was not till the Mahomedan invasion of Egypt and North Africa, nearly seven centuries later, that real contact was made between the shores of the

Mediterranean and the interior of the Soudan. The vast desert of Sahara is spanned by two main roads, one on the west from Morocco, one farther east from Tripoli, and it was by these two great arteries that communication was established. The story of the Black empires of the west is one of great interest, but it has no place here. Its early chroniclers were Moors, and with the expulsion of that race from Spain in the sixteenth century, their writings were lost for the time being to Europe. Remembering the struggle which took place at that period between the Mahomedan Turks and the Christian races, the discovery of the New World, and the opening up of China and India to trade, and the constant turmoil in Europe itself, it is small wonder that the inhabitants of the fertile land which lay beyond the desert were left unmolested and forgotten by the northern races. Indeed the expulsion of the Moors from Spain caused indirectly the almost complete cessation of the intercourse which had been kept up for over 500 years between the inhabitants of the countries south of the desert and the Arab-Berber population of the Mediterranean coast. For the Moors, driven from Europe into Morocco, attacked and broke up the highly civilised Black Empire which had established itself in the interior, and becoming themselves decadent, lapsed into semi-barbarism, and adopted a life of nomadic robbery. After this, for over 200 years Negroland was cut off from all communication with Europe, isolated from the outside world as before by the desert to the north and the trackless forests to the south. It remained for Europeans in the nineteenth century to rediscover a country inhabited by races possessing a high degree of civilisation, acquainted through their Mahomedan religion with literature, history, jurisprudence, and the art of government, and endowed with many of the qualities which go to make a people fit to take their place amongst the nations of the world.

The quest of the Niger forms one of the most interesting stories of African exploration. It was the lodestone which for many years drew ardent spirits from the northern continent to the tropical regions of Africa. To Mungo Park belongs the credit of being the first European to discover and bring back news of the mysterious river, and to confirm the truth of its easterly course. The hardships which he endured, and the dogged determination with which he braved all dangers till he was at last rewarded by the sight of the great river, are recounted in the volume which he published on his return to England from the Gambia in 1797. The problem regarding the outlet of the Niger remained, however, still unsolved. A second expedition by Mungo Park in 1805 ended disastrously in his death and that of all his companions. Expeditions were fitted out and travellers despatched from Egypt, from Tripoli, and from the west coast to penetrate into the interior of Africa, but for many years every attempt ended in failure. Horneman, a German, despatched from Tripoli by the British African Association in 1799, succeeded in crossing the desert only to lose his life in the interior; another traveller, sent by the same Association from Morocco with instructions to proceed across the desert to Timbuktu, was murdered by his servant. Nicholls, starting in 1805 from Old Calabar in the Bight of Benin, died only a few weeks' march from the coast. Tuckie was despatched by the Government to the Congo, where he died. Ritchie and

Lyon were despatched in 1817 to Fezzan, where the former died, Lyon bringing back some hearsay information about the countries south of the desert. Peddie in 1816 followed Mungo Park's tracks and died. Major Gray and Dr. Dochard followed Peddie in 1818, only to die. In 1827 Major Laing succeeded in penetrating from Tripoli to Timbuktu, being the first European to enter that city, but was murdered on his way back. In 1825 Clapperton with four companions started from Badagry, near Lagos, for the interior, but all died except Clapperton's servant Lander, who made his way back to the coast carrying his master's Journal and papers. Such was the death-roll of Niger exploration, and yet the course of the mysterious river was undetermined. Ptolemy's theory of its being a tributary of the Nile was still adhered to by some authorities; others believed that it joined the Congo; others that it lost itself in a lake or marsh in the interior of the continent. One enthusiast went to the length of publishing a book, which he dedicated to the Duke of Wellington, devoted entirely to developing a theory that the Niger flowed through Lake Tchad till it reached another river flowing northward which emptied itself into the Mediterranean through the quicksands of the Gulf of Syrtis.[1]

Clapperton had crossed the Niger at Boussa, where Mungo Park had met his death twenty years previously. His servant Lander, on returning to England, pressed to be allowed to return to this spot and to follow the river down to its outlet. Receiving a small grant from Government, he started with his brother for the West

[1] *A Dissertation on the Course and Probable Termination of the Niger*, by Lt.-Gen. Sir Rufaire Donkin, G.C.B., F.R.S. London, 1829.

Coast in 1830, and, marching inland by the route previously followed, embarked in a native canoe and began his voyage down stream. A month later they found themselves drifting in a southerly direction, and reached a point where the waters of the Niger were joined by another large river, called by the natives the Binué or Benué, flowing in from the eastward. The banks of the river were now hilly, unlike the flat plains through which they had been passing, and there were few villages. "Everything was silent and solitary," writes Lander; "no sound could be distinguished, save our own voices and the plashing of the paddles with their echoes: the song of birds was not heard, nor could any animal whatever be seen, and the banks seemed to be entirely deserted and the magnificent Niger to be slumbering in its own grandeur." One can imagine the feelings in such circumstances of the brothers, drifting they knew not whither, in intolerable silence and loneliness on the bosom of a river which had caused the death of so many men who had endeavoured to wrest from it its secret. Two days later a large village came in sight, and as soon as the canoes made their appearance they were hailed from the bank by "a little squinting fellow," dressed in an English soldier's jacket, who kept crying out as loud as his lungs would permit him, "Halloa, you Englishmen, you come here." On landing they discovered that this was a messenger of the Chief of Bonny, on the coast, who had been sent up to buy slaves. There was no longer any doubt where the mouth of the Niger lay. It was those so-called "Oil Rivers" flowing into the Bight of Benin, where Europeans had been for centuries trading in slaves and palm oil, without ever dreaming that these rivers and creeks were merely the delta of that great river whose course Mungo Park had lost his life in attempting to discover.

After enduring many hardships and narrowly escaping many dangers, the Landers arrived at the port of Brass, where they found an English brig, and eventually reached England on June 9, 1832, and reported their great discovery to Lord Goderich, the Colonial Secretary. The mystery of the Niger was at last solved, after a lapse of nearly 2500 years since its existence had first been recorded by Herodotus.

Meanwhile the countries of Equatorial Africa lying to the west of Lake Tchad had been explored by an expedition sent by the British Government in 1821 across the desert from Tripoli. Major Denham, R.E., and Captain Clapperton, R.N., had followed the caravan route, being escorted by 200 Arabs armed with matchlocks, and reached the kingdom of Bornu in safety. They had observed everywhere signs of the pitiless slave traffic which was even then being carried on between the interior and the Mediterranean coast. Halting one evening at sunset near a well in the desert, Major Denham had been shocked at the sight of more than one hundred skeletons lying round the spot, some of them with the skin still remaining attached to the bones. Reaching the neighbourhood of Kuka, the capital of Bornu, "we were about," writes Major Denham, "to become acquainted with a people who had never seen, or scarcely heard of, a European; and to tread on ground, the knowledge and true situation of which had hitherto been wholly unknown. . . . We advanced towards the town of Kuka in a most interesting state of uncertainty, whether we should find its Chief at the head of thousands, or be received by him under a tree, surrounded by a few naked slaves." His doubts were soon set at rest, for on approaching the outskirts of the town the expedition found a body of several thousand cavalry drawn up in line, and they were received by the Sheikh's first general, "a negro of noble aspect, dressed in a figured silk *tobe* and mounted on a beautiful horse." The Sheikh's bodyguard were armed with lances, and clothed in coats of mail composed of iron chain which covered them from the throat to the knees, dividing behind and falling on each side of the horse; and they wore helmets or skull-caps of the same metal with chin pieces, their horses being also protected by plates of iron, brass, and silver, just leaving sufficient room for the eyes of the animal.

Denham and Clapperton explored the principal cities of Bornu and Hausaland, and visited the markets of Kuka, Kano, Katsina, and Sokoto. From the ruler of Bornu and the Sultan of Sokoto they had received letters addressed to the King of England, expressing a desire to open up trade and to have British consuls established in their dominions. A high state of civilisation was found existing in these countries, mosques and schools being established in all the principal cities, and large armies of bowmen and spearmen obeying the orders of the sultans. A perpetual state of warfare was carried on, the Mahomedan States raiding the pagan tribes which inhabited the country farther south. Full reports were brought back to England by the travellers, who published an account of their journeyings and of the countries which they had visited.

The discovery by Lander of the outlet of the Niger

in the Gulf of Guinea demonstrated to Europe the existence of a great navigable waterway, leading from the coast into the heart of the continent, and giving access to the Mahomedan empires of Equatorial Africa by a far easier and more practicable route than the difficult and dangerous journey from the north across the desert. A great impetus was given to the attempts to develop a considerable trade with the tribes living on the banks of the lower reaches of the Niger. No sooner had the Landers returned to England and published an account of their discovery than an expedition was fitted out by a trading firm to explore the various creeks of the Niger delta, with a view to discovering their possibilities as a market for European goods, and in 1832 two steamships were despatched to the mouth of the Niger for this purpose. Very little was effected, however, and the crew suffered severely from the effects of the climate, only nine of the original forty-five who started from Liverpool surviving to return with the expedition two years later. As a trading venture it was, in fact, a complete failure, but, on the other hand, a considerable amount of useful knowledge was gained, and a great portion of the Lower Niger and the Benue rivers was mapped and charted. A few years later certain philanthropic persons, who were interested in the subject of slavery and eager to stamp it out from the African continent, took up the question of the Niger, and a movement was set on foot to which both Government and private individuals subscribed. In furtherance of this movement an expedition was fitted out and despatched to the Niger in 1841. It comprised a party of 145 Europeans, numbering amongst them doctors, missionaries, botanists, geologists, and naturalists, and the three steamers of which it was composed were officered by the Royal Navy. No trading whatever was to be allowed; its main object was the suppression of the slave trade, and the commander of the expedition, Captain Allan, R.N., was instructed to demonstrate to the Chiefs the advantages of free labour, to make treaties for the abolition of slavery, and to purchase land for forts and for the institution of a model farm, for which latter purpose all the necessary agricultural implements were provided. Two years later the expedition returned to England, after suffering the loss by sickness of 49 out of the 145 Europeans who started, having achieved little except the purchase of a small strip of land at the confluence of the Niger and Benue rivers where they had instituted, but subsequently abandoned, their model farm.[1]

These two disastrous expeditions of the years 1832 and 1841 could not fail to convey to the minds of those at home the seeming impossibility of ever establishing communication by means of the Niger delta with the interior.

For some years nothing further was done towards opening up communication with the interior. But Denham's and Clapperton's discoveries had not been forgotten, and in 1850 the British Government decided to send out, by way of Tripoli, another expedition to traverse the same route as the one followed by those travellers nearly thirty years previously. The command was entrusted to a Mr. Richardson, and he was accompanied by two German gentlemen, Doctors Barth and Overweg. Starting from Tripoli in March 1850, they crossed the desert and reached the Hausa States,

[1] This strip of land, however, was destined to play a very important part in the history of Nigeria, for it became the site of Lokoja, the first administrative headquarters of Northern Nigeria, and is now a large and thriving town.

where Richardson died, the remaining two pushing on to Kuka, the capital of Bornu. Here they separated, Overweg proceeding to explore round Lake Tchad, Barth striking south to Adamawa and Yola—a large pagan district ruled over by a Mahomedan chief, subject to Sokoto. He reached and crossed the Benue river, past whose junction with the Niger, 300 miles lower down, Lander had drifted twenty years before, and he sent a report to England recommending that this river should be used to establish communication between the coast—and therefore the ocean—and the states in the interior. Barth subsequently spent four years in exploring from Lake Tchad to Timbuktu, visiting the principal towns in the Hausa States on his way, and finally returned to England by way of the desert route and Tripoli, reaching London on September 6, 1855. His Journal giving the account of his travels was published in five volumes in 1857, and contains the most minute description of the country, the people, their history and their customs, and is a model of painstaking research. His expedition placed at the disposal of the British Government the fullest information concerning the countries that lay to the west of Lake Tchad, and supplemented the information brought home twenty years previously by Denham.

Meanwhile McGregor Laird, the indomitable and indefatigable Liverpool merchant who had taken out the first expedition by sea to the Lower Niger in 1830, had revived the project of exploring and opening up to trade those waters, and in 1854 he induced the Government to allow him to contract, to build, and equip a suitable vessel to place on the river.

A steamer named the *Pleiad* was therefore built

for the purpose, and equipped with every care. The expedition was placed under the charge of Dr. Baikie, R.N., and was accompanied by a surgeon and zoologist. No precautions were omitted which might help to safeguard the health of the members of the expedition, and, above all, a liberal supply of quinine was taken, which was administered daily both to officers and crew. Trade goods were also put on board, since the object of the voyage was to open up trade as well as to explore. To these two objects a third was added, of a philanthropic nature, for a native clergyman with a staff of native missionaries were sent out under the auspices of the Church Missionary Society, so that in this somewhat curious combination of interests, science, commerce, and the church each had its representatives. The *Pleiad* ascended the Niger as far as its confluence with the Benue river, and then ascended the latter and navigated it for a distance of nearly 250 miles, returning directly the river began to fall. They were, on the whole, well received by the natives with whom they traded, and a considerable amount of information was collected on the ethnology and natural history of the country. But perhaps the greatest triumph of all was the fact that the *Pleiad* returned to England after spending four months in the delta, without the loss of a single member of the expedition. It was thus proved that trade on the Lower Niger, and by means of the Niger with the countries in the interior, need not necessarily be carried out with the loss of nearly all those engaged in it, as had seemed probable from the experiences of previous expeditions. It was shown that, with proper precautions and a free use of quinine, Europeans were perfectly able to stand, at least for short periods, the climate of the Niger delta and its neighbourhood.

Three years later Laird induced the Government to enter into a contract with him by which, in return for an annual subsidy, he undertook to place and keep on the Niger a steamer to ply between Fernando Po and the Middle river, and Dr. Baikie was sent out as Consular Agent with orders to establish himself at the confluence of the Niger and Benue rivers. Trading stations were established at three points on the river, but these soon incurred the hostility of the natives, who considered that their privileges were being interfered with. Steamers were fired on, and in 1860 one of the factories was sacked and burnt. Although punishment was inflicted the following year by a British gunboat which was despatched up the river, Laird's death at this juncture, coupled with other causes, removed the mainspring of commercial activity, and the trading stations were abandoned. Baikie, who had founded on this strip of land—which had been acquired in 1841 for the model farm—a settlement which was named Lokoja, continued to exercise his functions as Consular Agent, and established friendly relations with the natives, but he was now almost completely cut off from communication with the coast. Occasionally he was visited at Lokoja by a British gunboat patrolling the river in pursuance of the Government's Anti-slavery Crusade, but the river was practically abandoned by merchantmen. He was, however, successful in establishing close communication with the Mahomedan Emir of Nupe, a vassal of the great Fulani Empire of the north, and with him he effected a commercial treaty. This Emir, in fact, sent a letter to the Queen with a present of a horse, declaring in this letter that he was desirous of establishing regular commercial intercourse with England, and guaranteeing to protect any English merchants who might enter his dominions. Government, however, at this time had its hands full in India and elsewhere, and proved apathetic about West African affairs. In 1868 the Consular Agent was withdrawn from the Niger, though the Consul at Fernando Po (whose headquarters were subsequently moved to Old Calabar on the coast) continued to exercise his jurisdiction at the mouth of the delta. Opinion at home at the time was strongly averse from undertaking any responsibilities whatever in the interior, and the general feeling is expressed in a report submitted in 1865 by a representative Committee of the House of Commons, which sat to investigate the affairs of the West African possessions. The following Resolution was submitted to the House of Commons and adopted on June 26, 1865: "That all further extension of territory or assumption of Government or new treaties offering any protection to native tribes, would be inexpedient, and that the object of our policy should be to encourage in the natives the exercise of those qualities which may render it possible for us more and more to transfer to them the administration of all the Governments with a view to our ultimate withdrawal from all, except probably Sierra Leone."

The policy of the British Government was therefore plainly stated. It was to withdraw as speedily as possible from all attempts at establishing any sort of political control in West Africa. This policy was from now onwards steadfastly pursued for a period of close on twenty years, till events forced Great

Britain to reverse the decision to which she had come, and to take action which ended by thrusting on her the responsibility for the administration of territories in West Africa exceeding half a million square miles in extent.

CHAPTER II

CHARTERED COMPANY ADMINISTRATION

"The contact with white races cannot be avoided, and it is more perilous and more injurious in proportion as it lacks governmental sanction and control. . . . Chartered Company government is not necessarily bad in its direct results. It is, in fact, little else than private despotism rendered more than usually precarious in that it has been established for the sake of dividends. A 'managing director' may be scrupulous and far-sighted, as Sir G. T. Goldie in the Niger Company."—*Imperialism*, by J. A. Hobson.

A period of stagnation now ensued in the region of the Niger. Trading vessels continued as before to visit the coast in large numbers and purchase from the natives supplies of the palm oil, which forms one of the chief ingredients in the manufacture of soap, and is consequently in great demand in the markets of Europe. As the years went by enterprising merchants from time to time pushed their way up the rivers and creeks, and instituted a barter trade with the natives. But these attempts were individualistic, and the competition which they caused proved harmful alike to the natives and to the traders themselves. Disputes arose, which were often settled with difficulty, the only official to whom they could be referred being the British Consul at Fernando Po, who exercised a somewhat vague consular jurisdiction over the Oil Rivers district. It was clear that if commerce were to make any headway, and if trade with the natives were to be placed on any sort of satisfactory basis, some kind of organisation was imperative. The British Government held aloof, and had frankly expressed its intention of taking no part in the affairs of those regions. It was one of those situations which occur from time to time in the history of every nation when a man with clear ideas, steady purpose, and courageous initiative is needed to take the lead, and fortunately in our nation such a man is not often long in coming forward.

In 1877, Mr. Goldie Taubman, an officer of the Royal Engineers, who was interested in African exploration and had already travelled in the regions of the Upper Nile, came to the Niger with his brother, intending to ascend the Benue river and strike across the continent to the valleys of the Upper Nile. The serious illness of his brother obliged him to abandon this project, but his interest in the Niger problems had been aroused, and he conceived the idea of acquiring a charter for a Company, and thus opening up those regions to trade, and securing for Great Britain an influence over the inhabitants whereby law and order might be introduced, and an end be put to the slave-raiding and inter-tribal wars which devastated the country. The first step, he saw clearly, was to amalgamate the various trading interests on the river, and by so doing to put a stop to the cut-throat competition which was proving so disastrous from every point of view. With this object he approached the various firms which had established themselves on the river and, mainly owing to his efforts, these agreed to unite their several interests, and in 1879 they formed themselves into a Company, called the United Africa Company, an event which it is not too much to say revolutionised the situation on the Niger. Three years later the Company was re-formed under the name of the National African Company, and a large extension of trade, which had languished since the unhappy ventures in earlier years, gave immediate proof of the soundness of the policy of united and organised effort which had been pursued. Addressing, twenty years later, the shareholders of the Company, Mr. Goldie Taubman—now Sir George Taubman Goldie—used these striking words:

"In an unsettled country, where the foundations for the security for native life, liberty, and property are being laid by the efforts of a small number of British subjects, scattered amongst dense populations of turbulent savages, and where the conditions of progress are hampered by climatic and physical difficulties, it is of the utmost importance that these efforts should be united, instead of being wasted in internal jealousies and struggles, which not only retard the progress of civilisation, but must ultimately destroy what has already been effected. I am not ashamed to confess my personal responsibility for the conception and execution of this policy of united effort from the year 1879—three years before the foundation of this Company—down to the present day. It seemed to me that thus alone could the Niger Territories be won for Great Britain, and British influence be maintained there during the period of foundation and pacification. My colleagues have throughout entrusted to me the carrying out of this policy, and eighteen years' experience has convinced me of its soundness, so long as the administering power in those regions remains in the invidious position—unparalleled in our generation—of a trading company liable to competition with other Europeans within its jurisdiction."

So marked was the success of the Company, that it was not long before foreign competitors appeared on the scene, and two important French firms established themselves on the Niger, with the sympathy and encouragement of the French Government and the French Press. The Company decided that immediate action must be taken if the Niger trade were to remain in British hands, and British influence to maintain itself in those regions. It accordingly determined to purchase the French interests, and concentrate the entire trade in its own hands. It therefore approached the French firms, with the result that in 1884 they accepted shares in the British Company, and withdrew from competition, leaving the trade of the Niger entirely in British hands. It is doubtful whether this result would have been achieved had it not been for the fact that French disasters in Tonkin had brought about a temporary reaction in the Colonial policy of the Republic, which would otherwise scarcely have consented at such a juncture to see its flag disappear from the Niger. Hardly had the Company secured their position in this manner when Germany startled the world by adopting a new and vigorous Colonial policy on the African continent, and in 1884 declared a Protectorate over the Cameroons and Togoland, two portions of the west coast lying not far from the Niger delta. A scramble for Africa ensued amongst the European Powers, which led immediately to the assembling of the Berlin Conference in October of that year, when representatives from fourteen Powers met to consider the various questions which had arisen on that continent. Thanks to the Niger Company the

British representative at this Conference, which was attended by Sir Goldie Taubman representing the Company, was able to declare that the entire trade of the Middle and Lower Niger was in British hands, and that the British flag flew alone on those waters. Consequently, when by international agreement the Conference declared the Niger open to free navigation, it was Great Britain that was entrusted with the duty of carrying out the necessary regulations, and she at the same time notified to the Powers the assumption of a Protectorate over that part of the coastal regions known as the "Oil Rivers." Prince Bismarck, at the termination of the Conference on February 25, 1885, used the following words: "The resolutions which we are now engaged in formally ratifying, secure for the trade of all nations free access into the interior of the African continent. . . . The arrangements provided for in these resolutions for the navigation of the Niger are on the whole such as to present for the trade and industry of all the nations, the most favourable conditions for their development and security." What had been insisted upon by the Powers, and readily admitted by Great Britain, was that the navigation of, and transit over, the waters of the Niger to the interior should be free to all nations, precisely as was the case with the Danube and other rivers, without the riverside states being thereby in any way deprived of their territorial rights on the banks.

The years that followed the Berlin Conference witnessed in this portion of Africa an international rivalry of the keenest description. Some of the foremost of the European Powers entered on a hard-fought struggle to obtain a footing and extend their influence over various regions of the African continent. In the neighbourhood of the Niger, where the contest was by no means least severe, the curious spectacle presented itself of a small commercial Company left to uphold its interests—and therefore those of the nation under whose flag it fought—against those of two powerful foreign Governments. This Company had secured for Great Britain the country at the mouth of the Niger, but other Powers fixed their attention on those great Mahomedan empires in the hinterland which had been discovered to Europe by British enterprise. "We knew," said the Chairman of the Company subsequently, "that by far the most valuable region of Equatorial Africa was that known as the Hausa States, forming roughly the northern and less accessible half of our present territories. They are extremely fertile; they are the most popular lands of large extent, not only in tropical Africa, but in any part of that continent; and when the Pax Britannica is established there, and the constant slave-raiding is abolished, their population will be speedily quadrupled. They are inhabited by races—partly Fulah, partly hybrid, but mainly Hausa—very different from those of most parts of Negroland; races which possess a considerable degree of civilisation, and above all are very industrious. . . . The ultimate wealth of every country must mainly depend on the industry of its inhabitants, and in this all-important respect the Hausa States have an immense advantage over all other parts of tropical Africa."

It was known that Germany was contemplating the despatch from its new Protectorate in the Cameroons of an emissary to extend if possible her influence into these regions, whence sixty years before Clapperton had brought a letter from the Sultan asking

Great Britain to appoint a consul in his dominions. The Company acted with foresight and promptitude and despatched an envoy to Sokoto, who, in 1885, obtained from the Sultan a treaty recognising the status of the Company, and giving it jurisdiction over his territories on the banks of the Benue and Middle Niger, and certain rights of political influence and commercial privileges over the remainder of his empire.

It cannot be said that during the succeeding years the Company adopted a "dog-in-the-manger" policy. In the settlement of the boundary between the hinterland of the German Cameroons and the Company's territories, it consented to give up the greater portion of a district which formed an outlying province of the Sokoto Empire, and where the Company actually possessed a trading station, though Germany had at the time no shadow of interest there. Indeed the Company—throughout the negotiations which were carried on by England during these years both with Germany and France, when friction at times developed into dangerous proportions—justly claimed that in pressing their rights they had been "most careful to avoid, either by active agitation or by passive resistance, creating difficulties for Her Majesty's Government, who have, in dealing with Foreign Powers, to consider the interests of the Empire as a whole." The difficulties with Germany were finally overcome, and agreements were signed by the two Governments, the last of which, in 1893, definitely determined the boundaries between the Cameroons hinterland and the Niger territories, and put an end to all disputes.

Some considerable time before this result was achieved, however, the British Government had decided on a step which had become necessary directly the National African Company found itself pressed on all sides by foreign rivals acting under direct orders of their respective Governments. As early as the year 1881, the Company had applied for the grant of a charter, but had been refused mainly on the grounds that it was too small to be entrusted with such responsibilities. Since then, however, it had become a much larger and more important concern, and with a view to meeting the objection, had raised its capital to a million sterling. But the main consideration which induced the Government to look favourably on the request of the Company for a charter, was that as a mere trading concern it had no authority to enter into sovereign right treaties with native Chiefs, and in view of the claims which were being pressed by France and Germany it was incumbent on Great Britain either to take over the administration of the Niger Districts herself, or to delegate it to a Company, or to abandon the territories altogether. The parting of the ways had arrived and public opinion had changed since the Resolution of 1865, already referred to, had been passed and adopted in the House of Commons. Great Britain was no longer prepared to resign to other nations a position which had been procured for her at the cost of so many lives, and so much enterprise and energy. Nor was she yet prepared to undertake the arduous task of setting up all the complicated and expensive machinery of a Government administration. She recognised that the National African Company had at its head men who could be entrusted with the responsibilities of administration, and who possessed both the knowledge and machinery necessary for the purpose. In July 1886, therefore, a Charter was bestowed on the Company, which henceforth became the Royal Niger Company, and the Government in so doing assumed the ultimate responsibility for entering into political relations with the regions explored sixty years before by Denham and Clapperton, as well as the intervening territories down to the coast line.

By virtue of this Charter, the Company was empowered to govern, to keep in order, and protect the territories of the Chiefs, with whom it had concluded sovereign right treaties, and, subject to the sanction of the Secretary of State, to acquire new territories. It was authorised to levy Customs duties to defray the cost of administration, such duties being subject to the sanction of the Secretary of State, to whom a full account of all administrative expenditure was to be submitted. It was given jurisdiction over foreigners and British subjects throughout its dominions. It was to discourage and gradually abolish slavery, to tolerate the religion of the inhabitants, and uphold as far as possible their native laws and customs, and to treat them with justice. Various provisos were also made to prevent any monopoly of trade, and to ensure free access to its markets for all traders.

The Charter differed fundamentally from most of those granted in other quarters of the world, for under it the Company remained a trading concern, as well as undertaking administrative duties. Sir George Goldie had himself suggested that the Company should be given a Charter somewhat analogous to that granted to the British North Borneo Company, which does not itself trade, but for various reasons Government decided otherwise. Its status was therefore curious. It occupied, in fact, two positions, which, though mutually dependent on and indeed essential to each other, were in many respects distinct. One may be described as the financial position: receiving no pecuniary assistance from Government its capital was the property of the shareholders, for which the latter had a right to expect a fair and remunerative return. The other position might be described as political or governmental: in this it stood as the delegate or trustee of Great Britain in the vast region covered by its treaties, or which fell within the sphere of influence secured to it by international agreement. The Customs duties on imports and exports which it was authorised to levy were to be fixed with due regard to the interests of the British and foreign traders; their amount and character were to be investigated and sanctioned by Government, and the sums received from them were to be expended solely on administrative expenses, an annual account of the latter being submitted to Government. These were to be paid by the Company itself, exactly in the same manner as they were paid by other traders, British or foreign. "Ours is the only Chartered Company of our time," stated the Chairman in commenting on the position of the shareholders in 1897, "which is forbidden to earn profits on its capital out of Customs duties or other taxation, the entire revenues so raised having to be expended for public purposes."

It speaks volumes for the financial skill with which the Company was conducted that, from the outset, it paid its shareholders a steady dividend, averaging some 6 per cent, although it had to compete in surrounding territories with foreign concerns in many cases either directly or indirectly subsidised by their respective Governments. It may be remarked in passing that, although the system of Government subsidies undoubtedly gave foreign merchants and firms an advantage over an unsubsidised British possession like the Niger where the whole cost of administration was met by taxation on trade, it could hardly benefit the home Governments from whose exchequers the subsidies were paid. Moreover it is probable that an unsubsidised concern profits in the long run from the energy evoked and the liberty fostered by independence of State subsidies and State interference. The avoidance of dry nursing is wholly in accordance with the traditional policy of the British nation, and it is mainly this policy which has fostered the qualities of initiative and sturdy independence which have been characteristic of the race the world over.

The first duty which devolved on the Company as a result of the bestowal of the Charter was the organisation of the machinery necessary to carry out its new functions as a governmental body. The arrangements for the effective performance of these new functions were rapidly carried into execution. An Agent-General was appointed with a staff of executive officers acting under him, and he was responsible to the directors for carrying on the political duties of the Company on the spot. For the maintenance of law and order courts of justice were instituted and a force of constabulary raised and equipped. A Chief Justice was therefore appointed by the Company who presided over a High Court. A force of constabulary was organised under British officers, on the same principles as those already existing on the Gold Coast, and at first numbered about 400, though as the responsibilities of the Company increased it was strengthened until it eventually reached a total of 1000. This force was distributed in detachments throughout the territories, according to local requirements. A force of native police was also organised for civil duties, and gaols established. Administrative headquarters were fixed at a central point on the river, some distance below the confluence of the Niger and Benue rivers.

The Board of Directors in London had as their Chairman and Governor Lord Aberdare, with Sir George Goldie as Deputy-Governor. With two such men at the head of affairs there was no fear that the political and administrative responsibilities of the Company would be neglected, or sacrificed on the altar of commercial advantage.

As soon as the machinery had been created, and this was done with marvellous rapidity, the Company set to work to carry out its administrative duties. Treaties were concluded with the numerous Chiefs on the banks of the Benue and the Lower and Middle Niger, and in July 1888 the Governor was able to report that the Agent-General had made treaties with no less than 235 riverside states and tribes, giving the Company territorial rights over the regions bordering the whole of the Lower Niger and its tributaries, and of such parts of the Middle Niger and Benue and their numerous affluents as did not fall under the sovereignty of the Sultan of Sokoto, from whom it had already obtained concessions completing its jurisdiction along the banks of those waters. The Governor warned the shareholders, however, that progress would not and could not be rapid. "With 300 tribes," he said, "who have been for countless generations plunged in idle barbarism, whose sole idea of wealth has been the holding of slaves, whose main occupation in life has been to obtain such slaves by inter-tribal warfare, or by kidnapping, it would be absurd to expect that these practices could be completely suppressed within a few years. We have succeeded beyond our expectations ; but much time must elapse, much hard work be done, before that sense of security in life, liberty, and property can be attained, without which any extensive introduction of agriculture would be impossible." But it was not in the semi-savage regions bordering on the rivers that the far-seeing directors of the Company placed all, or even the major part of their hopes. "We can hardly impress too strongly on our shareholders," continued Lord Aberdare, "the fact that our hopes of future prosperity rest far less on the lower regions of the Niger which first attracted British enterprise, and which even now yield the greater part of our trade, than on the higher and inner, and recently explored regions acquired at great expense of money and energy, but which, being so recently occupied and imperfectly developed, are at present rather a loss than a gain."

The introduction of law and order and the prevention of inter-tribal war and devastating slave-raiding, which hindered civilisation and paralysed development in the interior, could not be effected without an enormous expenditure of money which the Company had not at its disposal. The two functions of the Company—commerce and administration—were mutually dependent, since it was commerce alone which could supply the sinews wherewith law and order could be introduced. And on the Niger, unlike India, "there was no pagoda tree," as the Governor remarked, "to be shaken, with the accompanying shower of rupees. We do not, so far, raise from the natives one penny of direct revenue."

It was uphill work, and the Company's hands were

very full in these early years of struggle. German and French rivalry called for every quality of energy, tact, foresight, and rapid decision possessed by the directors —and, fortunately, none of these qualifications were lacking—while the pacification of the numerous tribes within its own borders was a task of no mean order, and the little force of constabulary was none too large for its execution. Besides this, the Company was the target for perpetual attacks in the Press and in Parliament. It was accused of monopolising trade, of imposing ruinously high and oppressive duties on imports and exports, of violating the Charter, of acting with high-handed injustice towards foreign traders. In reply the Company pointed out that they were debarred by their Charter from imposing any dues not first sanctioned by Government, or from establishing a monopoly; and that they were willing and anxious to submit to any inquiry as to their methods. In fact, inquiries were instituted in their territories, both a German commissioner and later a British Government commissioner investigating causes of complaint on the spot, with the result that a satisfactory report was rendered by both, the Company affording every assistance. Yet the attacks did not diminish till the Under-Secretary had stated in the House of Commons, after full consideration of the Report submitted by the special commissioner who had been sent out to investigate, "The administration of the Royal Niger Company is . . . in the main highly satisfactory as to progress, system, and observance of the Charter."

No sooner had the Company settled the difficulties with Germany on its eastern frontier, than it encountered difficulties of a similar and even more dangerous nature with its French neighbours on its western borders. Chauvinist Parisian papers had in the 'eighties revived the dream of a vast French African empire, stretching from the Mediterranean to the Gulf of Guinea, and from the Atlantic to Egypt. Great Britain had, on the contrary, deliberately pursued a "Coastal" as opposed to a "Continental" policy, with the result that her coast colonies were in danger of being enclosed and shut off entirely from the markets of the interior. The National African Company alone had aimed at securing a hinterland, and with this object had concluded treaties with Chiefs on both banks of the Niger to a distance of nearly 1000 miles from the sea. At the time there appeared to be no danger of coming into contact with the French, whose Mediterranean colony of Algeria was separated from the Hausa States by the whole breadth of the desert, whilst her possessions in Senegambia were separated from the Middle Niger by a vast distance. The only possible point from which danger might arise was the hinterland of Dahomey, a state where France possessed a sphere of influence. To guard against this the Company, with that painstaking foresight which characterised all its operations, had concluded a treaty with the small pagan state of Borgu which lies on the western bank of the Niger. In 1890, with a view to determining the northern boundary of the Niger territories, the French had proposed that a line should be drawn from the Niger eastwards to Lake Tchad, a distance of some 800 miles, and had agreed to its being deflected so as to include the kingdom of Sokoto, with whose Sultan, as has been recorded, the Company held a treaty. An important declaration was therefore signed the same year between the French and British Governments, whereby the latter agreed to recognise the sphere of influence of France "to the south of her Mediterranean possessions, up to a line from Say on the Niger to Barrua on Lake Tchad, drawn in such a manner as to comprise in the spheres of action of the Niger Company all that fairly belongs to the kingdom of Sokoto, the line to be determined by the commissioners appointed."

This term "sphere of influence," first employed at the Berlin Conference of 1884, was somewhat vague, and was instituted with a view to preventing any collision between European Powers, who were endeavouring to extend their influence over regions which they neither occupied nor administered. The claim on which such pretensions were based was, as a rule, the existence of a treaty or treaties with the Chiefs occupying such countries, and although a suggestion had been made by Great Britain at the Conference that any such treaties should be followed by effective occupation before the claim received international sanction, this suggestion was not adopted. Hence it was perfectly possible for any European Power to obtain international recognition of its sphere of influence over a vast tract of country to which it had done no more than merely send an emissary to conclude treaties with the local Chiefs. It is obvious that such an arrangement, conceived as it was with the best intention of avoiding international disputes and conflicts, gave an enormous impetus to the art of treaty-making with African Chiefs—an art which was by no means difficult to acquire and which had its fascinations for ambitious servants of the various Governments.

In 1893 France proclaimed a Protectorate over the kingdom of Dahomey, which, as has already been mentioned, lay to the west of the territories administered by the Royal Niger Company, and, as the Company had foreseen, proceeded to push their claims to the hinterland, with a view particularly to obtaining a footing on the navigable waters of the Niger. With this object French treaty-making expeditions were soon forcing their way into the interior, and the little state of Borgu, which lay on the western bank of the Niger, became the object of attention. Borgu, however, was claimed by the Niger Company on two grounds: first, that it lay south and east of the town of Say, and hence was in their sphere of influence by virtue of the agreement as to the Say-Barrua line before mentioned; second, that they already held a treaty with the dominant Chief. Learning, however, that the French claimed that this Chief—with whom the Company had concluded the treaty—was subordinate to another Chief who lived at Nikki (a small town about 200 miles west of the Niger) the Company determined to place their claims beyond dispute by despatching an expedition to Nikki to conclude a treaty. At the moment, therefore, that the French were despatching an expedition northward into the interior from Dahomey to Nikki to conclude a treaty on which they could base a claim to the kingdom of Borgu, the Company despatched Captain Lugard by way of the Niger to the same town with the same object. When the French arrived at Nikki it was only to find that Captain Lugard had concluded a treaty for the Company on behalf of Great Britain, and had actually quitted Nikki with the treaty in his pocket some days before their arrival. A swarm of French expeditions now entered the territories claimed in this neighbourhood by the Niger Company, and, in the absence of resistance, became practically masters of the small triangular section which lay between the meridian of Say, the Middle Niger below that town, and the 9th parallel of latitude. The Company acted with great self-restraint, recognising the dangers to which precipitate action on their part might expose both themselves and the peace of the Empire. Their case was so overwhelmingly strong that they felt confident that it could safely be left to the result of diplomatic action between the Governments concerned. They considered that the Agreement of 1890 had absolutely secured to them the territory in dispute, and numberless extracts from the French Press, published at the time of that Agreement, could be quoted to support the contention that the same opinion had previously been held in France as well. For instance, the *Journal des Débats*, in commenting on the Agreement in 1890, had remarked: "South of Say, and of the parallel which passes through it, are territories which appear relatively rich and prosperous . . . they will not be ours." The *Temps*, four months after the Agreement of 1890, published a map showing everything east of the meridian of Say (including, of course, the triangular section on the west bank of the Niger) as British.

The little pagan state on the banks of the Niger became, in short, a theatre where the representatives of two European Powers stood face to face, and the tension appeared at one time so dangerous as to threaten the peace of Europe—French and English outposts occupying adjacent villages, the flags of the two Powers floating within a few yards of one another. Wise counsels however prevailed, and the dangerous situation was brought to a close in June 1898 by an

Anglo-French Agreement, signed at Paris. By this Agreement a compromise satisfactory to both Powers was arranged, and a paper boundary laid down. Say was given up and the line carried south to another point on the Niger some 200 miles farther down stream; from this point a line was drawn southwards to form the westernmost boundary of the Niger Company's territories, and to include the greater portion of the state of Borgu. The line constituting the northern boundary of the empires of Sokoto and Bornu remained practically as before.

The Anglo-German Agreement of 1893 and the Anglo-French Agreement of 1898 effectively put an end to the international struggles in which the Chartered Company had been engaged for more than twelve years. In reading the history of those anxious years it is impossible to withhold a feeling of admiration for the patience, courage, foresight, and skill which characterised the actions of those who were responsible for the policy of the Company. It must be remembered that at the time the Company was formed the policy of the British Government was strongly opposed to extending its influence in the region of West Africa, and both the Foreign and Colonial Offices doubtless felt themselves bound by the decision of the House of Commons Committee of 1865. Nor did West African merchants themselves up to 1885 realise that trade interests alone did not constitute political rights. It was therefore necessary to bring about a revulsion in public opinion so far as West Africa was concerned, and to do so it was necessary to find an instrument outside Parliamentary control and unaffected by the contests of parties. This instrument was supplied by the Company, and it was unquestionably its action in securing the rich territories at the back of its coast regions which gave an impetus to other British West African Colonies, and thereby saved them from becoming completely hemmed in by foreign Powers and being cut off from the markets of the interior. This alone will always constitute a sufficient claim for the Royal Niger Company to be remembered in connection with the modern history of Africa.

While the Company had been engaged in these dangerous and difficult international complications, other serious difficulties had arisen in their own borders, which at one time threatened their very existence. It will be remembered that, in the neighbourhood of the confluence of the Niger and Benue, there existed a province known as Nupe, ruled over by a Mahomedan Emir,—a Fulani, owing allegiance to the Sultan of Sokoto. The bulk of the inhabitants were pagans, though in a high state of civilisation, but the Emir also claimed a considerable number of less advanced pagan tribes towards the south and west on both banks of the river. The establishment of the Company on the river had brought them into close communication with the Emir of Nupe, with whom they made every endeavour to establish friendly relations, and at first with success. Treaties had been concluded, both in 1885 and 1890, with his suzerain, the Sultan of Sokoto, and he had welcomed the establishment of trading stations at points on the river situated within his territories. It was, however, soon evident that he had no intention of desisting from his habits of devastating his pagan dependencies by slave raids, and of oppressing his subjects. To the Company's protestations he turned a deaf ear; to friendly advice he paid no heed; threats he treated with scorn, and finally with insolence. Meanwhile his constant slave-raiding expeditions were paralysing the efforts of the Company, and it was not long before the latter realised, that if its obligations as regards the prevention of slave-raiding were to be carried out, it must be by force. The situation was critical. The Emir was reported to be able to put into the field close on 30,000 men, a third of whom were mounted. The Company had at its disposal less than 1000 constabulary, of whom a little over half could be collected for an expedition of a military nature, the remainder being necessarily retained at their various posts on the two rivers. Yet advice, protestations, and threats having failed, nothing was left but to put a stop to further misgovernment by force of arms. Advantage was taken of the Nupe army being dispersed, half of it having crossed the river on a slave-raiding expedition. Every possible precaution was taken to ensure success and to avoid a failure, which would have endangered the very existence of the Company. Every detail was carefully thought out, and in January 1897 a force of about 550 constabulary left Lokoja, Sir George Goldie accompanying it in person.

Outside the walls of the Emir's capital at Bida it was assailed by the Nupe army, estimated at from 10,000 to 15,000 men, mostly mounted, and led by the Emir himself, but these were quickly routed and the town entered the following morning. The Emir, who had fled, was declared deposed, and the heir-apparent, who had accepted the terms of the Company, was installed in his place. The southern portion of Nupe, which had suffered so severely from the raids and oppression of the late Emir, was pronounced a free country under the protection of the Company, and the legal status of slavery was declared abolished throughout Nupe. Sir George Goldie then proceeded with an escort to Illorin to treat with the Mahomedan Emir of that province, who was likewise a Fulani, owing allegiance to the Sultan of Sokoto. The escort was attacked, though half-heartedly, and after a mere show of resistance, the Emir tendered his submission and signed a treaty under similar terms to those granted to Nupe. By this short expedition the Niger Company demonstrated throughout their territories that they had behind them a power which it was futile to resist, and that henceforth slave-raiding, oppression, and misgovernment would not be tolerated in the territories over which they exercised control.

On his return to Lokoja Sir George Goldie received from Lord Salisbury a telegram, heartily congratulating him and all concerned in the expedition. "The arrangements which brought about the defeat of the Foulahs and capture of Bida," ran the words, "appear to have been admirably devised and brilliantly executed." Even more gratifying were the extraordinary demonstrations of joy of the native population at their deliverance from the Fulah yoke. Several communities sent letters expressing their gratitude to the Company for "freeing their country from oppression and slavery."

This affair, coupled with the serious complications with the French which were taking place at the same time on the north-west frontier of the Company's territories, induced the British Government to put into execution a project, the necessity for which had been rapidly growing apparent, and to raise an

Imperial local military force on the Niger. The task was entrusted to Colonel Lugard, who left England with a staff of officers in March 1898, and soon had under his command a considerable force, locally recruited, consisting of two battalions of infantry, two batteries of artillery, and a company of engineers, the whole being designated the West African Frontier Force. It was independent of the Royal Niger Company, and had its headquarters at Jebba, some 500 miles up the Niger.

The raising of this Imperial Force foreshadowed a further step which the Government had in view with reference to the affairs of the Niger territories. In addressing the shareholders of the Royal Niger Company in July 1896, Sir George Goldie had said: "The true work of the Company for the last ten years has been establishing a state of things which will offer sufficient security for the creation of a vast commerce with, and the much-needed communication in, the rich regions of the Central Soudan. When that work is completed the time will have arrived for the absorption of the Company in the Imperial Government, a process which was contemplated when we first applied for the Charter." The complications arising from the free navigation of the Niger, and the international struggles created by two great colonising Powers striving to establish their influence in countries claimed by the Niger Company, had throughout made the latter's position under the Charter extremely unstable.

The conclusion of the Agreement with France in 1898 had put an end to the foreign complications which had harassed the Company for so many years—complications in which they had manfully held their own against the weight of a foreign Government. It was evident, however, that such large territories, bounded as they were on the one side by French and on the other side by German Protectorates, could no longer be left in the hands of a Chartered Company, but that the responsibility must be definitely and directly assumed by the British Government. In June 1899 Lord Salisbury addressed a letter from the Foreign Office to the Treasury in which he stated that he had for some time past had under consideration the question of approaching the Royal Niger Company with a view to relieving them of their rights and functions of administration on reasonable terms. He had arrived at the opinion, he said, now that the ratifications of the Anglo-French Convention of June 14, 1898, had been exchanged, and that the frontiers of the two countries had been clearly established, that it was desirable on grounds of national policy that these rights and functions should be taken over by Her Majesty's Government. "The state of affairs created by this Convention," he wrote, "makes it incumbent on Her Majesty's Government to maintain an immediate control over the frontier and fiscal policy of British Nigeria, such as cannot be exercised so long as that policy is dictated and executed by a Company which combines commercial profit with administrative responsibilities."[1] Lord Salisbury therefore requested the Lords of the Treasury to endeavour to come to an early settlement with the Company.

On the receipt of this letter negotiations were at once set on foot between the Treasury and Sir George Goldie as the Governor of, and acting on behalf of,

[1] Letter from the Secretary for Foreign Affairs to the Secretary to the Treasury, June 15, 1899.

the Niger Company, and an Agreement was concluded, subject to the sanction of Parliament, which was set out in a Treasury Minute dated June 30, 1889, copies of which were submitted to both Houses of Parliament.

By this Agreement, the Lords of the Treasury having directed that an Order should be submitted to the Queen in Council revoking the Charter on a date to be specified in such Order, it was arranged that from the date of revocation the Company should be relieved of all its powers and duties, and should assign to Her Majesty's Government the benefits of all the treaties, and all its land and mining rights of whatever sort and however acquired, retaining its plant and trading assets, its stations and waterside depôts, with customary rights of access, buildings, wharves, workshops, and the sites thereof. Government would take over from the Company its war materials and buildings for administrative purposes, and so much of the Company's plant, including steamers, buildings, and land at stations, wharves, stores, etc., as was specified in certain schedules attached to the Minute. In return for this, Government assumed entire liability for the annual payment of a sum representing the interest at 5 per cent on £250,000, the public debt of the Niger territories, which had hitherto been a charge on the administrative revenue of the Company, and undertook to pay a sum of £150,000 as the price of the Company's rights which have been described above, and as compensation for the interruption and dislocation of the Company's business, resulting from the revocation of the Charter: also a further sum of £300,000 in repayment of sums advanced by the Company from time to time for the development and extension of the Niger Territories, in excess of the revenue obtained from customs duties and applied to the necessary expenses of the ordinary civil administration of the territories.

There was a further clause in the Agreement to which attention will be directed later on, though at the time little general notice was taken of it. By it Government undertook to impose a royalty on all minerals which might be worked within a certain defined area, which comprised the greater part of the Protectorate, provided that such minerals were exported from a British port or passed through a British custom house; but it undertook, for a period of ninety-nine years from the revocation of the Charter, to pay to the Company, or its assigns, one-half of the receipts from any royalty so imposed.

The date on which Government was to assume the direct administration of the territories which the Royal Niger Company had thus acquired for it was subsequently fixed as the 1st of January 1900. It was decided to divide the territories into two portions, the southern to be attached to, and administered by, the Oil Rivers Protectorate transferred from the Foreign Office to the Colonial Office, and to be known henceforth as the Protectorate of Southern Nigeria. The northern, which included the territories on both banks of the Benue river north of the 7th parallel of latitude, and the whole of the Middle Niger and the northern states up to the Anglo-French boundary, containing an area of close upon 320,000 square miles, was to be called the Protectorate of Northern Nigeria, with a separate and distinct administration under a High Commissioner.

From the 1st of January, therefore, the Royal Niger Company reverted once more to its original rôle as a trading concern, having surrendered its political and governmental rights and responsibilities into the hands of the Imperial Government, for whom it had acquired a territory close on half a million of square miles in extent. After a lapse of eleven years it is now possible to estimate the manner in which it had acquitted itself in the task of Empire-building, and the verdict of every fair-minded man must be that it performed its self-imposed and difficult mission with infinite credit, both to itself and to the country whose delegate and trustee it had been.

In its dealings with foreign nations it had shown, throughout a series of most difficult and complicated situations, due to international rivalries and jealousies, tact, foresight, tenacity, and judgment, coupled with a self-restraint and level-headedness which were wholly admirable. The same qualities had been exhibited in its dealings with the natives with whom it had been brought into close contact, and over whom it had been empowered to exercise a supervision. Amongst these the name of the Company stands high to this day for justice, and fair and sympathetic dealing. It was all-important that the feeling engendered amongst the natives towards the first Europeans with whom they were brought into contact should be one of respect and confidence. That this result was achieved by the Company no one can now deny, and the new Administration set up by the British Government reaped the benefit of it.

There remains the question as to whether, in entrusting the development of this vast region to a commercial company, the Government acted in the best interests, primarily of the inhabitants and secondly of itself.

Lord Cromer, the value of whose opinion on a subject of this nature none will deny, has recently laid down a principle which, he maintains, lies at the root of all sound administration. "The principle," he writes, "is that administration and commercial exploitation should not be entrusted to the same hands. State officials may err, but they have no interests to serve but those of good government, whereas commercial agents must almost of necessity at times neglect the welfare of the subject race in the real or presumed pecuniary interests of their employers."[1] It is fair to say that Lord Cromer qualifies this weighty dictum with the remark that although he personally holds strongly to this opinion, it is not universally accepted; and he quotes "a very able and competent authority, Sir Charles Lucas," as saying that, "on the whole, the second birth of Chartered Companies is one of the most hopeful signs of the times."[2]

Another advocate for the development of unexplored regions through the agency of commercial companies, states the case as follows: "The policy of granting Charters to powerful commercial associations has been criticised both in the Press and Parliament of England; but no better means have been suggested for substituting legitimate trade in a large way for the traffic in slaves which is now being everywhere checked. The rapid development of such legitimate commerce lies far beyond the resources of individual enterprise, and if it be not rapidly developed, the suppression of the slave trade must be followed by evils of the worst

[1] *Ancient and Modern Imperialism*, by the Rt. Hon. Earl of Cromer.
[2] *Ibid.*

character. The natural growth of the population, no longer kept under by the raids of the slave traders, must cause a further depreciation in the value of human life, and in the absence of regular employment the increasing number of idle hands must bring about a corresponding increase in the practice of witchcraft and of cannibalism in the extensive regions where anthropophagy is still rife. Hence, after the abolition of the slave trade, these practices must continue to flourish until the chiefs discover by experience that their subjects are more valuable as producers than as food for the market, or as victims of the witch doctor. In the present transitional stage of the social relations, the regeneration of Africa lies to a large extent in the hands of properly organised Chartered Companies, powerful and enterprising enough to run railways through the country, and to launch steamers on the navigable inland waters. In this sense the Congo State itself may be regarded as a huge trading association chartered by the Berlin Congress in the name of humanity."

While expressing the greatest diffidence in putting forward an opinion on a question concerning which such experienced and able authorities have stated their views, it seems only right to suggest that one or two factors—more especially the personal element—appear to have been somewhat overlooked in these generalities. Is it absolutely true that State officials have no interests to serve but those of good government, while commercial agents must almost of necessity regard only the pecuniary interests of their employers? Have not State officials private interests, which they may be at times tempted to serve? For instance, may they not at times be tempted to seek for the credit which may accrue to them by the exaction of a large revenue from the country they are called upon to administer, and may not this revenue be obtained by harsh, unjust, or excessive taxation? And may not a Chartered Company, whose employers are in the last resort the State, have other than pecuniary interests to serve?

A charge of this very description was dealt with by Sir George Goldie in an address to the shareholders of the Royal Niger Company on the 16th of July 1897, in words which deserve quoting. An unprejudiced and honourable organ of public opinion had laid down, he said, the doubly ambiguous premise that the *first* duty of a Council or Board of Directors—"as honest men"—was to promote the interests of their shareholders, and had thence drawn the inference that they would necessarily sacrifice all legal and moral obligations to the *pecuniary* interests of their shareholders. "I would ask," he said, "whether this principle of *first* duty applies only to Directors of Chartered Companies, or whether it is equally applicable to editors of newspapers, statesmen, and persons generally who are entrusted with the material interests of individuals or nations; for if so, our conceptions of public life will have to be modified. In the second place, as regards your interests, I would point out that, when you accepted a Charter, you took upon yourselves a public trust, which has, we venture to assert, been faithfully as well as zealously discharged. We may be mistaken in our theories, ineffective in our methods, feeble in our execution, for we are not infallible, but we have always recognised that we have two equally imperative duties towards you—one being the furthering to the utmost of your pecuniary interests, and the other the faithful discharge of the public obligations which you had voluntarily assumed. In fulfilling this latter duty to the best of our ability, we believe that we have also been promoting your permanent pecuniary interests by convincing Her Majesty's Government and public opinion, as a whole, that you were not unequal to the responsibilities placed upon you. In Chartered Companies, as in all other institutions, honesty is, in the long run, the best policy."

I would suggest that two things are necessary to prevent a commercial company, charged with administrative functions, from misusing its powers. The first is that its actions should be subject to Parliamentary control and open to the influence of public opinion. The second is that those who are directly responsible for its activities should be men of integrity and standing, distinguished for their sense of honour, justice, and fair-dealing. Given these two conditions there is no reason why a commercial body should not administer and bring under control a newly-acquired country, with as scrupulous an exercise of justice and equity as a body of State officials; nay more, the elasticity which they possess owing to their relief from the excessive rigidity and bureaucratic impediments more or less necessary in a Government department, will probably enable them to do so more rapidly and effectively than the latter could hope to do. If, however, either or both of these conditions be lacking, as has till recently been the case in another part of the African continent, Lord Cromer's dictum will probably be justified, and good government will be sacrified for commercial gain.

The Royal Niger Company may fairly claim that both these conditions were fully satisfied. It has already been shown how completely its actions were subject to Parliamentary and departmental control, and to criticism by the Press and the public. With respect to the personal element as represented by the characteristics of those who controlled the policy and were responsible for the actions of the Company, it is only necessary to recall the names of the first Chairman and Governor, Lord Aberdare, and of the Deputy-Governor, Sir George Goldie, who on succeeding in 1895 to the Governorship, was replaced as Deputy-Governor by Lord Scarborough. By them, not only was the policy of the Company maintained at a high level, but a standard was set which permeated the entire staff and ensured an observance of equity and justice in its dealings with the natives every whit as whole-hearted as was their zeal in furthering the commercial interests of its shareholders.

It is well to recognise at once that the activity of European nations on the African continent and more particularly in the equatorial regions, during the latter part of the last century, has been due to more than one cause. That it was mainly prompted by a desire for fresh markets and a field for commercial enterprise may at once be conceded. But it would be unfair and unjust not to recognise as well that it was prompted also by a real and genuine desire for the welfare of the inhabitants, by substituting an era of law and order for the pitiful condition of insecurity and inter-tribal warfare in which they lived. It is quite impossible for any one who has not lived and travelled in the regions of Equatorial Africa to realise what this condition was. Perpetual slave raids and internecine wars, with their concomitant miseries, were the established order of things: the strong preyed upon the weak; whole towns were blotted out in inter-tribal warfare, the inhabitants being either killed or carried off into slavery, and it is one of the commonest sights in African travel to come across the crumbling walls of some deserted town which only a few years before had been the home of a thriving community.

It is doubtful whether any Government administration could have introduced law and order into such a region with as much rapidity as a commercial company: it is certain that it could not have done so without a far greater expenditure of money; yet in the interests of the natives themselves, rapidity and economy were essential. The danger of entrusting a commercial company with the exploitation of a new country is both apparent and real, but its advantages must also be considered. And it may fairly be claimed that the danger can be reduced practically to a vanishing point by a system of checks which, in these days of rapid communication and constant ventilation of public opinion through the medium of the Press, it is perfectly possible to devise.

Virtus post nummos may have been, as Lord Cromer states,[1] the watchword of every class of society in the days of the Roman Empire, but it is not so now, and the revolt against a purely commercial basis of morality gains adherents every day. Even men whose actions are guided by this principle—and it is idle to deny that the twentieth century sees many such in positions of power and responsibility—would be ashamed publicly to admit it, and would be the first to condemn it vehemently in others.

History will in time to come pronounce a verdict as to the actions of Great Britain in Nigeria, and it is

[1] *Ancient and Modern Imperialism.*

neither possible nor profitable to discuss what that verdict will be. But if it is admitted that, by undertaking the administration of the countries lying on the banks of the Lower and Middle Niger and thence to Lake Tchad, she achieved the result of diminishing by ever so little the sum total of human misery, the verdict cannot be wholly unfavourable. And if credit be allotted, by no means the smallest share must be given to the Chartered Company which acted as pioneer, and to whose far-sighted Directors is due the existence of Nigeria as a British Protectorate.

CHAPTER III

DESCRIPTION OF THE COUNTRY AND ITS PEOPLE

"The great province of Kano stādeth eastward of the riuer Niger almost fiue hundred miles. The greatest part of the inhabitants dwelling in villages are some of them herdsmen and others husbandmen. Heere groweth abundance of corne, of rice, and of cotton. Also here are many deserts and wilde woodie mountains containing many springs of water. In these woods grow plenty of wilde citrons and limons, which differ not much in taste from the beste of all. In the midst of this prouince standeth a town called by the same name, the walles and houses whereof are built for the most part of a kinde of chalke. The inhabitants are rich merchants and most ciuill people. Their king was in times past of great puissance, and had mighty troupes of horsemen at his command. . . . The inhabitants of Zeg Zeg [Zaria] are rich and have great traffique unto other nations. Some part of their kingdom is plaine, and the residue mountainous, but the mountains are extremely cold, and the plaines intolerably hot. And because they can hardly indure the sharpness of winter, they kindle great fires in the midst of their houses, laying the coles thereof under their high bedsteads, and so betaking themselues to sleepe."—LEO AFRICANUS, vol. ii. pp. 8, 31.

NORTHERN NIGERIA comprises, roughly speaking, the countries lying on both banks of the Middle Niger and the Benue rivers, and the regions extending from these to Lake Tchad, which forms its extreme north-eastern corner. It is bounded on the east by the German Protectorate of the Cameroons, the line separating the two having been fixed by various international Agreements. On the north and west it is bounded by the French possessions in the Central Soudan and the hinterland of Dahomey; on the south by the British colony of Lagos and Protectorate of Southern Nigeria. The southern portion is partly low-lying, partly broken up by ranges of hills—chiefly of laterite and granite—rising in some places to considerable heights, especially in the centre of the Protectorate, where a great rocky plateau, averaging 4000 feet in altitude, forms the watershed in which rise rivers which fall respectively into the Niger, the Benue, and Lake Tchad. Along the northern border runs a wide strip of open upland country, stretching from the Niger across to Lake Tchad, varying in elevation from 1000 to 2400 feet above sea level. Here the climate is drier, the heat more temperate, and the air purer and fresher than it is in the river valleys farther south.

The year is divided into two seasons—the rainy and the dry. The former begins about April with a few violent hurricanes of wind and rain, which become more frequent and less violent as the year advances, till towards the month of July rain falls almost every day, and by the end of September the rivers are in full flood and tracts of the country under water. In October the steady rain is succeeded once more by violent storms or tornadoes, which finally cease about the end of the month, and the dry season sets in, not a drop of rain falling for a period of nearly six months, when the April tornadoes begin once more.[1] During the months of January and February the temperature reaches its lowest point, and a steady wind blows from the north-east. This wind, known locally as the *harmattan*, occasionally blows with great violence for several days in succession, filling the air with tiny specks of sand from the desert, blotting out the view, and covering everything with a fine dust. At night the temperature in the northern districts falls at these times to within a few degrees of freezing-point, and

[1] There is occasionally a slight fall of rain about the end of December, but it is never more than a fraction of an inch, and does not occur every year.

the air remains bitterly cold till the sun is high in the heavens.

It is in April, immediately the first shower falls, that the natives plant their corn, having previously cleared the parched soil of weeds and the remains of last year's crop, and prepared it for sowing. The method of preparation is to dig a shallow trench with a rough native hoe,[1] piling the earth up to form a ridge alongside. As a rule millet is planted in the furrow, and guinea corn (*sorghum vulgare*), the staple food of the country, in the ridge. The former ripens rapidly and is usually harvested early in July; the guinea corn, which grows in some places to a height of ten feet and more, ripens more slowly, and is not as a rule ready for harvesting till November. After harvest, during the dry season, the natives are engaged in stacking their corn, and threshing what they require. Cotton is picked from December onwards: tobacco, onions, cassava, and sugar-cane are cultivated throughout the dry season in fields beside the streams, from which they are often irrigated by a bucket and well system, similar to that used in India and Egypt. It is during the dry season also that the mud walls of their towns and houses are repaired, grass cut and tied into bundles for thatching, and roofs mended. Advantage, in fact, is taken of the short spell of leisure from farming operations to put the home in order before the rainy season comes round again and agriculture once more claims all the time. This, too, is the great season for hunting, when the dry grass has been burnt down and the game takes refuge in well-known covers. Many a youth who is too poor to buy

[1] Ploughs are unknown, all field work being done by means of iron hoes of native manufacture.

a portion of the meat of a bullock which has been killed in the market and divided for sale amongst the butchers, takes down his bow and arrows and sets out in the faint starlight just before dawn, bringing back in the evening enough meat for the whole family and one or two neighbours as well.

Pagan tribes in every conceivable stage of civilisation inhabit the country on either side of the great Benue river, "the Mother of Waters," as its name denotes, which, rising in the hills of German Adamawa, flows westwards, and after entering Nigeria pursues its course through a deeply wooded valley for a distance of over 450 miles, till it unites with the Niger at a point some 340 miles from the sea. During the dry season the river becomes a slowly moving current, which wends its way in a channel through long stretches of sand, with a depth in places of no more than two or three feet. At this time it is navigable in its upper reaches only by native "dug-outs"—flat-bottomed canoes hollowed out of the trunks of trees. But with the advent of the rainy season the river begins to rise, till about September, at the height of the season, when the various tributaries are daily pouring their contributions into it, the water rises and fills the entire space between the banks, in many places nearly a mile apart, and for about six weeks steamers can make their way up stream for a distance of over 500 miles from the confluence. The Benue thus forms an immense highway, running from east to west throughout the southern portion of the Protectorate, navigable all the year round for canoes and barges of light draught, and at high water for steamers as well.

Several tributaries give access to the interior, and

during the high-water period the larger of these can be ascended for considerable distances by launches and steamers of light draught; the Gongola, for instance, which flows in from the north, is for some weeks navigable up to a distance of nearly 150 miles, giving access to the kingdom of Bornu and the province of Bauchi.

Numerous tribes inhabit the countries bordering on the Benue. The most important of them is that of the Munshis, who inhabit an extensive tract of country on either bank, and exhibit a higher state of civilisation than most of the other pagan tribes in this locality. They are divided into a number of clans, which indulge not infrequently in internecine warfare, and the whole tribe has a reputation for truculence and impatience of control. They are splendid agriculturists and spend much time on handicrafts as well, manufacturing chairs and stools, and displaying some art and much ingenuity in wood-carving. The Munshi has a reputation for courage and independence which has preserved his country to a great extent from Mahomedan slave raids. Most of the villages of this tribe are surrounded by a ditch, the earth of which is thrown up to form a rampart and topped with a stockade; for the main desire of the Munshi is to be let alone. They have little or no desire at present to trade, and for costume are more than satisfied with the simple and somewhat exiguous loin-cloth worn by both sexes.

Farther in the interior, in the hills that extend from west to east at a distance of about a hundred miles from the north bank of the river, pagan tribes of a much lower type are to be found. Many are cannibal, and in many no clothing whatever is worn by either sex. Here we begin to get an idea of what primitive man was like.

Absolute insecurity is the day-to-day reality, which of necessity dominates the actions and habits of the people. There is practically no cohesion, no organisation. Villages of little beehive-shaped mud or grass huts are perched on seemingly inaccessible heights, or cunningly hidden in a maze of dense tropical vegetation. At early dawn the men, carrying their bows and arrows—from which it is never safe for them to be parted—sally out to the fields at the foot of their fastnesses to cultivate their crops, whilst the women pick their way down to the springs to fill the earthenware waterpots which they carry on their heads. Towards sunset the men may be seen making their way back up the steep rocks to their homes on the summit, with their bows still slung over their shoulders, and carrying in their hands the hoes which form their sole implements of agriculture.

Each village is entirely self-supporting, for no trade of any sort is ever indulged in, unless it be in salt, a little of which is obtained from time to time by barter. They are almost invariably at war with a neighbouring tribe or village, the probable cause being that some of their women have been carried off. A tribe may unite to ward off an attack, or even to raid another community, but except at such times each village holds aloof from the other, and in the village itself there are usually several petty chiefs each with his following, sometimes consisting merely of his own household. The man with the most influence is not as a rule the nominal chief, but the witch doctor, whose power over the superstitious people is directly proportionate to his success in imposing upon their credulity. An unexpected calamity whose cause cannot be traced, or an epidemic of sickness, or a sudden death, will immediately be attributed to black magic, and suspicion will fall upon some unfortunate member of the community. A hasty conference will be held in the village meeting-place beside a big rock or under a shady tree, and the suspected man or woman if convicted will immediately be sold away into slavery. At the time when all the corn has been harvested and gathered in, and each household has packed away in its little mud granary the supply requisite for the following year, the surplus will be collected, and with it large supplies of native beer will be brewed. Then follow drinking-bouts and orgies, lasting often for several days at a time. Many heads will be broken, and knives and swords used, often with fatal results.

Probably nowhere in Africa—possibly nowhere in the world—can be found such a variety of tribes, or such diversity of languages. In one small area, covering not more than a few thousand square miles, it was recently estimated that between sixty and seventy different languages are being spoken by the various tribes. Allowing for the number which may be found on closer investigation to have a common origin, and to be rather dialects of a single tongue than separate languages, this gives an idea of the complexity of the task of administration in such a locality, and affords a proof of the habits of isolation and independence which separate the petty communities one from the other. It is rare to meet a native in such parts who knows his way beyond the next village. The outside world is utterly unknown to him. He is aware that it exists, but of those who inhabit it, or who they are or what they do, he is totally ignorant.

At certain places this network of independent pagan tribes has been penetrated by Mahomedans from the north, who at the beginning of last century made their way down as far as the Benue and established themselves in some cases as rulers over large provinces. The most important of these is Yola, where nearly a hundred years ago a Mahomedan Emir established himself, and carved out a large province extending over a wide tract of country on either side of the Benue, some 450 miles above its confluence with the Niger. This province, which to-day forms the extreme south-eastern corner of the Protectorate, affords an interesting example of what the traveller Barth, who visited it sixty years ago, calls "a Mahomedan Kingdom, engrafted on a mixed stock of pagan tribes."

The Mahomedan conqueror founded and established himself with his followers in the town of Yola, in a swampy plain about 3 miles to the south of the Benue, with which it is connected by an inlet. In former days the province extended far to the eastward and was named Adamawa after the Mahomedan conqueror Adama, who established it out of the ruins of several ancient pagan kingdoms. The greater part of Adamawa is now, however, in German territory, a large tract of country having been handed over by the Anglo-German Agreements of 1886 and 1893. The inhabitants of the town of Yola itself are mostly Mahomedans, and there is a large mosque close to the Emir's residence, but the outlying districts are almost entirely pagan. Adamawa was till recently, up to the time in fact when British and German influence were established, the great hunting-ground for slaves. Of it Barth wrote in 1851: "Slavery exists on an immense scale in this country; and there are many private individuals who have more than a thousand slaves. . . . I have been assured that Mahomed Lowal (the Emir) receives every year in tribute, besides horses and cattle, about 5000 slaves." Slaves, in fact, constituted the chief export of the country, though large quantities of ivory were also exported, there being numerous herds of elephants in the interior.

The conditions of the northern part of the Protectorate, away from the valleys of the great water-troughs, were totally different. Two great Mahomedan empires, Bornu and Sokoto, divided between them the broad plateau 800 miles in length, which lies between Lake Tchad and the Niger. These were the countries which Denham and Clapperton had explored in 1823-24, as already recorded. Their condition forms a striking contrast to that of the pagan tribes. In place of hidden huts, we find great walled cities containing a dense population; in place of the naked pagan, we find the cultivated follower of Islam, clothed in flowing robes; in place of the witch doctor, the grave and learned judge, well versed in Koranic law and jurisprudence; in place of superstition and pagan rites, mosques and schools; in place of ignorance, knowledge; in place of disintegration, cohesion.

Picture a tribal raid by the naked savages that inhabit the rocky fastnesses north of the Benue, and then turn to Barth's description of the Bornu army, setting out on an expedition—cavalcades of horsemen, each squadron under its officer, clad in gorgeous attire; the heavy cavalry wearing a casque very much like our knights of the Middle Age, but of lighter metal, and ornamented with gaudy feathers; the costume of the officers, a cloak of red or yellow, wrapped in a picturesque manner around the upper part of the body, exposing to view an inner garment of richly coloured silk.

The kingdom of Bornu at the time of the inauguration of the British Protectorate lay on the western border of Lake Tchad, and including its pagan dependencies extended over an area of nearly 30,000 square miles, with an estimated population of over a million. As it now exists it is the remains of a vast empire, which extended at one time in an easterly direction to the borders of Egypt, and northwards as far as the hinterland of Tripoli. A written chronicle of its history has been kept since the early part of the sixteenth century, previous to which there is nothing to rely on but oral tradition, though information is to be gleaned from the writings of Arab and Moorish historians considerably earlier. There is little doubt that the kings of Bornu originated from a Libyan tribe, that is to say, they were of Berber origin; and when we first hear of them about the beginning of the tenth century, they occupied the country of Kanem, east and north-east of Lake Tchad, and are described as of a red or light complexion, as we should have expected. A change of dynasty occurred about 1080 A.D., when Islam was first introduced from the direction of Egypt, and there followed a period during which the kingdom rose to great eminence and extended its borders far and wide, probably from the Niger to the Nile, and northwards across the desert to Fezzan. At this time Bornu was in close and constant communication with Egypt and with the countries on the Mediterranean coast. The whole history of Bornu from its earliest days up to the time of the British occupation is one of never-ceasing warfare. The same may indeed be said of any or every African tribe or nation, but Bornu was, by its central position, peculiarly exposed to attack on all sides, and periods of victory, when it pushed out its borders in all directions, alternated with periods of humiliating defeat, when it was driven back on its central position on the borders of Lake Tchad. Its importance and far-reaching fame as an empire may be judged from the fact that its name appears on a Portuguese map as early as 1489. It reached the highest pitch of its greatness about the middle of the sixteenth century and kept up frequent intercourse with Tripoli, from which it imported a large number of muskets and Arab horses; it was no doubt the presence of musketeers in his army that enabled the celebrated King Edris, who resigned during the latter years of that century, to subjugate the entire surrounding country in a series of successful campaigns.

After the death of this king the greatness of Bornu began to wane, and steadily declined, till at the beginning of the nineteenth century the then much-reduced empire found a difficulty in holding its own against the Fulah Empire of Sokoto, which was at that time rising on its western borders. At this juncture, when the once powerful kingdom was on the point of being brought under a foreign yoke, there arose a stranger—a nationalised Arab—who, in saving the last remains of the kingdom, founded a new dynasty. This remarkable man, named Alameen-ben-Mahomed-el-Kanemi, was born in Fezzan of Kanem parents, though on his father's side descended from a Moor. After visiting Egypt he came to Kanem, and soon earned for himself, by the extreme correctness of his life and the benevolence of his disposition, the respect and affection of the people. Conceiving the design of freeing Bornu from the invaders, he collected a following, and in a series of well-planned and courageously executed campaigns drove the Fulahs from the country. Raising the green flag, the standard of the Prophet, he refused all titles but that of "Servant of God," and proceeded to clear the whole country of the invaders, and to reward the faithful followers who had assisted him. The Sultan remained a figure-head, the whole of the real power resting in the hands of the Sheikh, who assumed, in fact, the position of a dictator.

Sheikh Mahomed-el-Kanemi died in 1835, leaving forty-three sons, of whom he named Omar, the eldest, as his successor. Meanwhile, the members of the old dynasty had still continued to be nominated to, and to hold, the titular office of Sultan, the entire power remaining, however, in the Sheikh's hands. Some ten years after Omar's accession, the then Sultan determined to make an attempt to oust the Sheikh, and to possess himself of the power of which the sultans had been, except in name, deprived so long. Allying himself with a neighbouring chief, and taking advantage of the absence of part of the Bornu army on a distant expedition, he raised the standard of revolt, but was defeated and slain. This event put a final end to the sultanate of Bornu, and the Sheikh henceforward assumed the office as well as the power, though he and his descendants retained the title of Sheikh or Shehu, which the ruler of Bornu holds to this day.

Besides the Bornuese themselves and the various subject pagan tribes, there are scattered throughout

Bornu large numbers of Shuwa Arabs, speaking almost pure Egyptian Arabic, and leading a more or less nomadic life. They are great breeders of cattle, and bear a strong resemblance both in features and habits to some of our gipsy tribes. They were said, in Denham's time, to be able to put into the field 15,000 warriors, mostly mounted—a useful addition to the Bornuese army.

Arabs and Tripolitan merchants were to be found in Kuka, the capital of Bornu,—a large walled town situated some miles to the west of Lake Tchad before the date of British occupation—and there were always a number of pious Moslems who had performed the pilgrimage to Mecca. There were many learned men who could read and write Arabic with ease, and possessed books and manuscripts in that language.

Both Denham in 1824 and Barth in 1855 concluded with the rulers of Bornu on behalf of Great Britain a treaty of a vague description, but after Barth's mission Bornu was not again visited by a European till the Royal Niger Company in 1890 despatched one of its officials to the country with a view to concluding a treaty with the Sheikh. He was well received by the Sultan, who was, however, prevented from concluding a political treaty with the Company, owing to the strong influence of some thousands of Senussi Arabs, who flocked into Kuka. Hence, when the British Protectorate of Northern Nigeria was formed, Bornu, although included in the Protectorate by virtue of the various international Agreements which had been made, did not stand in any treaty relation to Great Britain.

West of Bornu lie the Hausa States, stretching right away to the Niger and beyond it. The origin of the Hausa race lies in obscurity. They themselves have a tradition that their forefathers came originally from Bagdad; but most Islamised African tribes claim to come from the East, on account of the prestige which they imagine such claim to confer. It is practically certain that the Hausas are not indigenous to the region in which we find them now, but are immigrants of comparatively recent date. Their language shows some relationship with both the Berber and Coptic, and, whatever its origin may be, shares with Arabic and Swahili the honour of being one of the three most important tongues spoken throughout the continent of Africa. Some of their old pagan rites and beliefs handed down from bygone generations bear a remarkable resemblance to the customs of the Phoenicians. The Hausas also resemble the latter in another particular, for they are, like them, born traders, and travel far and wide over Africa on trading expeditions. Though black they have not the thick lips nor the flat noses of the typical negro, still less have they the straight features of the Arabs. Everything points to their being the result of a mixture of several races, and the probability is that their origin is to be found in a blending of immigrants from the East with an aboriginal negro race, the greater part of whom were driven by the invaders south into the hilly fastnesses north of the Benue, or still farther into the equatorial forests. It will be remembered that, in the story related by Herodotus, the Nasamone youths after crossing the Great Desert found "black men of diminutive stature." If the story be true, it would seem to point to the fact that the strip of land bordering the desert was at that time peopled by a race totally unlike the tall sturdy races which inhabit it to-day; and the description of the "diminutive black men" recalls at once the accounts given by explorers in recent times of the pigmy races found in the forests of the Congo region. We know that from the earliest times waves of immigration have rolled from Central and Western Asia in to Europe, sweeping as far as Egypt and the shores of North Africa. It is unlikely that these great disturbances of population had no effect on the rest of the African continent and exercised no pressure westwards from the direction of Egypt and Abyssinia, even if the Great Desert proved an effective barrier to any movement southwards. We know that Islam was introduced into the districts bordering on Lake Tchad from the direction of Egypt in the eleventh century, and there is no reason why, during the preceding centuries, there should not have been large movements of population along the same route. Again, there may have been immigration from the Mediterranean littoral southwards to the fertile lands of Equatorial Africa, in spite of the immense barrier set up by the "Sea of Sahara." Herodotus speaks of a black people in the Atlas Mountains and the oases of the Sahara who were hunted by the Garamantes or Berbers in scythed chariots. The Carthaginians were well acquainted with the products of tropical Africa, and exchanged the famous purple cloth, the blue bugles, and the speckled beads of their Tyrian colonists for slaves, gold-dust, and ivory, the Berbers acting as middlemen. The latter would have familiarised the Phoenician colonies on the Mediterranean with accounts of the fertile well-watered lands which lay to the south of the desert barrier. "There is hardly anything which has been said of Phoenicia," writes a well-known authority in this connection,[1] "which could not be applicable in the present day to the cities of Hausaland." The same writer points out that the religion which was in existence in these parts before the inhabitants were converted to Islam was an enlightened paganism which bears many resemblances to what we know of the worship of Astarte, Jupiter Ammon, and Isis, and is wholly different from the fetishism of the coast tribes. It may be that the Hausa race resulted from immigrations both from the north, that is to say from the Mediterranean shores, and from the east, or Egypt: that immigrants came from time to time from both directions and, intermarrying with the women of the aborigines and driving the men farther south, formed in course of time a mixed race, just as the English race to-day is composed of various elements—Danes, Jutes, Saxons, Celts, Normans, and others. A suggestion has recently been made that the Hausa race resulted from an immigration of mixed Abyssinians, Copts, and Arabs, which possibly took place into what is now Hausaland from the ancient city of Meroë, which was situated on the Nile south of the Nubian Desert.[2]

That some such immigration took place is far from unlikely, but all attempts at discovering the early ancestry of the Hausas must, in the absence of tangible clues, remain at present pure conjecture. Through the mist of the past we can only dimly perceive fleeting pictures of vast movements of tribes and nations, driven hither and thither by war and the pressure of population, seeking new lands, with

[1] Lady Lugard: *A Tropical Dependency*.

[2] It will perhaps be remembered that some authorities hold that Meroë was an older civilisation than that of Egypt itself, and that Egypt, in fact, derived its civilisation from it.

occasional glimpses of commerce connecting for a time countries separated by immense distances. When history begins to shed a fitful light on the scene, we still find no repose: tribes roll one upon another like the waves of the sea, and these human currents intermingle to form fresh combinations, the characteristics of whose various elements are barely discernible.

The Fulanis, known also as Fellata, Fulahs, Pulbe, Puls, and by various synonyms, are unquestionably the most remarkable and interesting of all the tribes and nations of Equatorial Africa. Their origin is as obscure as that of the Hausas, but they differ fundamentally from the latter in almost every particular. The true Fulani is not negroid. His complexion is fair, his features regular, his hair long and straight. He speaks a language which resembles no other African tongue, but which has been stated by more than one authority to resemble that spoken by gipsies, and to be akin to the Indo-Germanic stock. He is nomadic, and is primarily a cattle-owner, driving his herds from pasture to pasture. It is partly for this reason that the suggestion has been made that the origin of the Fulani is the same as that of the Hyksos or Shepherd Kings, who crossed from Arabia and invaded Egypt about 2000 years before our era, and were expelled some 500 years subsequently. However this may be, it is generally believed that the Fulani came from the East, possibly from India, possibly from Arabia, but curiously enough he is first known in Africa in the extreme west, not far from the shores of the Atlantic, and in historical times his movements have been from west to east. Fulanis [1] have always kept aloof

[1] The root of the word, "Ful," signifies red or ruddy, and denotes the complexion of the race.

from other races, and have looked upon themselves as a "white race," infinitely superior to the negro. Their pride of race has been justified, for, in practically all the principal kingdoms of Equatorial Africa, a Fulani has at one time or another played a leading part, and the race has always produced scholars and statesmen from amongst its members.

There are many authorities who attribute the founding of the earliest known West African empire, that of Ghanata in the neighbourhood of the valleys of the Gambia and Senegal, to a race in which Fulani blood predominated. The founding of this empire takes us back to approximately the third century of our era. Other authorities take us back still farther and identify the Fulanis with the Leucaethiopes mentioned in the celebrated *Periplus* of the Carthaginian general and explorer, Hanno, who conducted a navigating expedition round the coasts of Africa, and found these people in the neighbourhood of the Gambia. These light-complexioned Africans of whom Hanno wrote on his return to Carthage could not have been Berbers, still less Arabs, and it is by no means impossible that the theory which identifies them with the Fulanis is correct. If the Fulanis came originally from India or the East, it is certainly strange that they should first be found in the extreme west of the African continent; but the only other explanation of the presence of a white race close to the Atlantic shores of Africa—putting aside the improbable theory that they were a white indigenous race—is that they were a remnant from the submerged continent of Atlantis, which is generally considered to be a myth, and need not therefore be discussed. We pass therefore from these fascinating but dangerous regions of conjecture to the more solid realms of history, which take us back to a comparatively recent period, less than a thousand years ago, when Fulanis were undoubtedly settled in the country about the sources of the Niger. When Arab influence spread along the northern shores of Africa and thence pushed its way across the desert, carrying with it the green flag of the Prophet, the Fulani race was one of the first to accept the new religion, and not content with adopting it amongst themselves they proceeded to disseminate it far and wide throughout Equatorial Africa. Thus we find Fulanis preaching the doctrines of Islam in Bornu and the Hausa States as early as the beginning of the thirteenth century. It is evident from the records of history that there must have been from the earliest times considerable differences in social status amongst the members of the tribe, a fact always indicative of an advanced state of civilisation. There was the uneducated nomadic class, wandering from place to place with its flocks and herds, holding itself strictly aloof from other races and thus preserving to the fullest extent its racial features and characteristics. This class remains to the present day nomadic, exclusive, uneducated, speaking its own tongue, and in many cases retaining its old pagan beliefs. It is to these "Cattle Fulani," as they are termed nowadays, that we must turn if we wish to see the light complexion, the long and pointed noses, and the regular features, which were the obvious characteristics of the race before it intermarried with the negro and negroid peoples of Africa. The intelligence and the administrative capacity which are equally characteristic of the race must be sought in the Fulanis of the aristocratic class, who have risen far above the herdsmen, and in so doing have mingled their blood with the ruling families of negroid tribes, and while retaining their intellectual qualities, have lost many of their distinctive physical traits, and adopted to a great extent the customs and even the language of those with whom they have coalesced.

From the fifteenth century onwards we constantly hear of Fulanis occupying positions of eminence in the African empires of that period, besides forming kingdoms of their own. The members of the aristocratic class seem always to have been characterised by an independence of character and an intellectual ability which marked them out for rule, while the nomadic element showed the same spirit of independence which they preserved in their wandering life, paying a cattle tax, but owning no allegiance to the Chiefs in whose territories they pastured their herds.

Towards the end of the eighteenth century we find Fulanis scattered throughout the Hausa States, and the educated classes occupying positions chiefly as teachers and priests. Many of these had performed the long and arduous pilgrimage to Mecca, and had in that cosmopolitan centre mingled freely with co-religionists from every quarter of the globe, and imbibed some of the learning and ideals of the civilised world. Amongst the Fulani pilgrims was one Othman dan Fodio, into whose spirit entered at the holy shrine a burning zeal for reform; he returned to his home in Hausaland with his soul on fire to purify the faith which, he realised, existed there to a large extent in a debased form, being often little more than a veneer over pagan beliefs and customs. On his arrival from Mecca he wrote letters to the rulers of Timbuktu, of Bornu, and of the Hausa States, commanding them in the name of the Prophet to put down the gross abuses that existed; to discard the wearing of ornaments and fine apparel; to enforce rigorously the laws of the Koran; to abolish amongst their subjects the drinking of intoxicating liquors; and to conform to the usages of Islam. It was not long before he was surrounded by ardent disciples whom his doctrines attracted in large numbers, till at last, in 1802, the pagan king of the Hausa state of Gober, in which Othman had settled, became alarmed at the danger which he foresaw, and summoning the reformer to his presence, administered a severe public reprimand. This acted as a spark to the inflammable material which is always created by religious enthusiasm, and the infuriated reformers immediately declared Othman a sheikh, and raised the standard of revolt. At first they met with little success, but before long large bodies of zealous adherents flocked to Sheikh Othman's banner, a *jehad* or Holy War was declared and was carried into every quarter of the Hausa States. The movement has been always described in history as a Fulani conquest, sometimes as an invasion. It was in no sense the latter, and can hardly be called the former, for the Fulanis formed but a small part of the conquering forces, though in nearly every case they provided the leadership. Priests who had for many years been settled in the various Hausa States, preaching the doctrines of Islam, and attracting to themselves the most intelligent and ardent elements of the Hausa race, flocked to Sheikh Othman's camp and received from him a flag wherewith to return to their districts and rouse their followers to the Holy War. There is no doubt that for some time past Hausaland had been in a state of transition from paganism to Mahomedanism. Islam had indeed been introduced many centuries before, and Katsina had a Mahomedan king in the seventeenth century, while the neighbouring state of Bornu had been ruled by Moslems since the eleventh century. The rivalry between Islam and paganism had continued throughout the centuries, victory continually inclining towards the more enlightened faith.

Othman dan Fodio, after his success in stirring up a jehad, founded and established himself in the town of Sokoto, handing over the active military and administrative duties to his brother Abd Allahi and his son the celebrated Mahomed Bello. As the rulers of the various states were defeated and expelled, and nominees of Othman's assumed their offices, the empire thus formed was divided into two portions: the westernmost, which stretched down the Niger as far as its confluence with the Benue and included the provinces of Nupe and Illorin, was entrusted to Abd Allahi, who established himself at Gando; the eastern and more important states, including Katsina, Kano, Zaria, Bauchi, and others, were handed over to Bello, with headquarters at Sokoto. Thus it came about that the whole of the northern part of the Protectorate of Northern Nigeria was found divided between the two great Mahomedan empires of Bornu and Sokoto; for Gando, with its subordinate states of Nupe and Illorin on the east and west banks of the Middle Niger, though nominally independent of Sokoto, became eventually in practice dependent on it.[1]

These important events have been lightly sketched,

[1] There was also the small pagan state of Borgu—or as much of it as had been saved from the French—on the west bank of the Niger, independent of Sokoto. I omit mentioning it in order to save confusion.

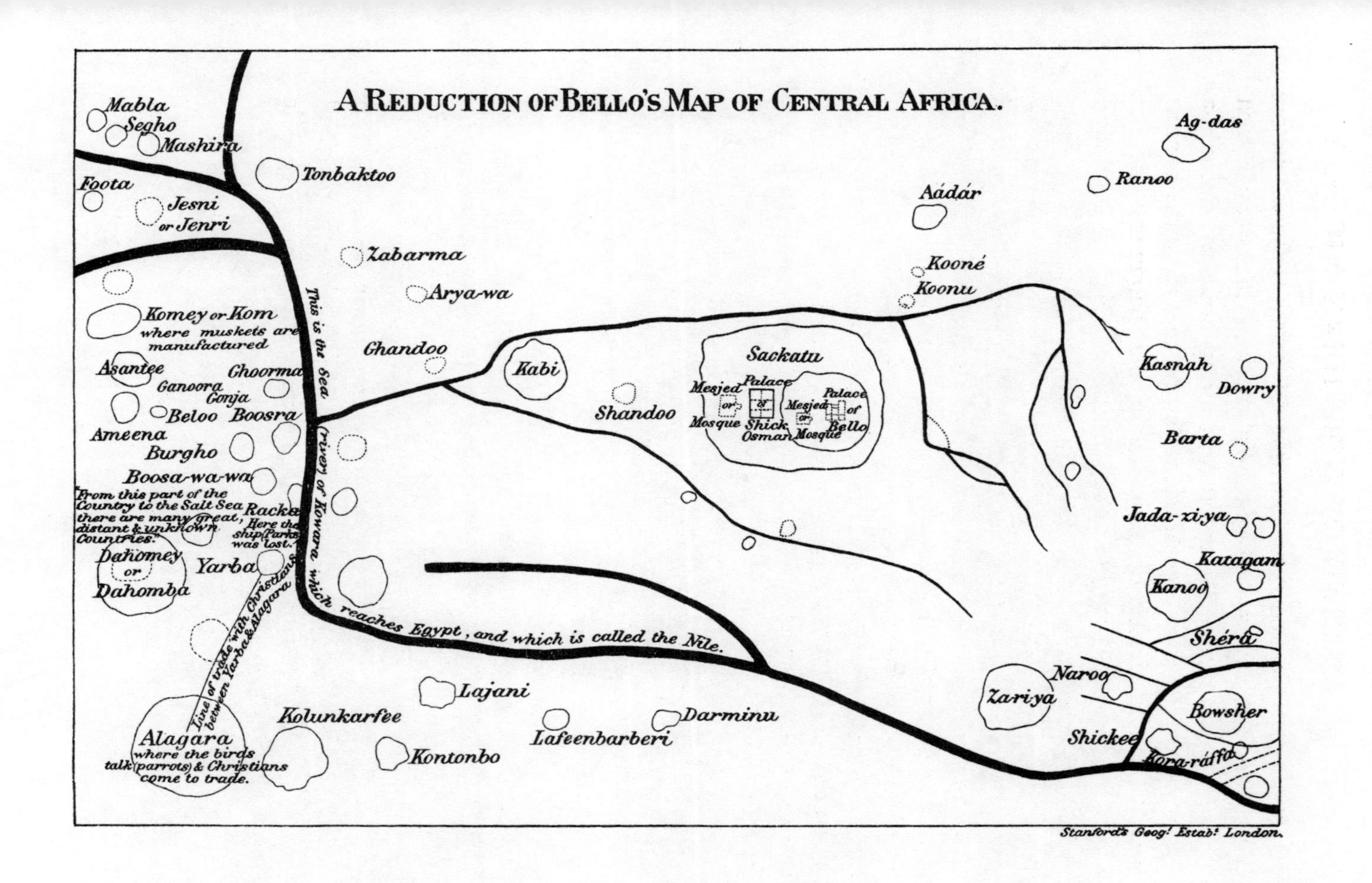
A Reduction of Bello's Map of Central Africa.
Mabla
Segho
Mashira
Foota
Tonbaktoo
Jesni or Jenri
Zabarma
Arya-wa
This is the Sea (river) of Kowara which reaches Egypt, and which is called the Nile.
Komey or Kom where muskets are manufactured
Ghandoo
Asantee
Ghoorma
Ganoora
Gonja
Beloo
Boosra
Ameena
Burgho
Boosa-wa-wa
"From this part of the Country to the Salt Sea there are many great, distant & unknown Countries."
Racka
Here the ship (Parks) was lost.
Dahomey or Dahomba
Yarba
Line of trade with Christians between Yarba & Alagara
Alagara where the birds talk (parrots) & Christians come to trade.
Kolunkarfee
Kontonbo
Lajani
Lafeenbarberi
Darminu
Kabi
Shandoo
Sackatu
Mesjed or Mosque
Palace of Shick Osman
Mesjed or Mosque
Palace of Bello
Aádár
Kooné
Koonu
Ag-das
Ranoo
Kasnah
Dowry
Barta
Jada-xi-ya
Katagam
Kanoo
Shéra
Naroo
Zari-ya
Bowsher
Shickee
Kora-ráffa
Stanford's Geog! Estab! London.

all detail being avoided, because it is only necessary for our purpose to get a general view of the state of affairs that existed in these regions at the moment when British influence was established over them. The religious upheaval set in motion in the early years of the nineteenth century by Sheikh Othman dan Fodio ended, as has been shown, in the welding together of a number of independent Hausa States under Fulani leadership. Yet each state retained for practical purposes its virtual independence, and the various Fulani Mallams[1] became the founders of dynasties, each in his own state. Each looked to the Sultan of Sokoto as his spiritual chief, and acknowledged his temporal power to a limited extent, but as time went on the descendants of the Mallams began to look upon themselves, and be looked on by the people, as hereditary rulers succeeding by right to the throne of their fathers. This was the condition of the Sokoto Empire when the British Protectorate was proclaimed.

[1] A "Mallam" is a priest or educated man, religion and education being almost synonymous terms in semi-civilised Mahomedan communities.

CHAPTER IV

FIRST YEARS OF THE ADMINISTRATION, 1900-1901

"Already the desire of exchanging whatever their country produces for the manufactures of the more enlightened natives of the North exists in no small degree amongst the natives : a taste for luxury and a desire of imitating such strangers as visit them, are very observable : and the man of rank is ever distinguished by some part of his dress being of foreign materials, though sometimes of the most trifling kind. It is true that these propensities are not yet fully developed : but they exist, and give unequivocal proof of a tendency to civilisation, and the desire of cultivating an intercourse with foreigners."—DENHAM, vol. ii. p. 171.

THE decision of the Government to revoke the charter of the Royal Niger Company, and to undertake the administration of the territories which had been acquired, necessitated a careful and detailed inquiry into the expenditure which this would entail, and the staff and administrative machinery which would be required.

This resulted in much correspondence between the Foreign Office, the Treasury, the Colonial Office, and the Council of the Chartered Company, and already in July 1898 a Committee had been appointed, consisting of representatives of all these, to discuss and report on the various questions under consideration. These questions concerned three separate but contiguous Administrations, namely :—

1. The Colony and Protectorate of Lagos, under the Colonial Office.

2. The Niger Coast Protectorate, under the Foreign Office.
3. The Niger Territories, under the Royal Niger Company.

The local conditions of these three countries were so entirely dissimilar that it was considered inexpedient to make any immediate attempt to combine them under one administration. Their eventual amalgamation, when all the unexplored and undeveloped regions had been brought under control, was, however, the aim consistently kept in view, and it was recognised that their administration as separate units was of a purely temporary nature.

It was decided that Lagos Colony and Protectorate[1] should remain as it was, under a Governor responsible to the Secretary of State for the Colonies. The Niger Coast Protectorate was to be extended so as to include the portion of the territories of the Royal Niger Company which lay between a point on the Niger some 280 miles from its mouth, named Idah, and the coast. The new Protectorate thus formed was constituted under an Order in Council dated the 27th of December 1899, and named the "Protectorate of Southern Nigeria," the administration being transferred from the Foreign to the Colonial Office. The remainder of the territories of the Royal Niger Company were, by an Order in Council of the same date, constituted the "Protectorate of Northern Nigeria," likewise under the Colonial Office.

The revenues of the Coast possessions were derived from Customs duties on exports and imports,

[1] By an Order in Council issued at the end of 1899, the Protectorate of Lagos was extended to the boundaries of Northern, and the Protectorate then known as Southern Nigeria.

and the revenue for administrative purposes of the Royal Niger Company had, it will be remembered, been derived from the same source.

Under the new arrangement the Protectorate of Northern Nigeria would have no coast line, and all goods imported into it from overseas would necessarily pass first through either Lagos or Southern Nigeria, and pay Customs duties at their ports. The recommendation of the Committee was, therefore, that the tariffs of Lagos and Southern Nigeria should be assimilated and brought into force along the whole coast; that goods on which duty had been paid in either Protectorate should be free to pass into the other or into Northern Nigeria[1]; and that, since it would be impossible to determine precisely what proportion of the Customs revenue was derived from the duties on goods for consumption in Northern Nigeria, the Customs receipts should be allotted in such proportions as the Secretary of State should from time to time direct.

The Committee were of opinion that it would not be prudent for the present to impose any form of direct taxation on the natives, but thought that a village tax in some form or other might be gradually imposed in the future. It was recognised that some sort of compensation, which could most appropriately be derived from a scheme of internal taxation, would be necessary for Chiefs who, owing to British intervention, had been or would be deprived of their means of livelihood, of which the principal one was slave-raiding.

The next step was to form an estimate of the staff

[1] Except trade spirits, the importation of which into Northern Nigeria was absolutely prohibited.

that would be required to set up an efficient administration in the new Protectorate, and of the funds necessary to meet all the expenses.

Early in 1899, therefore, Colonel Lugard, who—as Commandant of the West African Frontier Force which he had raised in March 1898—was fully conversant with local conditions in the Niger Company's territories, was instructed to prepare estimates for a civil establishment to administer the proposed Protectorate. A large number of Departments, Political, Secretariat, Treasury, Judicial, Police and Prisons, Medical, Marine, Public Works, Postal, Transport, etc., would be required, and for each of these an estimate had to be framed, setting forth the numbers of staff, the salaries of each individual, and all necessary expenses. The task was immediately taken in hand by Colonel Lugard, and an estimate was presently forwarded by him to the Colonial Office. Every item was carefully checked, and every expense eliminated except those shown to be absolutely necessary. After many revisions, the final estimate was found to reach the total of £86,000.[1] Below this figure it was absolutely impossible to form any estimate which would allow of adequate machinery for the administration of the contemplated Protectorate, and it was accepted by the Treasury, together with a further

[1] I use round numbers. The actual sum was £85,938, distributed as follows:—

	£	s.	d.		£	s.	d.
High Commissioner's Office . .	£4,860	10	0	Judicial . . .	£2,482	10	0
Political . .	9,429	5	0	Police and Prisons .	2,531	5	0
Stipends to Chiefs .	3,350	0	0	Medical . .	10,289	5	0
Secretariat . .	2,239	15	0	Marine . . .	18,236	0	0
Treasury . .	3,604	15	0	Workshops . .	2,585	0	0
Postal . . .	1,574	5	0	Store and Issue .	3,880	0	0
Telegraphs . .	6,603	0	0	Public Works .	8,763	0	0
Printing . .	520	0	0	Miscellaneous .	4,360	0	0
				TOTAL	£85,938	15	0

sum of £50,000 required for the purchase of river steamers and of buildings to be sent out and erected for the use of the civil staff. These two sums, therefore, amounting to £136,000, represented the total which it was estimated would be required to defray the cost of administration and expenditure in the new Protectorate during its first year of existence, exclusive of the military force, which was to be maintained as before by a special Parliamentary grant.[1] To meet it Parliament voted a sum of £75,000, the balance to be made up by a grant from the Protectorate of Southern Nigeria, representing the share of the Customs duties which the Secretary of State considered due to the Northern Protectorate. In this manner the funds necessary for the administration of the Protectorate during the first year were assured, and it remained to select the staff arranged for in the Estimates. The choice of the Government for the arduous and difficult post of first High Commissioner fell on Colonel Lugard, who had held the post of Commissioner in addition to his duties as Commandant of the W.A.F.F. since the beginning of 1898, and who had already in Uganda and elsewhere made his mark as an administrator. To assist him Government secured the services, as Deputy High Commissioner, of Mr. William Wallace, C.M.G., who had been for many years in the employ of the Royal Niger Company, latterly as Agent-General, in which capacity he had gained an unrivalled experience of the natives and of local conditions.

A Political Department was formed, consisting of officials of various grades, their number being fixed

[1] This amounted to £200,000, so that the estimated expenditure of the Protectorate during its first year, including both military and civil, was £336,000.

in the first Estimates at nine. From the outset it was decided that the method of administration should be one of indirect rule through the native Chiefs themselves, and to accentuate this policy the newly-appointed political officers were named "Residents" instead of "Commissioners," a term which was in general use in other Colonies and Protectorates, where more direct methods of administration were employed.

A Secretariat was formed, consisting of a Secretary to the Administration with three assistants, charged with the duty of attending to all routine correspondence of the Protectorate.

The accounts were dealt with by a Treasury Department, consisting of a Treasurer with four assistants and six native clerks. With this was subsequently incorporated the Accounts Branch of the West African Frontier Force, which had been in existence since the formation of that Force, and numbered five accountants.

Communication with the coast depended solely on the river, and a Marine Department—consisting of a Superintendent, two assistants, three European Masters and three European Engineers, besides a large native staff—was charged with the important duty of maintaining the vessels to be used for this purpose. The Government had purchased from the Royal Niger Company a nucleus fleet consisting of one stern-wheel steamer, five launches, two pinnaces, and two hulks,—the stern-wheel steamer being the only one of these capable of carrying cargo. The Company had not been anxious to part with these vessels, but they were of absolutely vital importance to the Government, since the river was the artery on which the very life and existence of the new Protectorate depended, and its navigation was the sole means of importing material and carrying on postal and other services. Orders for two more stern-wheel steamers were issued as soon as the Protectorate came into existence, but they were not actually placed on the river till the following year.

A staff of eight doctors, five lady nurses, and ten male nurses and dressers formed the Medical Department, which was subsequently increased by the transfer to it of the medical officers of the West African Frontier Force, the whole becoming a branch of the General West African Medical Service.

A Chief Justice was appointed to preside over the Supreme Court, and an Attorney-General to act as legal adviser to the High Commissioner.

An Inspector, with an assistant, was placed in charge of the small force of civil police, and made responsible for all matters connected with the gaols, and the custody of civil prisoners and convicts.

A Post-master, with native staff, controlled the Postal Department, which was at first supervised by the Treasury, as was also another Department, named the Store and Issue, which consisted of a Store-keeper, with five assistants. This latter Department was responsible for the receipt, disposal, and storage of all civil and military stores, and was charged with the duty of tracing the responsibility for any losses that might occur.

A Director of Public Works was appointed with an assistant and a staff of executive engineers and European and native artificers. To this Department was subsequently entrusted the construction of telegraphs, for which a staff of linesmen and operators was employed.

Finally, Government workshops and a Government printing office were organised, each with its staff carefully detailed and estimated for.

Nor did the provision for all these many Departments complete the complicated task of preparing the Estimates for the new Protectorate. A number of minor and incidental expenses of a miscellaneous description were budgeted for, such as a provision for language gratuities to encourage civil officers to study the native languages: a small sum for recreation facilities, to improve the health of the officials by means of exercise, and to decrease the monotony and consequent depression which arises in such a climate. A sum was also placed on the Estimates to meet the expense of subsidies to be paid to native Chiefs, as it was considered right that the subsidies arranged by treaty and paid annually by the Royal Niger Company to the various Chiefs should be continued for the present at least.

One of the greatest expenses connected with administration by European races of tropical African countries is the frequency with which, for climatic reasons, officials have to be sent home on leave. Medical authorities maintain that a European should be sent home on the expiration of a year's service in West Africa, and since the journey to England from Nigeria occupies at least a month, and four months' leave in England is considered the minimum period necessary to regain health after a year's service in West Africa, it follows that an allowance must be made for the absence of every official from his post for six months out of each year and a half, or a third of his time. In other words, a staff must be provided 50 per cent in excess of the number actually required to be at work in West Africa, in order to allow of one-third being absent from the country on leave. In the original Estimates the total civil staff for all Departments amounted to eighty-five Europeans, of whom it might be counted that, under normal conditions, fifty-seven would at any given moment be serving in West Africa, while the remaining twenty-eight were absent on leave. Free passages to and from England were granted, and this in itself added very greatly to the expense of administration. The leave question also made it practically impossible to organise any Department with less than two Europeans, since each European must spend a portion of his time absent from the country and from his post, and it would be necessary for some one to act for him during his absence. When the constant coming and going from home of officials in West Africa is realised, and the frequency of sickness and invaliding, some idea may be formed of the extraordinary difficulty that lies in the administering of the country.

It was finally arranged that the transfer from the Niger Company to the Crown should take place on the last day of December 1899, and the Protectorate come into being on the 1st of January 1900. Colonel Lugard, therefore, arriving in Northern Nigeria at the end of December, took over the Administration from the Royal Niger Company. On the 1st of January 1900 the Union Flag was hoisted at Lokoja in place of the Company's, in the presence of a parade of all arms, and attended by all civilians. The date corresponded with a very critical period at the commencement of the South African War, and to this fact is due the comparatively small attention which was paid in England to the addition to the Empire of territories in tropical Africa covering more than 300,000 square miles, and entailing heavy responsibilities.

The first task which presented itself to the new High Commissioner was the pacification of the country, the prohibition of inter-tribal wars and slave-raiding, and the dispersal of armed forces; the next, the securing of the goodwill of the Chiefs and people, and the establishment of an efficient civil administration, combined with the strengthening of such as already existed in the native states themselves.

The means were at hand to deal with the first of these requirements, for an efficient military force was already in being. This was the West African Frontier Force, raised nearly three years before, as has already been related, by Sir Frederick Lugard himself. The first act of the High Commissioner was to take over the Niger Company Constabulary, and after calling for volunteers required for Southern Nigeria and the Gold Coast, to incorporate the remainder in the West African Frontier Force, thus bringing it up to strength. Fifty of the number were also selected and detailed for the work of civil police. The redistribution of the garrisons throughout the Protectorate—such of it, that is to say, as was effectively occupied—was arranged, and steps were taken to prevent the importation of alcoholic spirits into the Protectorate by the establishment of a cordon of military posts along the southern frontier to the west of the Niger. At the very outset, however, the High Commissioner made it clear that he had no intention whatever of introducing a policy of mere military occupation, or of administration under martial law. On the contrary, his policy was to set up at the earliest possible moment a civil administration, with civil police to preserve order. "In my view," he wrote in his first Annual Report on the new Protectorate, "civil police, under efficient control, backed, of course, by force in the background (as, in fact, it is in every country, however civilised), should, as soon as possible, supersede military occupation, setting free the troops for their proper work, viz. the breaking down of organised resistance and the garrisoning of central towns, where their discipline and efficiency can be maintained."

This was the keynote to the policy pursued from the very first days of the new Administration. The country was to be rescued from the state of anarchy, inter-tribal warfare, and perpetual slave-raiding in which it had been engaged for so many centuries, not by a series of military expeditions, but by the creation of an efficient staff of administrative officials to get into close touch with the people, and help them to govern themselves on their own lines, so far as these were compatible with modern ideas of justice and liberty. "Capable officers can do much more by getting in touch with the people," wrote Sir F. Lugard, "than can be effected by a series of punitive expeditions and bloodshed."

Of such political officers, however, the number was at the outset wholly inadequate for the work to be done. There were, in fact, but nine,[1] and although the majority of these had been some years in the country and were well acquainted with its conditions, they were too few to administer the entire Protectorate.

[1] These were Mr. (afterwards Sir) William Wallace, C.M.G., Mr. Hewby, C.M.G., both formerly in the service of the Royal Niger Company; Major J. A. Burdon, late Commandant of the Niger Company Constabulary; the Hon. D. Carnegie, all appointed in January; and five more appointed during the course of the year.

They were placed at important centres on the Niger and Benue rivers, until such time as the arrival of more political officers from England might enable the High Commissioner to divide the Protectorate into provinces, each with its civil administrative staff.

Apart, however, from the paucity of staff, there was another circumstance which prevented the High Commissioner from at once setting up a civil Administration in the districts other than the actual banks of the river, and which called for immediate action. This was the condition of the caravan roads from the interior. West Africa knows not the use of wheels. From time immemorial commerce has followed mere tracks or paths, and trade goods have been transported either on the heads of human beings or on the backs of animals—the camel, in the desert and its neighbourhood; the horse, the mule, the pack-ox, and the donkey elsewhere. The trade routes have always been well defined. From the Hausa States, year by year, caravans had brought down to the coast large supplies of their produce, following beaten tracks. Hausa traders, banded together for mutual protection under a chosen leader, had started at the beginning of each dry season from the great emporium of Kano and its neighbourhood, driving before them their herds of cattle and live stock, and their pack-bullocks, ponies and donkeys laden with salt or natron from the interior, leather goods and cotton fabrics; and behind these followed a long file of slaves or sturdy freemen carrying immense loads of the same goods, the women of the party balancing on their heads cooking utensils and food, neatly tied up with nets of string. Each trader was armed with spear and knife, usually with bow and arrows as well, and regular advance and rearguards were formed by each caravan. Each night a halt was made near some stream, rough shelters of grass or leaves constructed in a clearing, and guards set; while the men collected firewood and lit fires, the women untied their loads and threshed and ground the corn, and as darkness fell the evening meal was prepared and eaten. In the Mahomedan states the roads were fairly safe, and regular camping-grounds were set aside for the caravans close to the walls of the large towns, fees being exacted by the Emirs and Chiefs.

In the pagan belts, however, through which the caravans were obliged to pass, they were liable to constant attacks from the pagan tribes, which in many cases looked to the looting of a caravan as the normal method of procuring their annual supply of salt, and considered it a just retaliation for the slave-raiding to which they were subjected by the Mahomedan Chiefs. Two of the latter, whose territories lay on either side of the main caravan route from Kano to the Niger, had been particularly active in raiding the pagan tribes which inhabited the country through which this route passed. They were the Emir of Bida and the Emir of Kontagora. The former had been deposed by the Royal Niger Company in 1897, as already related, but had returned after the withdrawal of the British force, ousted the Emir installed by Sir George Goldie, and begun slave-raiding and devastating the country with increased vigour. These two Emirs had hampered trade, not only by their raids, but by exacting excessive tolls from the caravans which traversed their territories. It was absolutely necessary to bring them to book, and to take steps to introduce law and order permanently into their provinces, and to safeguard the trade routes which passed through them. This could best be achieved by placing a permanent garrison in some central position on or near the main caravan route, and Sir Frederick Lugard determined to select for his administrative headquarters some suitable site which would satisfy this condition.

It was further of importance that the new headquarters should be removed some distance from the unhealthy valleys of the Niger and Benue. A tributary of the Niger, the Kaduna, rising in the highlands of Bauchi and falling into the Niger about 120 miles north of the confluence of the latter with the Benue, appeared to offer the best means of communication with the interior. The pagans in this vicinity had the previous year sent representatives to the Niger Company asking for protection, and the High Commissioner determined to send patrols to survey and report on the country lying on either side of this river. In May 1900, therefore, a strong patrol of the West African Frontier Force was directed to proceed up the Kaduna in order to survey the country and discover if there were any site on or near its course suitable for the administrative headquarters of the Protectorate. Two smaller patrols were at the same time despatched to follow up the course of two other rivers, with instructions to meet the larger patrol at a given point on the upper Kaduna. These patrols were instructed to avoid all hostilities, and to make every effort to win the confidence of the people whose territories they traversed. The orders of the High Commissioner were carried out with satisfactory results, the patrols uniting at the point indicated, and they returned in August with the topographical and other information which they had collected. One of the small patrols was attacked by a pagan tribe under the impression that it was a caravan, thus demonstrating in a very practical manner the truth of the reports as to the state of affairs on the trade routes.

The Kaduna was found to be navigable for a distance of about eighty miles, after which the channel was obstructed by rocks and rapids, which made navigation impossible. At the highest navigable point was a town called Wushishi, under the slave-raiding Emir of Kontagora, who had built and was in the habit of using it as a war camp or an advanced post from which he conducted raids into a large pagan tribe which lay to the east. A company of the West African Frontier Force was left here as a garrison, and occupied a defensible position on a knoll overlooking the town.

At this critical moment, when all available troops were needed to deal with the turbulent Emirs—who, anticipating the event of European control with the prohibition of slave-raiding, had begun early in the year devastating the pagan tribes in their immediate vicinity—the Ashanti War broke out, and Northern Nigeria was immediately called upon to provide a contingent. The total number despatched to Ashanti was no less than 1200, leaving the Protectorate so short-handed that it was only with the greatest difficulty that the necessary garrison duties were carried on, and it was quite impossible to deal with the slave-raids of the Emirs. The little outpost of Wushishi lay exposed to attack from both sides, and so serious did matters become that the High Commissioner himself—hearing in July that the two Emirs had planned a combined attack on the garrison—hurried there with what reinforcements he could gather. Meanwhile the raids were carried on up to the very banks of the Niger, and to within a few miles of the temporary headquarters at Jebba, and endeavours were made by the Emirs to get the natives to rise and expel the white men, whose troops they said had been exterminated in Ashanti. The officer in command of the small garrison at Wushishi during these anxious months was engaged in a series of skirmishes with the horsemen of Kontagora and Bida, in which he held his own as much by his personal gallantry as by the aid of his scanty detachment. On one occasion, after meeting and dispersing the gatherings of Bida horsemen, he pursued them up to the walls of the town, and entering the latter with only thirty men, endeavoured to arrest the Emir with his own hand; in this, however, he was unsuccessful, and, badly wounded, only escaped by the greatest good fortune.

Nor were these the sole operations in which the troops were engaged during this first eventful year of the new Protectorate. Early in the year an expedition against the powerful Munshi tribe on the north bank of the Benue had been necessitated owing to an attack made by them on a party constructing the telegraph line from Lokoja to Ibi: while another punitive expedition had been caused by the murder of a political officer[1] close to Lokoja.

In December, however, the return of the troops from Ashanti relieved the situation, and enabled the High Commissioner at last to deal with the two Mahomedan Emirs who had been devastating the country. An expedition was at once organised, and early in January it marched on Kontagora. The town

[1] The Hon. David Carnegie.

was captured, the Emir—known far and wide as Nagwamachi, the Destroyer—escaping with a handful of followers. A company of the West African Frontier Force was left as a permanent garrison, and the remainder of the force marched to the Kaduna river, meeting everywhere with demonstrations from the villagers, who were overjoyed at the fall of "The Destroyer." On their upward march they had passed through a district absolutely depopulated by this Emir.

Meanwhile, the High Commissioner had sent messages to the Emir of Bida, desiring him to meet him at a point on the Niger with all his principal chiefs. The Emir, however, sent in response one small party under a minor official. The High Commissioner thereupon sent a second message, bidding the Emir to meet him at a point on the Kaduna river, whither he was proceeding, assuring him that, no matter what the result of the interview, his safe return would be guaranteed. Again, however, only a small party under the same subordinate official arrived at the rendezvous. The High Commissioner therefore determined to proceed to Bida himself, taking with him as escort the troops which had just returned from Kontagora. He sent messages that not a shot would be fired unless he were attacked, but that the time had arrived when matters must be finally settled between himself and the Emir. The latter, however, elected to fly without awaiting the High Commissioner's arrival. Sir Frederick Lugard entered the town, and the troops being formed in a hollow square in the open ground in front of the Emir's "palace," the High Commissioner proclaimed as Emir, before the assembled people, the man whom

Sir George Goldie had four years before installed in the same place, and who was the rightful heir to the office. With due ceremony the new Emir was presented with a "letter of appointment," on which were inscribed in English and Arabic the conditions on which he was henceforth to hold the Emirate. These were, briefly, that he should rule justly and in accordance with the laws of the Protectorate, that he should obey the High Commissioner, and be guided by the advice of the Resident; and that minerals and waste lands should be the property of the Crown.

These conditions were accepted in full by the new Emir. A Resident was left at Bida, with an adequate garrison, and the High Commissioner returned with the remainder of the troops to headquarters.

The results of these two brief expeditions may be summarised as follows. Two of the most powerful of the Mahomedan Emirs had been deposed because, after repeated warnings, they would not desist from laying waste the country and carrying off the people as slaves. Their towns had been preserved from destruction: the loss of life had been confined to the slave-raiders themselves, the peasantry suffering not at all. Slave-raiding in these districts had been absolutely abolished, for the garrisons left at the capitals were sufficient to check any attempts at its renewal. No interference had been made in local customs, and a Resident had been appointed to act as adviser, and to see that the administration of the countries was carried on with justice and without oppression.

The policy adopted was one which has long been advocated in dealing with native races. It was that of utilising and working through the native Chiefs themselves, availing itself of their intelligence and knowledge, and insisting only on their observance of the fundamental rules of justice and humanity. Residents were appointed, who, although empowered to deal directly with the people, were instructed primarily—in the Mahomedan states at least—to limit themselves to advising, assisting, and encouraging the Chiefs and officials in governing the people on their own lines, provided only that in doing so they did not transgress civilised and modern notions of justice and humanity.

It will be remembered that Bida, and also Kontagora, were provinces of the Empire of Sokoto, in which a partly pagan and wholly indigenous population was ruled by Mahomedan Emirs of an alien race—the Fulani. It has been seen that in many cases pagan people had petitioned to be freed from their Fulani oppressors, and had appeared delighted at the latter's overthrow. It may be wondered why under such circumstances the policy was not adopted of removing the Fulanis from their governing positions, and appointing instead Chiefs from the people themselves. The answer is that it was considered that the Fulani race was possessed of such a genius for rule and so much intelligence, that their continuance in positions of responsibility was best for the people, provided that their power for evil were held in check, as in fact was assured by the appointment of a Resident, with an adequate force behind him. To conserve the existing machinery, to preserve all that was best in it, and patiently to eliminate all its evils and abuses, was, in short, the aim in view. It was frankly an experiment, as Sir Frederick Lugard stated in his first Report. "I am anxious," he wrote, "to prove to these people (the Fulanis) that we have no hostility to them, and only to insist on good government and justice, and I am anxious to utilise, if possible, their wonderful intelligence, for they are born rulers, and incomparably above the negroid races in ability."

It is still more or less of an experiment, but after ten years it may, I think, claim to have justified itself by the success with which law and order have been introduced into these vast regions of Northern Nigeria, with the minimum of disturbance of existing conditions, and of discontent and unrest amongst the people, both of the ruling and of the peasant classes.

The pacification of the country on both sides of the Kaduna, and the establishment of settled government throughout the Emirates of Bida and Kontăgora, opened the way for the removal of administrative headquarters to a more central position inland. Directly Sir Frederick Lugard had completed his arrangements at Bida he set out to select a site for the new capital, taking with him the Director of Public Works, a senior medical officer, a trained surveyor, and a small escort. It was of urgent necessity to begin the erection without delay of a headquarters station, for it was impracticable to go on living—in the words of the High Commissioner—"as it were from hand to mouth," with the temporary expedients which had been adopted at Jebba and Lokoja. Selecting Wushishi, therefore, as a base, the High Commissioner made a rapid survey of the neighbouring country.

The river was found to lie in a deep valley, but above Wushishi its bed consisted of large boulders, and was broken during the dry season into a series of clear streams and waterfalls, connecting stretches of deep blue pools. To the east lay a fairly level undulating plateau, surrounded by a semicircular range of hills, formed of quartzite rocks, and intersected by deep gorges and valleys. From these hills numerous streams of clear water made their way into the basin of the Kaduna. After a rapid but thorough exploration of the ground a site was selected which offered many advantages. It lay about a mile from the bed of the Kaduna, on the banks of a tortuous stream which guaranteed an ample supply of good water. Some fine trees grew on the spot, and the neighbourhood was well-wooded, affording an abundant supply of fuel. Its distance from the Kaduna bed, though not as great as might have been hoped, was still sufficient to promise a fair expectation that it would be more or less free from mosquitoes (mostly of the anopheles genus) which infest that valley. Finally, there were no obstacles from an engineering point of view to the construction of a small rail or tramway, to connect it with the nearest navigable point on the Kaduna.

Having selected the site, a rough plan was made by the High Commissioner, in consultation with the Director of Public Works and the medical officer, showing the way in which the proposed station was to be laid out. Materials for the dwelling-houses, twenty-one in number, including Government House and a hospital, had already been sent out from home. They were of wood with corrugated iron roofs, and were to be raised some four feet from the ground on masonry pillars. The public offices, court-house, gaol, and magazine were to be built of bricks made on the spot. The location of the line to connect the new site with the river was put in hand at once, and the High Commissioner left for Lagos to confer with the

Governor of that colony, and with the High Commissioner of Southern Nigeria.

The first year of the Protectorate had been one of strenuous activity and immense responsibility for the High Commissioner and all concerned. The initial organisation of each of the numerous administrative departments had alone entailed the working out of endless complicated details, harassing in the extreme. The inadequate staff which had been rendered necessary by the paucity of funds had hampered efforts and thrown upon the High Commissioner personally so much detail work that, as he reported, he had been unable to accomplish as much in other directions as he might otherwise have done. Yet the record for the year is astounding, both in its volume and its variety.

That portion of the Protectorate which was effectively occupied had been divided into nine provinces, each with a Resident in charge, assisted by a small civil staff. These provinces so formed were: (1) Illorin, (2) Kabba (with Lokoja), (3) Middle Niger, (4) Lower Benue, (5) Upper Benue, (6) Nupe (Bida), (7) Kontagora, (8) Borgu, (9) Zaria.

In each of these provinces a Provincial Court had been set up, presided over by the Resident in charge, while Native Courts, under the supervision of the political officer, had been instituted wherever possible.

A Supreme Court, presided over by the Chief Justice, held original and appellate jurisdiction over all non-natives; Judges of the Inferior Courts being Commissioners of the Supreme Court within its jurisdiction.

In the provinces, Residents—through the Provincial Courts—held jurisdiction co-existent with the Native Courts over natives, limited only by the necessity for confirmation by the High Commissioner of all serious sentences.[1] They were compelled by the proclamation to render every month to the High Commissioner a "Cause List," giving full details of every case tried in their courts. The Cause Lists operated as appeals, and the High Commissioner, advised by the Attorney-General, could refer any case to the Supreme Court.

In practice, where it was possible to set up a Native Court, that tribunal would deal with most cases of ordinary crime by natives, and practically with all civil cases between natives.

Provincial Courts would deal mainly with cases in which non-natives were concerned, Native Courts having no jurisdiction in such cases. They would also try offences by natives against specific laws of the Protectorate which were foreign to native law and custom, such as those connected with slavery, liquor, firearms, etc.

The Supreme Court administered strict law; Provincial Courts administered English law, modified by native law and custom; Native Courts administered—in Mahomedan states—Koranic law; in pagan states, native law and custom.

Throughout the Protectorate, therefore, English law was administered, modified in certain cases by native law and custom, and also by specific laws, issued by the High Commissioner under the Protectorate seal in the form of Proclamations. These were drawn up by the High Commissioner, with the aid of his legal officers, and were submitted to the Secretary of State for his approval, and required the Royal assent before they became law.

During the first year seventeen such proclamations

[1] The limit was fixed at sentences of over six months' imprisonment.

were enacted. Some of these were of a more or less formal character, to bring the new Protectorate into line with Colonial Office regulations; others, however, were of very great importance, and laid the foundations of the policy which was to be pursued throughout the coming years. The Supreme Court and Provincial Courts, as well as Native Courts, were set up by Proclamation within a few weeks of the establishment of the Protectorate; a Liquor Proclamation prohibited the importation of all trade liquor into the Protectorate, or its possession for sale; a Firearms Proclamation gave effect to the obligation of the Brussels Act, and prohibited the possession of arms of precision except by permit and licence.

Finally, two Proclamations of immense importance to the future welfare of the country were enacted. These concerned the status of slavery and the question of land.

The Land Proclamation made the acquisition of land by a non-native from a native illegal without the consent in writing of the High Commissioner.

The Slavery Proclamation was directed principally against the enslaving of any person; as regards domestic slavery, it abolished the legal status, and declared all children born after April 1, 1901, to be free.

There were many troublesome questions which harassed the High Commissioner during the first years of the Protectorate. Besides the endless details, many of them trifling in the extreme, which he was daily and hourly called upon to settle in the initial development of the several Departments, each with an insufficient and overworked staff, the military situation, with the Protectorate denuded of troops by the Ashanti War, caused at times a heavy anxiety. His attention had again and again each day to be diverted from some weighty international problem on the border, or the drafting of complicated legislation, to some trivial but necessary decision as to the salary of a native artificer, or the respective seniority of a couple of officials. Rest or time for recreation there was none. Perpetual anxiety and overwork were the normal conditions of the High Commissioner's life in those days, and considering the climate and the primitive conditions of food and housing that prevailed, it is a marvel that any constitution was found strong enough to carry through the work without a breakdown. To those who know the history of the first few years of the Protectorate of Northern Nigeria, the work accomplished, both in the soundness of its broad general principles and the minute accuracy and care with which each detail was worked out, will stand as a monument to the tireless energy and devotion to duty of the man in whom the entire responsibility centred.

In the spring of 1901 Sir Frederick Lugard proceeded home on leave of absence, Mr. William Wallace assuming administrative charge of the Protectorate until his return in the autumn. The same year a second contingent of troops, between 600 and 700 strong, was sent from the Protectorate to the Ashanti War, leaving in April and returning in October. In the latter month a contingent 300 strong was further sent to Southern Nigeria to assist in an expedition against the Aro tribes in that Protectorate, this being the third occasion within two years on which Northern Nigeria was called upon to provide a contingent for operations outside the Protectorate.

Meanwhile affairs in the Protectorate itself were by no means satisfactory. There was considerable unrest owing mainly to the hostile attitude adopted by the Mahomedan states along the northern border. Every effort to enter into friendly relations with these had so far failed, and they remained sullenly aloof. Two letters had been sent by the High Commissioner to the Sultan of Sokoto, but no answer had been received. Bornu and Bauchi were *terrae incognitae*. Nothing remained at present for the Administration but to consolidate its position in the south, and to leave the north for further consideration.

During the summer of 1901, therefore, the work on the new site for the headquarters was pushed rapidly forward. The location for the light line which had been sanctioned to connect it with the navigable Kaduna was completed, and material was forwarded directly the rainy season set in and the rivers rose. "West Africa," wrote the High Commissioner in his Report for 1901, "does not bear a reputation for rapidity in work, but I venture to think that it would not be easy to find a parallel for the work done by the Crown Agents and Messrs. Shelford in England, and Mr. Eaglesome in Africa, in this comparatively small undertaking. In May the final sanction for the line was given, and the rails were rolled in Leeds and the first steps for the location were made in Africa, and before Christmas the first train steamed into Zungeru" (the new capital). The gauge of this surface-line was 2 feet, and its length was 10 miles, and it was subsequently extended another 10 miles to a more convenient terminus on the river. Arrangements for the shipment of material were made in England by the High Commissioner himself. By means of this line materials for the necessary building were rapidly transported to the new site, and erected according to the plans already arranged. During this time the civil and military staff had been living as best they could, doubled up in quarters, and occasionally in tents. At out-stations, Residents and others lived in mud huts of native pattern, designing and superintending the erection of these when they could spare the time from their other multifarious duties.

In the east of the Protectorate, 400 miles up the river Benue, matters had reached a crisis during the summer of 1901. It may be remembered that a Fulani Chief—owing allegiance to the Sultan of Sokoto—ruled over a pagan country, with his capital at a town named Yola, which had first been visited by the traveller Barth in the 'fifties. This large and populous district was virtually a slave reserve, and every year enormous numbers of pagans were enslaved and sent northwards in large caravans. "There is probably no part of the Dark Continent," wrote the High Commissioner, in 1900, of this district, "in which the worst forms of slave-raiding still exist to so terrible an extent . . . nor are they even provident of their hunting-ground, for those who are useless as slaves are killed in large numbers, the villages burnt, and the fugitives left to starve in the bush." The Emir of Yola was one of the worst types of the Fulani ruler, well educated, but possessed with a religious fanaticism which rendered him extremely intolerant of European "infidels," and addicted to the constant practice of slave-raiding. He and the neighbouring Emir of Bauchi carried on a regular traffic in slaves, which were imported from German territory in great numbers and sent throughout the Hausa States. In 1901 in spite of his treaties with the Niger Company he had compelled the latter to haul down their flag on the trading-hulk which they used as a depôt since he had refused to allow them to have a station ashore. Warnings and threats having proved of no avail, and complaints having been received from various native traders, it was decided to send an expedition to Yola, and in September of 1901, taking advantage of high-water, a force of some 400 men was despatched. The Emir, who was reported to be hardly sane, would not listen to reason, or to the conciliatory offers made, and the force attacked the town. Considerable resistance was encountered, two French cannons, which had been presented some years before by a French adventurer, being used with some effect, but the town was eventually stormed, and the Emir fled with a small following.[1] The acknowledged heir was installed in his place on the usual conditions of appointment, and a Resident was left in charge with a small garrison.

A situation of a very different description prevailed in Bornu, caused chiefly by French activity in the region of Lake Tchad. A brief historical retrospect is needed to appreciate the events that were taking place in that region.

Those who have read the Life of General Gordon will be familiar with the name of Zubehr Pasha. One of the latter's most able lieutenants was a man named Rabeh. When Zubehr's son, Suliman, revolted in 1878 against the Egyptian Government and was defeated and induced to submit, Rabeh held out, and with a few soldiers established himself at a place between Darfur and Wadai. Here he gradually formed an independent dominion, conquering the neighbouring Chiefs, and in the course of a few years became so

[1] He was eventually killed by some of the pagans whose tribes he had so systematically raided for slaves.

strong that he was able to treat with contempt the overtures made to him by the Mahdi and his successor the Khalifa. In 1891 Rabeh came into collision with the French in Wadai and was forced westward: he established himself on the banks of the river Shari and soon became the rival of the Sultan of Wadai, engaging the latter in a series of conflicts with varying success. In 1893 he invaded Bornu, defeated the ruling Sheikh and occupied the capital, Kuka. Various attempts were made by the Bornuese army to oust the invader, but in each case they were defeated and the leaders slain. Rabeh now established himself as ruler of Bornu and transferred his capital to Dikoa in the German sphere of influence, introducing taxes to provide for his army, and conducting a series of expeditions against neighbouring Chiefs. In 1897 a French mission under M. Gentil arrived from the French Congo to establish a Protectorate over Wadai, and French troops before long came in contact with Rabeh. An attempt to open friendly negotiations with him failed, and on the 17th of July a small French force of native soldiers with five Europeans was overwhelmed by Rabeh and annihilated, only three wounded escaping. The French now organised a large expedition, and on October 29 attacked Rabeh, and after eight hours' severe fighting defeated him, the losses on both sides being heavy. For the next few months no fighting took place, but in the meanwhile the French prepared three converging missions to co-operate in the neighbourhood of Lake Tchad. Early in 1900 one of these missions, marching from Zinder (north of Hausaland) on Lake Tchad, installed as ruler of Bornu the nephew of the man whom Rabeh had defeated and slain seven years previously. At this time Bornu, although part of the new Protectorate of Northern Nigeria and recognised internationally as within the British sphere of influence, was not occupied or administered by the British. In March, Rabeh's forces engaged the French in a series of skirmishes in which both sides sustained severe losses, but on the 21st April the three French missions effected a junction, and the following day attacked Rabeh in a strongly stockaded position. After a battle lasting nearly three hours the French were victorious, completely routing their opponents and capturing their guns, Rabeh himself being among the slain. The command of Rabeh's forces now devolved on his son, Fadr-el Allah, who was at Dikoa with some 3000 followers. A series of skirmishes took place between Fadr-el Allah and the French during the month of May, some of them in British territory. Having driven Fadr-el Allah into the interior of Bornu, the French now withdrew to the fortified posts which they had established in their Protectorate.

These events had been watched with great anxiety by the High Commissioner of Northern Nigeria. The operations of the French so close to the borders of British territory, indeed within its very limits, threatened serious international complications. Yet, in the absence of any effective occupation of Bornu by the British, it was clearly impossible for the French to allow a paper boundary to afford a refuge from which a hostile army could conduct operations against their garrisons and devastate the country. The situation evidently called for the immediate occupation of Bornu by a British force. But the Ashanti War had denuded Northern Nigeria of all its available troops, and until they returned, no movement towards Bornu was possible. Fadr-el Allah's arrival in the interior of Bornu, however, presented a problem which demanded instant attention. Either he must be attacked and driven out, or a district would have to be assigned to him in which he might settle on terms of friendship. If matters were allowed to drift, the whole district would become a cockpit of war, and would be depopulated and ruined. With Bida and Kontagora actively raiding within a few miles of the Government headquarters, with the Hausa States sullenly hostile, and the whole country seething with unrest, the High Commissioner's situation, deprived of the bulk of his troops by the Ashanti War, was towards the close of 1900 sufficiently serious to cause grave anxiety. This was the situation when Fadr-el Allah added a fresh complication to the already difficult problem by appealing to the British for protection, promising to obey the orders of the Administration. The High Commissioner, believing strongly that co-operation and mutual assistance between Europeans were of vital importance in Africa, was naturally unwilling to accept overtures from a man who had been a moment before in conflict with a friendly European Power. Moreover he knew too well from past experience the methods of Nilotic Soudanese when unrestrained amongst a ruined and conquered people, and realised the danger of allowing so large and well armed a body of seasoned veterans to settle in British territory. On the other hand, Fadr-el Allah's messengers had been received in a friendly manner by the Resident on the Upper Benue, and had thus been led to hope for protection; while the absence of troops from the Protectorate made it advisable to avoid a conflict which would require a strong force at a great distance. In these difficult circumstances an officer was despatched in June 1901 to meet Fadr-el Allah and report on the situation. He was received with acclamation and treated with great hospitality, and conceived a high opinion of Fadr-el Allah, who appears to have been a most gallant soldier and a capable and determined ruler. He returned with a report wholly in favour of recognising Fadr-el Allah as Emir of Bornu.

While these negotiations were pending and the High Commissioner was considering what steps he should take, Fadr-el Allah had once more come into contact with the French, whom he appears to have attacked near Dikoa. A force of 230 French was despatched against him and pursued him into British territory, finally overtaking him at Gujba, 135 miles south-west of Lake Tchad, and therefore 160 miles within British territory. An eight-hour battle ensued, ending in the complete rout of Fadr-el Allah's forces, he himself being among the killed. Two days later his brother surrendered to the French with 400 rifles, 1500 guns, 1 cannon, and 200 horse, while 5000 Bornu captives were liberated. The French then withdrew to their own territory. Such was the situation at the close of 1901.

CHAPTER V

EVENTS IN 1902—OCCUPATION OF BAUCHI AND BORNU—MOVE TO NEW ADMINISTRATIVE HEADQUARTERS

THE immediate occupation of Bornu by British troops in order to rescue it from the state of anarchy into which it had fallen now became a clear necessity. The situation created by the French and Rabeh's forces had been discussed by Sir Frederick Lugard with the Secretary of State in England, and the latter had instructed the High Commissioner to visit the district on his return to the Protectorate towards the close of 1901. So many administrative problems were found awaiting him, however, that he was unable to proceed personally to Bornu. He therefore despatched an expedition some 500 strong under Colonel Morland—the commandant of the Northern Nigerian forces — with instructions to make full inquiries as to the action of the French and the causes which led up to it, and to ascertain whether the rumours of their having carried off natives of the British Protectorate and raised large sums of money had any foundation in fact.

The expedition left Ibi, on the Benue river, in February 1902, and marched northwards on Bauchi, being accompanied as far as that place by Mr. William Wallace, C.M.G., in political charge. A pagan tribe on the west of the road, which had been attacking caravans and murdering traders, had already been punished by a previous expedition and had tendered its submission. Bauchi was in a special degree the centre of the slave trade, and its Mahomedan Emir had the year before perpetrated a terrible crime in the treacherous sack of one of his own towns, whose inhabitants he had, in defiance of Koranic laws, massacred or carried off into slavery. The size of Colonel Morland's force, however, deterred the war party from active opposition, and the town was entered without fighting, the Emir seeking refuge in flight.[1] The leading officials were invited to choose a successor, and at once named the deposed Emir's heir, who was installed by Mr. Wallace with the usual ceremony and given the customary letter of appointment. A Resident was left in charge, supported by a garrison detached from the troops, and the expedition moved on in the direction of Bornu. Arriving on the banks of the Gongola river, they found the country seething with unrest, owing to the operations of a Mallam, or priest, who had some years previously set up as a Mahdi. This man, Mallam Jibrella, had been expelled fourteen years previously from a Mahomedan state farther north on a charge of witchcraft. After some years of wandering he collected a following in the territory of the Mahomedan Emir of Gombé and commenced a series of intrigues against that Chief. In 1894 the Emir marched against him, but was defeated and killed, whereupon Jibrella seized most of his dominions and gave himself out as a Mahdi. He ordered his

[1] He was captured by the Resident a few months later, and sent to Illorin, where he was permitted to settle under the surveillance of the Resident.

followers to wear the *jibbah*, and displayed a sacred banner on the frequent occasions when he harangued them. He was several times attacked by armies sent against him from Sokoto, Kano, and Bauchi, but managed to preserve his independence. At one time he was on terms of friendship with Rabeh, but subsequently quarrelled with him, and on more than one occasion he entered into conflict with Fadr-el Allah. At the time of the British expedition to Bornu Jibrella was firmly established in the neighbourhood of the Gongola and was on the point of seizing the town of Gombe, the capital of the Mahomedan province of that name. The advance of the British troops frustrated his plans, and he at once turned his attention to the new danger. While advancing across the open country on the road to Bornu, the British force was suddenly warned by its scouts of the presence of a body of some 600 foot and 100 horsemen behind a fold in the ground. Colonel Morland had just time to form a square, when he was charged in a fierce and determined fashion by a fanatical horde led by Mallam Jibrella in person. The sudden onslaught was only checked on reaching a distance of 50 yards from the square, when it was dispersed by the heavy rifle fire. The leader was pursued and eventually captured by an officer who rode 70 miles in seventeen hours to effect it. He was a white-haired old man of striking personality, seventy years of age, and had won the respect and admiration of our officers by his dash and pluck. He was sent to Lokoja, and maintained in honourable exile there.

On March 11, the expedition reached Gujba, the scene of Fadr-el Allah's defeat by the French a few months previously, and here a garrison was left, the remainder of the troops proceeding to the neighbourhood of Lake Tchad.

The situation was found to be as follows. After the defeat and death of Fadr-el Allah, the French had imposed a war indemnity of 50,000 dollars on the Sheikh[1] of Bornu, and the latter was detained by them in Dikoa, while his messengers were ransacking the impoverished and destitute country to obtain the money required. Colonel Morland sent messengers to the Sheikh telling him that he would recognise him as ruler of British Bornu if he came to reside in the country, and at the same time put a stop to the collection of any further payment to the French. The Sheikh accepted the offers with alacrity, returned with a large following, and took up his residence near the lake, pending the rebuilding of the old capital of Kuka, which had been destroyed by Rabeh. At this moment the arrival of a large German expedition caused the French to evacuate Dikoa and German territory and retire behind the river Shari. The presence of the troops of three European Powers in a district in the centre of Africa gave rise to much friction and unrest, and much valuable time was spent in trying to lay down a temporary frontier. In consequence of this state of affairs the High Commissioner advised His Majesty's Government of the necessity of proceeding with the delimitation of the frontier without delay. To this proposal the Secretary of State assented and a joint Commission was appointed.

In Bornu itself the re-establishment of the rightful ruler on his throne fulfilled the first condition to the settlement of the unfortunate country, so long dis-

[1] This was the title by which the ruler of Bornu has been known since the accession of the Kanemyin dynasty. See page 62.

tracted by devastating wars. A second company was left behind at the seat of government and a Resident appointed to take charge of the province. Over 1000 miles of country had been mapped, and an area of 60,000 square miles brought under administrative control with little bloodshed. Bornu showed signs at every step of the anarchy and war of which for so many years it had been the scene. The population was depleted, towns once large and prosperous were now only charred ruins, while brigandage and pillage were everywhere rife. To bring back peace and prosperity to the inhabitants was the task which lay before the newly appointed Resident.

The expedition under Colonel Morland began their return to headquarters in April, marching south by way of Yola. Several pagan districts were traversed to the north of the Benue, between Yola and Ibi, and the expedition was on several occasions attacked, but reached Lokoja in safety in June.

Meanwhile, a Resident had been appointed to take charge of a large district to the north of the Benue river, through which ran two important caravan routes from Kano and Zaria to the south. This district was inhabited mainly by pagan tribes in various degrees of savagery, and a portion of it, consisting of a long narrow strip running down from the interior to the Benue, owed a shadowy allegiance to the Fulani Emir of Zaria. The latter's deputy, an able but fanatical Mahomedan bearing the title of "Magaji," had established his headquarters at a town named Keffi, on the main caravan road from Zaria to the Benue and some four marches north of that river. Early in 1902 a Resident had been stationed at this town with a small detachment of troops, and a province named Nassarawa had been formed, comprising both the strip administered by the Magaji and the districts on each side inhabited by independent pagan tribes. In June 1902 the murder of a native missionary, added to other acts of repeated lawlessness, compelled the High Commissioner to despatch a small expedition against a town named Abuja in the western district which was a centre of brigandage and crime. The town was captured and most of the leaders of the marauding band arrested, while a new chief was installed in place of the former one, who was killed in the fighting.

Meanwhile there had been considerable unrest at Keffi, the provincial headquarters. The Magaji, a man of strong character and hasty temper, showed a similar determination to that exhibited in the Emirates of Bida and Kontagora, to resist the introduction of law and order and the prohibition of slave-raiding. The local Chief proved willing enough to assist the Resident in his efforts to check the lawlessness which prevailed, but the latter found himself continually thwarted by the Magaji, who maintained an armed following constantly engaged in robbing caravans and slave-raiding. As soon as the Resident had returned from the expedition in his western district he decided to summon the Magaji to his presence and discuss the situation frankly, feeling confident that he could induce the Magaji to listen to reason and so utilise his personality and influence in the pacification of the district. He therefore went to the house of the local Chief and sent a message to the Magaji, desiring him to attend. The latter peremptorily declined to do so. The assistant Resident was then sent to fetch him, but, being misled by a Government native agent, he entered the private apartments of the Magaji, who ordered his armed attendants to set upon him and throw him out. The Resident had now no alternative but to call up a detachment of troops. The Magaji, seeing that his arrest was imminent, rushed out of the house and shot down the Resident and the political agent who was with him, both being unarmed and unprotected. He and his followers then fled, but sent messengers that they would return presently and finish their work. Troops were hastily summoned from Lokoja, and pursued the Magaji to the confines of the province, but he made good his escape and hurried to Kano. News arrived subsequently that he had been received with much honour by the Emir of Kano, who assigned him a house and gave him presents, while he rode always at the post of honour on his right hand. There was no longer room to doubt the feelings towards the British régime which prevailed amongst the Fulani rulers of the Hausa States in the north.

It will be remembered that, when the town of Kontagora had been captured in January 1901, the Emir had fled northwards with a small following. Anxious to do all in his power to show the Sultan of Sokoto that the British Government desired to maintain the same friendly relations as had existed with the Niger Company, the High Commissioner had despatched a letter detailing the reasons why it had been necessary to depose the Emirs of Bida and Kontagora, and asking the Sultan to nominate an Emir to take the place of the latter, but he had received no reply. Later in the year the deposed Emir of Kontagora had collected a large force and proceeded to raid and harry the territories of the Emir of Zaria, which had not yet been occupied or administered. In January 1902 the Emir of Zaria appealed for assistance to the High Commissioner, who at once despatched a force to effect the capture of the deposed Emir. By a series of forced marches and the brilliant handling of a small troop of mounted infantry, the latter's war camp was surprised, and he himself captured without a shot being fired. Of his enormous following, amounting to nearly 20,000 persons, a large number were brought back to their homes in Kontagora, while a great many recently captured slaves were liberated, and found their way back to their own villages. The Emir himself was brought down to Lokoja, but after a time the High Commissioner, finding no one suitable to succeed him, reinstated him at Kontagora, where, under the Resident's guidance, he has since done good work. Many years must elapse before the district recovers from the devastating slave-raids to which it had been subjected. It is impossible for any one who has not travelled through and lived in districts in Central Africa which have suffered from slave-raids and internecine war to realise the condition to which they can be reduced by these means. One may travel for miles over fertile plains and see nothing but weeds and scrub growing up, with every now and then the ruins of some farmstead or village, forming a pathetic indication of the population which once called these crumbling walls their home.

After the capture of the Emir of Kontagora, a Resident with a small garrison was stationed at Zaria, since the Emir had by his appeal to Government ostensibly accepted British rule. Zaria is, however, but a short eighty miles from Kano, and Kano was by this time actively hostile and formed a focus of intrigue. Relieved of his fear of Kontagora, the Emir of Zaria now began to send messengers to Kano. The garrison was reinforced, but the intrigues continued. Moreover, with the craft of an oriental, the Emir despatched small parties of armed gun-men throughout his dominions to extort levies of tribute, giving out to the inhabitants that he was compelled to do this by the Government: in this way he hoped not only to increase his own gains, but to bring down the odium of the people on the British Administration. The murder of the Resident of Nassarawa province at Keffi was not of course chargeable in any way to the Emir of Zaria, though the murderer was one of his officials, but he was known to be sympathetic, and the High Commissioner detached that portion from his territories and made it independent.

For some months the Resident persisted in his attempts to get into touch with the Emir and gain his co-operation, but without effect. Finally, in September, he determined to bring matters to a head, and summoning the Emir and his chief officials, he informed him of all the charges against him, and announced that he had decided to take him to headquarters to be dealt with by the High Commissioner. The senior official was placed in temporary charge of the Emirate, and the Emir was sent under escort to Zungeru. Here he remained, pending the decision of the High Commissioner as to how the critical situation in Zaria and the Northern States should be dealt with.

The same month the High Commissioner was at last able to transfer headquarters from Jebba to Zungeru, the necessary buildings having been erected. The completion at the end of the previous year of the small section of light railway from the river to the new site had enabled the building materials to be sent up, and the laying out of the station and the erection of the buildings had been rapidly pushed forward. For the first time since the Administration was set up, public offices were available for the Treasury, the Secretariat, Government Printing Department, and others, and the increase of space and general improvement was an immense advance upon the previous makeshifts.

The problem of housing accommodation at out-stations presented many difficulties. The normal staff in each province might be calculated as three political officers, two military officers, with one or two more European non-commissioned officers, one medical officer, and one police officer. For all of these dwelling-houses were required, and in addition there was need of a strong-room for treasure and ammunition, a court-house and office, a guard-room and temporary gaol, besides the necessary minor buildings, such as clerks' houses, cook-houses, stables, etc. The soldiers of the West African Frontier Force hutted themselves, building either grass or mud huts, of the usual native design. For the rest, buildings of mud or sun-dried bricks, with roofs of thatch, had to be improvised. So long as they could be made strong enough to keep out the tropical sun and rain, they were sufficient for present needs, although the liability to fire was an ever-present danger. Nor were makeshifts of this flimsy description altogether suited for the storing of treasure or accommodation of prisoners. The need of lock-ups for prisoners condemned to short terms of imprisonment or awaiting despatch to the central gaol was urgent. In one province the Resident was obliged to resort to confining his prisoners in the native gaol in the town. The result was hardly satisfactory, for in his Report he states that one died, three fell ill with smallpox, and the remainder escaped.[1] The main difficulty in supplying out-stations with suitable buildings—or indeed with any other necessity—was one of transport. The Royal Niger Company had for this reason confined their activities to the neighbourhood of the navigable rivers. Their trading stations had all been erected at places on the banks of the Niger or the Benue where they could be reached without difficulty by water. When the administration of the Protectorate was assumed by Government, it was no longer possible to restrict operations to the navigable waterways. A few provincial headquarters could be reached by water—Lokoja, Ibi, and Yola—but the others were at least four days' march inland, such as Bida, Illorin, Kontagora, and Keffi, and in the absence of roads or wheeled traffic, all stores had to be transported on the heads of native porters or carriers. With the establishment of Residents in Bauchi, Bornu, and Zaria matters became still more serious with regard to the transport of necessary stores. These stations were twelve and fourteen days' march from the nearest river port, and apart from the cost of transporting stores over such long distances there was a great difficulty in obtaining sufficient carriers. The lack of transport was indeed the difficulty which faced the new Administration at every turn, and much of the unwritten history of the early days of the Protectorate is concerned with the makeshifts which had

[1] No official report, however, exists of the delightful incident, when, at one station in the Protectorate, a deputation, headed by the prisoner with the longest sentence, called on the Resident one evening to report that a storm had carried off the roof of the gaol, and that they would not consent to remain unless better quarters were provided.

to be employed to circumvent the various troubles to which it gave rise. It hampered the telegraph construction, which was so urgently needed to link the various provinces to headquarters, for it was by this means that troops could be rapidly summoned to any threatened point. In the absence of transport the wire was hung on trees cut in the bush and erected in place of the usual iron poles, but this temporary expedient led to frequent breakdowns, especially during the tornado and rainy seasons. The fortnightly mail service which was established with difficulty throughout the Protectorate was often delayed by the impossibility of finding carriers or runners to transport the mail-bags. There was, in short, hardly a Department in the Administration which did not suffer from the chronic difficulty of transport, and those officials whose duties lay in out-stations in the interior will not easily forget the hardships and discomforts which were directly due to it. Even water transport was beset with difficulties, for it was only during the brief flood season that steamers could ascend the upper reaches of the navigable rivers, and the depth of water depended on the rainfall, which was variable. Bulky stores, such as railway, building, or telegraph materials, had to be collected and stored at convenient points, ready to be pushed up rapidly the moment the river rose. Towards the close of the high-water season, as the rivers began to fall, the utmost precaution had to be taken lest vessels should be left high and dry at some interior port. Sandbanks, sunken rocks, and floating or submerged tree trunks were a perpetual menace to ships, and caused endless trouble to the Marine Department, whose workshops were never idle.

The construction of roads from the waterways into the interior early occupied the attention of the High Commissioner, but in a country with a tropical rainfall, roads fit for wheeled transport are expensive and difficult to construct, and funds for the purpose were not available. Moreover, the presence of the tsetse fly in the lower regions made the use of animal transport practically impossible, even had cart roads been constructed. Clearly the problem of communication was one of the most difficult of all those with which the Administration was faced.

Thus political problems, administrative problems, transport problems, housing problems, international problems, all presented their difficulty. But the problem which overshadowed all others was that of finance, with which was intimately connected trade and commerce, on which, in fact, it hinged. The Committee of 1898 had recorded their opinion that direct taxation would not at the outset be advisable, and the High Commissioner in his Report for 1901 had concurred, stating his opinion that "the Protectorate had not yet reached the stage of development when direct taxation was advisable." The native Chiefs had, however, been in the habit of receiving from their subordinate towns and villages tribute or dues in kind, in many cases in slaves, and the Mahomedan Emirs had looked to the result of their slave-raids for the greater part of their income. This, in fact, was the *causa causans* of their hostility to the new Administration, for they recognised at once that the prohibition of slave-raiding struck a blow at the main source of their incomes, and threatened them with something like financial ruin. For this reason the High Commissioner in the same Report wrote : " It is an achievement by itself to restore the equilibrium by legitimate means, viz. by affording them facilities for collecting a fair revenue from their subordinate villages without calling on them at present to pay a portion of this to Government." He maintained, however, the absolute right of the Government to levy a tax in return for benefits conferred, and merely postponed the step until such time as the population should have accepted a coin currency, and obtained, by the opening up of the country to commerce, the means wherewith to pay their dues. There was no reason, however, why direct taxation should not be applied to native traders, and the method of doing so will be dealt with later. As regards the remainder of the population, taxation might reasonably take the form of assistance in public works, as is in fact the custom in practically all communities at an early stage of civilisation, where labour is the main commodity.

CHAPTER VI

EVENTS IN 1903—OCCUPATION OF KANO AND SOKOTO

Two years of strenuous work had seen British influence in the form of a settled civil Administration extended over Bornu, Bauchi, Zaria, Kontagora, Borgu, and all the country lying south of these states, and on both banks of the Middle Niger and the Benue rivers. There remained at the end of 1902 the phalanx of Mahomedan states which lay along the northern border. So long as these remained independent of the Administration unrest must inevitably continue throughout the remainder of the Protectorate. Nor could the commerce so urgently needed to afford the native population the means of providing for their own administration be introduced until the caravan roads from the interior had been rendered safe. "Trade," wrote the High Commissioner, "cannot be established on a satisfactory basis until the Northern Hausa States are included in the 'Provinces' of the Protectorate, and the trade routes rendered safe for small traders." The relations between the states and the Administration must now be briefly detailed.

In the historical account of Northern Nigeria, it

has been shown how the religious uprising organised by Sheikh Othman dan Fodio in the beginning of the nineteenth century had knit together the Hausa States into an empire, owing an allegiance, mainly religious, but partly political also, to the Fulani Sultan of Sokoto. Othman had divided this empire into two parts, but it will simplify the situation to ignore this division—which was of little practical importance—and treat the empire as one under the supremacy of the Sultan of Sokoto. The result of the religious upheaval was to place on the throne of each Hausa State a Mahomedan Mallam, in practically every case a Fulani, who had received his "flag" from Othman, and was, in fact, the latter's nominee and depûty. Besides the Hausa States other pagan or partly pagan districts, such as Illorin, Nupe, and Yola, had been conquered in the flood of religious zeal and the stir of ambitious officials, and had been formed into provinces of the Sokoto Empire under Fulani Emirs. As time went by the descendants of the original "flag-bearers" had arrogated to themselves the status of ruling Chiefs, holding office by hereditary right, and each one had grown to consider himself more as an independent ruler than as a deputy appointed by the Sultan to administer a subordinate province. During the early days of British influence the exact relationship between the various Emirs and the Sultan of Sokoto was never clearly understood, indeed the holders of the offices were probably not agreed on the point themselves. Each state undoubtedly sent an annual tribute to Sokoto, consisting in many cases chiefly of slaves. Further, the Sultan of Sokoto nominated the successor to each vacancy, but only from amongst the members of the ruling family or families: and instances occurred where the Sultan deposed an Emir for malpractices, or on receiving a complaint of oppression from the inhabitants. In all other respects, however, the Emirs appear to have acted as independent rulers—making war, levying tribute, appointing or dismissing officers of State, and so forth. The Royal Niger Company made treaties with the Sultan of Sokoto as "Seriki-n-Muslimin"—Chief of the Mahomedans—with regard to the whole of his dominions, and paid him an annual subsidy for their rights throughout them; but it made war on the Emir of Bida and deposed him, while still maintaining friendly relations with Sokoto. The truth probably was that the Emirs were in theory merely deputies, administering provinces as representatives of the Sultan; but in practice they looked upon themselves as independent rulers, sending an annual tribute to the Sultan as Head of the Faith.

When Sir Frederick Lugard took over from the Company the administration of their territories he was anxious to continue the existing friendly relations with the Chiefs. He therefore drew up and submitted to the Secretary of State a Proclamation announcing the change, and declaring that the Government would be bound by the pledges given by the Company, and would expect from the Chiefs a fulfilment of the obligations into which they, on their part, had entered under the treaties. This document was translated into Hausa and despatched by a trusty messenger to Sokoto. The Sultan treated the messenger with contumely and returned no answer or acknowledgment. When the slave-raiding of Kontagora had forced the Administration to take military action and the Emir had been defeated, and had taken refuge in flight, the

High Commissioner, still hoping to secure the co-operation and friendship of the Sultan, had sent him a letter desiring him to appoint a successor—an act which was equivalent to the recognition of the Sultan's ancient prerogatives. Again no reply was received, but some sixteen months later (in May 1902) a brief and peremptory letter was received by the High Commissioner from the Sultan, bearing the latter's seal. It ran as follows:[1] "From us to you. I do not consent that any one from you should ever dwell with us. I will never agree with you. I will have nothing ever to do with you. Between us and you there are no dealings except as between Mussulmans and Unbelievers (Kafiri)—War, as God Almighty has enjoined on us. There is no power or strength save in God on high. This with salutations." Two months prior to the receipt of this, the High Commissioner had made a second attempt to secure the Sultan's goodwill by writing to ask him to nominate a successor to the deposed Emir of Bauchi. To this he received a reply very similar to the letter already quoted, though couched in language slightly less discourteous. It was obvious that the Sokoto Empire was determined to have no dealings with the new Administration, and was bent on resisting any interference by recourse to arms. It was useless under such circumstances to send the subsidy which had been paid by the Company during its administration, although sums to meet it had been provided in the Protectorate Estimates.

As regards the ethical question as to the right of the British Government to assume the administration of the Sokoto Empire, it must be remembered that

[1] See Appendix II.

the Fulanis themselves were an alien race who had usurped the power less than a hundred years before; and that they had devastated the country by constant war and slave-raiding, and that under their present rule neither life nor property was safe. The Company, and subsequently the Government, had both shown by their acts that they bore no hostility to the rulers as such, but that they insisted only on good government, and were willing to recognise the status of the Fulanis, provided only that they exercised their powers with justice and toleration.

As regards the states subordinate to Sokoto—Bida, Kontagora, Illorin, and Yola had been dealt with, and the present Emirs had accepted the Government's conditions, and the control of a Resident. Zaria had itself sought British aid, and a Resident had been placed in charge, supported by a garrison. Kano, Katsina, and the lesser northern Emirates were necessarily considered as integral parts of the Sultan's dominions, to which it was superfluous to send a separate communication. The attitude of the Emir of Kano was sufficiently indicated by his reception of the murderer of the Resident of Nassarawa province—the Magaji of Keffi—and during the summer of 1902 he was busily intriguing with the Emir of Zaria, and was said to have planned with the latter a combined attack on the garrison at that place.

Such was the situation at the end of 1902. It was evident that, all overtures having failed to secure the Sultan's co-operation by peaceful means, an appeal to arms was inevitable. The task was, as the High Commissioner wrote, not to annex new kingdoms, but to endeavour to fulfil the obligations and responsibilities to which Government had pledged itself with regard to the territory over which it had declared a Protectorate.

It was neither advisable nor possible to postpone action. An Anglo-French Boundary Commission had arrived at Lokoja on 1st November 1902 to delimit the boundary from the Niger to Lake Tchad, and this was an additional reason for effectively occupying the territory along whose borders they would pass, and safeguarding it from attack. Preparations were therefore made at the end of 1902 for an expedition to Kano and Sokoto, and supplies were collected at Zaria, which was to form the advanced base. To guard against any unforeseen contingency or unexpected check, reserves were ordered up from Lagos and Southern Nigeria by the direction of the Secretary of State, but the expedition was composed otherwise exclusively of troops in the Protectorate itself.

On the 29th of January 1903 a column, consisting of some 24 British officers and 700 men of the West African Frontier Force, left Zaria for Kano. On crossing the frontier they met scouts from the enemy, and arriving at a large walled town, they found the gates closed and armed men lining the walls. A summons to surrender being disregarded, an attack was made and the town stormed and taken. No further opposition was met with till the column arrived outside the walls of Kano. Here a formidable resistance was expected, as the walls, which were some 14 miles in perimeter, were from 30 to 50 feet high and about 40 feet thick at the base, with a double ditch in front. It subsequently transpired, however, that the Emir had gone some four weeks previously to Sokoto, ostensibly to salute the Sultan, taking with him about

2000 horsemen, and had left the defence of the town to two head slaves. After a fruitless attack on the main gate a breach was effected in a neighbouring one, and the town was stormed with little loss, the armed inhabitants taking to flight. The Emir's palace—a large walled enclosure or citadel, containing, amongst other buildings, a mosque, an arsenal, and a treasure-house—was occupied, and order restored. No looting whatever took place, and three days after the occupation of the town the market presented its usual appearance, except that the quarter set aside for the sale of slaves was deserted, the latter having been liberated on the arrival of the British force.

The fact that the whole of the inhabitants settled down at once to their usual avocations showed plainly that they realised that the expedition was directed against their rulers and not against themselves, and that its object was to replace the tyranny of an autocrat by a just and liberal administration.

A Resident having been left in political charge, with an adequate garrison, the expedition then proceeded to Sokoto, a march of some sixteen days. Letters had been sent to Sokoto and Katsina, informing them that the Government had no quarrel with them, provided they would receive its representatives in peace and carry out the conditions under which it was prepared to recognise and confirm them in their positions. After the fall of Kano the surrounding towns in that province all sent in their submission, and affirmed their wish for friendship. An answer was also received from the Emir of Katsina, to the effect that he had no desire for war, and was prepared to accept the conditions of Government.

Some six days after leaving Kano, a small reconnoitring party of mounted infantry was attacked by a force of 1000 horsemen and 2000 foot, which turned out to be the party which was returning from Sokoto with the Emir of Kano. The attack was beaten off and the force routed, and it was subsequently found that the Emir had fled the previous night, knowing that he was detested by his people, and fearing to be deserted by them in the fight.[1]

The expedition, meeting with no further opposition and being well received by all the villages *en route*, from which supplies were readily purchased, resumed its march to Sokoto, and on nearing the town was reinforced by a company of the West African Frontier Force, which had been garrisoning an independent state north-west of Sokoto. On nearing the town it was opposed by a force of about 1500 horse and 3000 foot, which fled, after a feeble resistance, leaving the town to be occupied by the British troops.

A few days later, the High Commissioner arrived from Kano, where he had followed the expedition, and had temporarily installed a new Emir. The same day the Waziri (Vizier) of Sokoto arrived in the camp with three other chiefs, and surrendered. As he had previously done at Kano, the High Commissioner summoned the Waziri and chief officials, and, after explaining to them fully the policy of the Government, invited them to nominate a successor to the Sultanate in place of the man who had fled. After a brief consultation they asked for the appointment of a man who had been elected in due form at the death of the previous Sultan, but who had been ousted by the

[1] He was subsequently arrested disguised as a trader, and sent into exile with a few attendants at Lokoja. The officer commanding the patrol which was attacked was awarded the Victoria Cross.

present ruler, now a fugitive. The High Commissioner found him to be a person of prepossessing appearance, intelligent, and likely to prove a ruler of the right stamp, whilst by birth he was in the proper succession. He therefore agreed to appoint him Sultan, and fixed the next morning for the installation. The troops were drawn up in a hollow square, and all the native officials as well as a great concourse of the inhabitants were present. The High Commissioner delivered an address setting forth the reasons which had forced the Government to undertake the administration of the country, and the policy which it intended to pursue. A murmur of deep satisfaction arose from the assembled masses when he announced the complete freedom of their religion, and when he had installed the new Sultan the priests recited a prayer.

The same afternoon the expeditionary force was broken up. A Resident was, as usual, appointed to take political charge, and a sufficient garrison was left with him, the High Commissioner starting for Katsina the following day with an escort of mounted infantry. Marching fast across an arid and often waterless tract which intervenes between the two towns, he reached Katsina in six days, and was met by the Emir. Summoning the Emir and his chief officials, he repeated the ceremony of installation which he had already performed at Sokoto, and explained the policy of the future. He added that since Katsina had always been looked on as the seat of learning and literature, he would be glad to give all possible assistance to education. Leaving a garrison to take up their quarters at Katsina, he then marched to Kano, where he formally installed, with the usual ceremonial, the man whom he had appointed temporarily as Emir a few weeks before. It is the custom at Kano that no king shall enter the royal enclosure by the gate used by his predecessor, so a great breach was made, prior to the ceremony, in the palace walls, and the local custom duly observed.

From Kano the High Commissioner marched to Zaria, and there installed as Emir, in place of the man who had been deposed the previous September, the rightful heir, who was the grandson of the original "flag-bearer," who had won Zaria for Othman. On the 14th of April the indefatigable High Commissioner was back once more at headquarters, having covered 800 miles in 38 days, and settled matters in Sokoto, Katsina, Kano, and Zaria—a fine record when it is remembered that this was the hottest season of the year, and that the sole transport available was native carriers.

The task of bringing these Mahomedan provinces into some sort of order after what appears to Western minds the chaos in which they had so long existed, was now in the hands of the Residents who had been appointed to take administrative charge of them. Their inclusion in the Protectorate had been brought about with a minimum of bloodshed and amazingly little disturbance. This fact alone is sufficient to prove that the bulk of the populace had been suffering from misgovernment and from the oppression of a small clique of somewhat ruthless officials. It would be a mistake to over-estimate the misgovernment and oppression which had existed, as Europeans accustomed to a highly civilised régime are far too apt to do. But it would be an equal mistake to ignore or to deny it altogether. Our justification for taking over the administration of Northern Nigeria is the belief that by our presence we can and do succeed in giving the vast mass of people a far better government under their own rulers than they would ever enjoy if the latter were left entirely to themselves.

Liberty and self-government are high-sounding words and are the ideals at which all civilised communities aim ; but it is imperative to realise that in a certain stage of civilisation—between, in fact, the very primitive and the highly developed—they inevitably cause, when unchecked, the oppression of the weak and ignorant by the strong and unscrupulous. That natives would rather be indifferently governed by their own Chiefs than well governed by an alien race is probably true. It was for this very reason that the policy was introduced in Northern Nigeria of maintaining the native rulers in their position, and using British Residents to advise and guide them, with power behind them to enforce that advice where necessary—an indispensable condition.

The peace which had settled so marvellously over the Hausa States since this brief expedition was not, however, destined to reign unbroken throughout the year. One element of unrest remained, in the person of the fugitive ex-Sultan of Sokoto. Sir Frederick Lugard had informed the new Sultan and his officials that he had no desire to punish or capture the ex-Sultan, and that if he chose to return and settle down quietly in one of his own towns he was at liberty to do so. The latter, however, did not accept this conciliatory offer. He was joined by the ex-Emir of Bida, the notorious Magaji of Keffi, and various other disaffected Chiefs and officials, and this party soon became a focus of unrest and disaffection in the south-eastern corner of the Sokoto Province. A small force was despatched from Sokoto to drive them out, and they passed eastwards between Zaria and Kano, the ex-Sultan giving out that he was about to proceed on a pilgrimage to Mecca.

The movement soon, however, assumed a dangerous aspect, since fanaticism was aroused and some thousands flocked to his banner. Troops were sent from Kano to break up the gathering, and followed the ex-Sultan in a south-easterly direction, being joined by a small column from Bauchi. Still pursuing, the force reached a walled town named Burmi, near the banks of the Gongola. This had been the headquarters of the fanatical Mallam Jibrella, who had attacked and been defeated by the Bornu column two years before. One of the sons of that chief had proclaimed himself "Mahdi" in his place and had established himself with a band of fanatical followers in the town. The small British force, ignorant of the hostile body, arrived before the walls of the town after a long march and requested supplies on payment in the ordinary way. These were at once refused, and the messengers were attacked and driven out; severe fighting took place, and the British force was obliged to withdraw, after having 64 of their small number killed and wounded. It fell back on Bauchi, and an expedition was at once organised from Lokoja. The ex-Sultan, who had previously passed through Burmi, now returned there and joined forces with the fanatical "Mahdi" and his followers. On the 27th July the expedition from Lokoja arrived and attacked the town: a desperate fight ensued, lasting till dusk, the commander of the British force being killed early in the engagement by a poisoned arrow, and the total casualties being over 80. The town was eventually stormed, and the fanatical inhabitants dispersed, after suffering heavy losses. Amongst the killed were the ex-Sultan of Sokoto and most of the disaffected chiefs who had joined him, including the Magaji of Keffi. This action put an end to the last remnant of active disaffection throughout the Hausa States. The "pacification of the country, the prevention of inter-tribal wars and slave-raiding, and the dispersal of armed forces" which the High Commissioner had set before himself as the initial task when he assumed charge of the Protectorate, had been completed. There now remained the second step—the "securing of the goodwill of the Chiefs and people, and the establishment of an efficient civil administration." Part of this had already been accomplished by the division of the Protectorate into Provinces and the appointment to each of a Resident in political charge, assisted by a small staff and supported by a garrison. The carrying out of the remainder lay in hands of the Residents, under the direction and guidance of the High Commissioner.

CHAPTER VII

ORGANISATION OF PROVINCES—CARAVAN TOLLS

"The inhabitants of that quarter of the globe have lived from the earliest times almost always cut off from the rest of the world. Protected by their sandy deserts they were scarcely accessible to the persevering toil of friendly caravans, never to the army of a foreign invader. . . . Nature, nevertheless, has provided in a remarkable manner that they should not remain total strangers to each other: she has not only given them fruitful inland countries, but stored even the immense sandy deserts themselves with treasures which have either excited the avarice, or been required by the necessities of mankind."—HEEREN, *Ancient Trade of Africa*.

It is interesting to note the different methods by which British administrators have set to work in various portions of the Empire to build up the Administrations entrusted to their care. In the Anglo-Egyptian Soudan, for instance,—a country whose conditions bear a striking resemblance to those in Northern Nigeria—the policy of a semi-military organisation was introduced as an initial stage. The Governors of the various provinces in that country were in the first instance military officers, in whose hands both the military command and political control were combined. In Northern Nigeria a different policy was pursued from the outset. The instant that armed opposition had been overcome, a civil official was placed as Resident in political control of each new province, having a handful[1] of native police to assist him in civil duties, and act as gaolers, court messengers, and so forth. The military forces were commanded by

[1] At first there were less than twelve in each province.

their own officers, who were directly responsible to the commandant at headquarters. In the event of disturbances occurring which necessitated the intervention of armed force, the Resident was entitled to call on the military for assistance. He indicated the object aimed at, and at the proper moment handed over the situation to the military officer, to take such steps as the latter deemed necessary. Directly the object had been attained, the Resident resumed the political direction of affairs, and the situation regained its normal aspect.

The inclusion of the Northern Emirates in the administration of the Protectorate led, in the opening months of 1903, to the formation of three new provinces, bringing the total number throughout the Protectorate to fourteen. The headquarters of some of these were separated from Zungeru, the centre of government, by distances of two and three hundred miles, and communication was maintained by a system of mail-runners, despatched fortnightly. The connection of the various provinces with the central authority by telegraph was also put in hand at once, the construction of the lines being pushed forward with the greatest possible rapidity. Under the circumstances, however, it was clear that considerable freedom of action, combined with a heavy responsibility, must remain with the Residents ; and although the general direction of affairs remained in the hands of the High Commissioner, the details and execution devolved of necessity mainly on the former. It was therefore essential that these should be men of the right stamp, and that their characteristics and abilities, and also their limitations, should be known personally to the High Commissioner, on whose shoulders rested ultimately the supreme responsibility for the welfare of the country and its inhabitants.

The political staff was appointed by the Secretary of State, applicants receiving their appointments at the Colonial Office, at first on probation for three years, at the end of which period they might be confirmed in them and placed on the permanent staff, provided that the High Commissioner's report on their services was satisfactory. No age limit was at first assigned to the appointments, and applicants belonged to a variety of professions—military, legal, medical, commercial, and many others. Before making an appointment the Colonial Office instituted a careful inquiry into the previous record of the applicant and of his various qualifications. The High Commissioner during his brief periods of leave in England made it his business to interview personally as many of the applicants as possible, and ascertain their qualifications in a practical manner. The termination of the war in South Africa in 1902 set free a number of men who possessed precisely those qualities which were needed in the administration of a new country, and the interest of the life attracted many applicants. Several of the officers who had been serving with the West African Frontier Force applied for transfer to the Political Department, and their knowledge of the country and its inhabitants made them valuable recruits. Indeed, so many military officers were at first appointed, that the High Commissioner in his Report for 1902 considered it advisable, in referring to the subject, to make the following comments: "Objection has in some quarters been taken to the appointment of military officers as civil Residents. Failing the supply of men with African administrative experience, I have found that selected Army officers are an admirable class of men for this work. They are gentlemen; their training teaches them prompt decision, their education in military law gives them a knowledge of the rules of evidence and judicial procedure sufficient when supplemented by a little special study to meet the requirements of a not too technical system of court work, and their training in topography enables them to carry out the surveys of all their journeys. Officers, more especially those who have served in India, have done some excellent work in Northern Nigeria, and their sympathy with and understanding of the people is certainly not less than that of the civilian. It is indeed a characteristic of the British officer that when in civil employ his rule is often marked by less 'militarism' than that of the civilian, and he is more opposed to punitive expeditions."[1]

The Universities were not long in coming forward with offers of facilities for the special training of graduates to enter the Colonial Service, and the Northern Nigeria political service did not fail to attract many young graduates to whom administrative work in tropical Africa offered interests and excitements hardly to be obtained elsewhere. The fact remained, however, that during the early years of the Protectorate, when the first impression on the native

[1] In *Ancient and Modern Imperialism* Lord Cromer has a note on the same subject. After quoting a passage from the work of a recent German traveller in India who writes: "Hard things are said at home of the English subaltern. You do not know him, you cannot judge him aright till you have seen him on the North-West Frontier," Lord Cromer comments: "The insufficient recognition sometimes accorded to these young men by a small section of their countrymen finds, I trust, some compensation in the high value attached to their services by those who, like myself, have seen them at work. They constitute, in my opinion, the flower of the youth of England. No other nation possesses Imperial agents to compare with them."

of Europeans and their administration was of such vital importance, the High Commissioner was obliged to rely on subordinates for the most part untrained and untried, who had to learn their work at the same time as they performed it.

And the work was not of a kind that could be mastered in a few weeks or months. The Resident combined in his own person practically every department of the Protectorate, except the military: indeed he was even at times obliged to assume the rôle of military commander, for there were many cases where an escort consisting of a handful of soldiers under a native non-commissioned officer accompanying a political officer through a pagan district was attacked, and the native soldiers, though in theory wholly responsible for the conduct of the action, naturally looked to the European who was with them for direction and control.

To enumerate all the duties and responsibilities of a Resident in charge of a province would be almost impossible. To begin with, he was responsible for law and order, and his first duty consisted in seeing that the Emirs and Chiefs and native officials carried out their administrative duties with justice and without oppression. To achieve this, his office must be open at all hours of the day, so that he might hear and investigate any complaint that might be brought, and deal with it, or refer it to the Emir, or Chief, or Native Court. Any report of crime, such as highway robbery or slave-catching, must be at once inquired into, offenders traced and arrested, the case tried by him in his Court-House, and the culprits punished. The Resident had also charge of the Civil Police and the gaol, and was responsible for the drill, discipline, accoutrements, etc., of the former, and for the maintenance of the prisoners, sanitation, and so on. He was the medium between Europeans and the native population, and was responsible for the provision of supplies and for fixing market prices. On him devolved the duty of arranging for transport for Europeans, or convoys of stores, passing through his province, either providing carriers or, in the Northern Provinces, purchasing, training, and maintaining transport animals with their equipment and attendants. He was likewise a Sub-Accountant, responsible to the Treasurer at headquarters for the correct accounting of all moneys received and expended throughout the province, rendering a monthly account, in which every item had to be supported by vouchers in duplicate, and appropriated to its proper head and sub-head under the Protectorate Estimates. He made arrangements for the provision of local labour and material for all buildings, laid out the Government stations, designed the houses, attended to sanitation and the construction of roads. He was Post-Master of the Province, and as such responsible for making up the fortnightly mail-bags, and for the despatch and receipt of all mails. He collected the revenue, and was personally responsible for all Government moneys; he compiled statistics of population, trade, crime, etc., and forwarded to headquarters, for the information of the High Commissioner, details of native organisation, tribal customs, languages, and taxation. It was his duty to traverse the whole of his Province and survey it, to prepare a map showing the various natural features, the towns and villages, and the tribal boundaries. In addition he was instructed to use every endeavour to encourage trade; to report on the output and possibilities of all products, sylvan, mineral, and agricultural; to promote the planting of trees of economic value; to encourage agriculture and to prevent deforestation.

These were the chief duties of a Resident appointed to take charge of a province. To assist him he had at first one or two junior political officers, half-a-dozen native agents and interpreters, and one or more educated native clerks from the Coast; a medical officer was responsible for the health of the Europeans and other Government employés, and advised on matters of sanitation. The great difficulty was to prevent the Resident being tied to his office at provincial head-quarters, and swamped by routine work and official correspondence. No one who has not experienced it can form any idea of the time and labour which are necessarily consumed by the minute and exact system of accounting in a Government office. To the novice the various Votes to which different expenditures have to be charged present a puzzle which at times seems almost insoluble, though in reality the system is simple enough to a trained accountant. Many a Resident who had spent a busy day from sunrise to sunset in his Court-House listening to complaints, trying cases, arranging for supplies and transport, and attending to the other multifarious duties which pressed on him, found himself obliged to work far into the night in the endeavour to extricate his accounts from some tangle, or to trace some petty error in addition which had thrown out the month's Balance. Yet no effective administration of the country could be carried on if the administrative officers were imprisoned in their offices immersed in routine work, and obliged to rely for their knowledge of the natives and affairs in the district on agents and interpreters by no means invariably trustworthy or intelligent. As Sir Henry Lawrence had said years before of India, "the work done by a Political Officer in his district, surrounded by the people, is infinitely superior to the work done in office surrounded by untrustworthy officials." If the administration of the Protectorate were to be carried on with any degree of success, an increase of staff was absolutely necessary; for unless there were sufficient political officers to enable Residents to leave their provincial headquarters and tour their districts, unscrupulous Emirs and Chiefs would be in a position to carry on a régime of gross oppression and injustice under cover of the authority and power secured to them by the Administration. Sir Frederick Lugard made urgent requests for an increase in the number of political officers, pointing out that so vast a country—one-third the size of British India—could not possibly be administered without an adequate administrative staff. "If the British nation," he wrote almost in despair in 1902, "is not prepared to bear the cost of an enterprise which promises good returns and already shows substantial progress, it were better that it had never undertaken it." The original number of political officers had, however, been steadily increased, and in 1903 a number of "revenue officers" were appointed, who were subsequently incorporated with the assistant Residents. The same year another great advance was made by the appointment of a batch of police officers, and a large increase was simultaneously made in the force of civil police. The object of this innovation was twofold: first, to increase the efficiency of the military force by relieving it of a number of petty detailed duties of a civil nature which it had up till then been called on to perform, to the detriment of discipline; second, to relieve the Residents of a large part of their more irksome duties, and give them time to attend to their important problems of administration and taxation. A police officer was attached to each province to take command of the detachment of civil police and to act as deputy-sheriff, having charge of the gaol and all civil prisoners. He also held the powers of a Justice of the Peace and could therefore deal with petty offences, and it was intended that he should investigate all crimes, arrest offenders, and prepare cases for trial before the Resident in the provincial court, acting himself as Public Prosecutor if necessary. The police force under him was armed with Martini-Henry carbines, and was to be given a semi-military training. It was to perform all prison duties, escort prisoners down country to the central gaol, and supply a small detachment to the Resident when he went on tour in a pagan district where an armed escort was considered necessary. A Chief Commissioner was appointed to command the whole force, with his headquarters at Zungeru, and all supplies, equipment, accoutrement, etc., were received at a central depôt, and issued thence to provinces as required. The system was by no means perfect, its chief objection being the dual control to which the provincial police officers were subjected, the latter being responsible partly to the Resident of the province and partly to their own Chief Commissioner at headquarters. It served its purpose, however, in relieving the Resident of a considerable amount of work, and the military of a number of detached duties.

The Resident in charge of each province was responsible directly to the High Commissioner. Routine correspondence was sent to the Secretariat, but all political matters were dealt with in letters and reports addressed to the High Commissioner himself, who thus maintained the closest possible touch with his Residents and the affairs of their provinces.

Orders and information were conveyed to Residents and others in the Government Gazette, which was published monthly, and printed copies of each new proclamation as it was enacted were sent to the provinces.

The policy of the High Commissioner was set out from time to time and communicated to Residents in a series of Political Memoranda, which dealt with such subjects as slavery, punitive expeditions, the status of native Chiefs, taxation, and native courts. They also explained various proclamations and the object of certain legislation; outlined instructions as to the proper methods of laying out stations and roads; gave lists of the various books and documents to be kept up in provincial offices; and generally familiarised Residents with the High Commissioner's views on all the most important subjects. It would be difficult to over-estimate the value of this system, whereby the High Commissioner was able to place on record and communicate to his political officers his views on the many administrative problems which presented themselves as the country became opened up. Receiving reports and information from every province throughout the Protectorate, he was able to form a general view of the situation and conditions, and to promote a continuity of policy through the medium of these Memoranda. "It is the duty of Residents," he wrote, "loyally to carry out the policy of the High Commissioner, and not to inaugurate policies of their own. The High Commissioner is at all times ready and anxious to hear, and to give full and careful consideration to the views of Residents, but when once a decision has been arrived at he expects Residents to give effect to it in a thorough and loyal spirit, and to inculcate the same spirit in their juniors."

At the end of every month,[1] the Resident in charge of each province submitted to the High Commissioner a full report of the work done in his Province, and all matters of interest connected therewith. The Report was divided into sections, such as General Administration, Judicial, Native Courts, Slavery, Trade, Departmental, Revenue and Taxation, Transport, Missions and Education, etc., and each subject was dealt with separately. To it were attached various statistical and other returns—such as Register of slaves freed, Summary of Caravan Statistics (showing Exports and Imports), Return of Revenue received, Summary of Cases tried in the Native Courts, Maps of the routes traversed on tour, and so on. Besides the Report and Returns to the High Commissioner, there were the provincial accounts to be despatched monthly to the Treasurer, with vouchers in duplicate, copies of cash-book, etc., the Cause List with a summary of every case tried in the provincial court during the month to the Attorney-General; a Transport Return to the Transport officer; Meteorological statistics to the Principal Medical Officer; and a variety of other documents. It will be seen that the office work was of no light description, and did not leave much time for the study of ethnology or native customs and languages. At the height of the caravan season the Resident was often employed collecting as much as thirty or fifty pounds each day in tolls, most of it in

[1] Subsequently changed to every quarter.

the smallest coins, for every penny of which he was personally responsible; in the intervals of counting money, he would be investigating a slavery case, or possibly making up the fortnightly mail-bag, and arranging for runners to take it to the next station. It was a time of tremendous stress, and for short periods many Residents were obliged to work as much as twelve and fourteen hours a day to prevent arrears from accumulating. They had, however, caught the enthusiasm which their indefatigable chief inspired, and they knew that if they worked hard, he worked harder still. For six o'clock saw the High Commissioner daily at work in his office, and he rarely left it except for meals till close on six in the evening, often spending the time after dinner in discussing important affairs of State with his headquarters officials. In 1903, however, the appointment of Revenue and Police officers came as a relief to the overworked political officers, and enabled them to turn their attention to other matters which now demanded it.

These increases of staff entailed a very considerable expenditure, and yet the only source of income for the Protectorate over and above a small sum collected for licence fees and other items, was the fixed contribution made from the revenues of the Coast Protectorates, which represented the supposed approximate value of the Customs dues on goods imported into Northern Nigeria through the coast ports. The balance was met by a Grant-in-aid from the Imperial Government. For the financial year ending the 31st of March 1902 this Imperial grant had been £280,000, the Southern Nigeria contribution £34,000, and local receipts £4,424, making a total revenue of £318,424. The estimated expenditure for the ensuing year, owing to the necessary increase in staff and other expenses caused by the extension of administration over the entire Protectorate, showed an increase of £37,000 over this total. It must be remembered, in considering the balance-sheet of the Protectorate, that the military force, whose cost (direct and indirect) absorbed a very large proportion of the revenue,[1] was not merely a local asset. It was liable for service in any part of West Africa, and large contingents had on three occasions been sent out of the Protectorate to take part in expeditions in Ashanti and Southern Nigeria. Nevertheless it was necessary to discover some source of internal revenue to meet the increased cost of administration and relieve the home Exchequer. The reasons against taking for the present any portions from the incomes which the Chiefs derived from their subordinate villages have already been given. But there were two classes of the population which had lost nothing from the prohibition of slave-raiding, and had gained enormously by the settlement of the country, the impetus given to trade, and the money which had been poured in. These were the native traders, and the canoemen of the navigable rivers. The High Commissioner's proposal, therefore, which was approved by the Secretary of State, was to impose a toll on the goods carried from the interior to the Coast and back by caravans, and a licence duty on the owners of canoes.

The method of assessing and collecting these taxes was simple. With regard to the canoes, all owners were obliged by Proclamation to register their canoes, which were classified according to size and carrying

[1] £132,000 was the direct charge on the Estimates for the W.A.F.F. during the years 1902 and 1903.

capacity, and an annual licence fee paid, varying, according to the classification, from five shillings to three pounds. Discs were issued to Residents to be affixed to each canoe as soon as it had been registered, showing its classification and serial number, and a receipt was issued from a counterfoil book for each payment made.

In a similar manner caravans were obliged by Proclamation to declare the goods carried by them at certain toll stations set up along the main caravan routes and notified as such in the Government Gazette. As these caravan routes passed in nearly every case through the various provincial headquarters, practically no new machinery was required, since political officers were able to register the goods and collect the tax themselves, aided by their staff of clerks, agents, messengers, and others. The toll was fixed at 5 per cent *ad valorem* in each Province traversed, up to a maximum of 15 per cent. The value of the goods was calculated at each Customs station; a schedule being prepared by the Resident and approved by the High Commissioner. The method of collection was as follows. On the arrival of a caravan at a toll station it encamped in the open space set aside for the purpose, and at once declared its goods—live-stock, loads of natron or salt, hides, and so forth—to the toll-collector, who checked them on the spot. The list was then prepared and taken to the Resident's office, where a Clearance Paper was made out in a counterfoil book, setting forth the name of the caravan leader, places whence he came and whither he was proceeding, value of each article, and toll due. This was signed by the Resident, and given to the caravan leader, who paid the toll in cash, and was then free to proceed on his journey. On arriving at the first toll station in the next province the same proceeding took place, the caravan leader being given a second clearance paper; if, in the meanwhile, he had sold a portion of his goods, he, of course, paid only on what remained, since the goods were checked afresh at each station. When a caravan had passed through three Provinces and received three clearance papers, it was free of further payment, since it had paid the maximum 15 per cent fixed by Proclamation.

These tolls were instituted early in 1903. The revenue for the financial year ending March 31 showed receipts under the heading Licences, Excise, etc., amounting to £7826, as against £631 collected the previous year. In the following year the receipts under the same heading advanced to £39,250.

The policy of raising revenue by means of caravan tolls was assailed from many quarters on the ground that it was an unwise burden on trade, which should have been fostered rather than taxed. The objection, sound enough in theory, overlooked practical considerations. To begin with, it was essential to raise a local revenue from some source, and that immediately, and these tolls taxed those who could most easily afford to pay and who had benefited most from the expenditure entailed by the occupation and administration of the country.

The system, moreover, enabled large sums to be raised with the minimum of expense and trouble, since the machinery for collecting the tolls was already in existence in the persons of the Residents and their staffs.

That the tolls did not hinder trade to any appreciable extent is clearly shown by the fact that the revenue from them increased year by year in spite of the fact that evasion became more frequent as the country became more settled and the by-roads secure. The tolls also had certain results which were of immense benefit to the development of the country. They enabled statistics to be collected of the bulk and nature of the trade which circulated through the country, and its value; for a full account was kept at every toll station of every article of merchandise which passed through during the year. Furthermore, they were an invaluable aid in the distribution of coinage to replace the cowrie shells which had hitherto been the only form of currency in existence, and which was so bulky that a man's load of cowries amounted in value to no more than a few shillings. Since traders were obliged to pay their tolls in coinage, a demand for this was created, and Government servants, officials, soldiers, and police who received their pay in current coin, found natives eager to accept it in exchange for food and local products.

Finally, the very attempts of traders to escape payment of tolls by evading the toll stations induced them to open up new routes and carry civilising influences into pagan districts which had never before seen a trader or come into contact with any individual outside the limits of their own tribes or villages. The caravan, in fact, corresponded to the peripatetic hawker or pedlar of Europe in the Middle Ages, and performed the same function in disseminating news, carrying into remote corners information as to the events taking place in other parts of the country. Within two years of the institution of caravan tolls, traders were penetrating into little-known pagan districts; caravans, hitherto banded together for purposes of self-defence, broke up into small parties which avoided the main roads and towns, and trickled through the country in tiny streams; the exclusive pagan, induced by the trader to exchange a little of his corn or honey for some of the salt which was such a necessity to him, received his first lesson in barter. It is difficult to exaggerate the effect which this distribution of trade produced in a short period of time in opening up the country and carrying some knowledge of the Administration into the remotest pagan villages. It was, however, never intended that caravan tolls should be a permanent institution. They were merely a temporary method of raising revenue while inquiries were being instituted into the native system of taxation by the Chiefs, which it was clearly recognised must be the basis of the future revenue of the Administration.

CHAPTER VIII

TAXATION PROBLEMS IN 1903–1904

THE beginning of the fourth year of administration saw the Protectorate under complete control, divided into provinces, each with its Resident in charge, assisted by a small staff and supported by garrisons occupying the chief strategical points. The principal Emirs had all been installed personally by the High Commissioner, and had accepted formally and publicly the conditions of appointment explained by him. The time had now arrived when they might with justice be called upon to contribute a portion of the expenses of administration from the revenues secured to them. Both the Secretary of State and the Treasury had concurred in the reasonable contention of the High Commissioner that an increased staff, involving a considerable expenditure, was necessary to make the Protectorate a revenue-producing and eventually self-supporting country, and for the financial year 1903-1904 the Imperial Grant-in-aid was increased to £405,000, which included £25,000 for telegraph construction—an undertaking recognised to be of urgent strategical importance. The estimated local revenue for the same year was £39,475,[1] a considerable

[1] The sum actually realised exceeded this figure considerably. It amounted to £53,726. Even so, however, the local revenue contributed little more than one-tenth of the total expenditure of the Protectorate.

advance over the total actually received in the previous year, which amounted to about £16,315. The increase was due to the large sums which it was rightly estimated would be produced by the caravan tolls and canoe licences, and also to certain small contributions which it was intended should be made by the native chiefs. To understand how these contributions were arranged for and from what source the chiefs derived their incomes, a glance must be taken at the various native organisations which existed throughout the Protectorate.

Speaking generally, three stages of civilisation were represented, more or less distinct, though often overlapping and merging into one another. To take the lowest first, there were the independent pagan communities, which had been able to set invaders at defiance and to maintain their independence. These had no system of taxation whatever; there was rarely any tribal organisation or acknowledged Chief. Each village was a self-contained community, every member of which enjoyed the same social standing, tilling his own field with his own hands, and supplying his own simple wants—the apotheosis, in fact, of socialism. Private property in land was an idea which probably never entered their heads, for land was plentiful, and every individual could have the use of as much as he needed. There might be disputes with another tribe or community regarding boundaries or territory, but these usually had their origin in questions of prestige, or hunting rights, rather than in land hunger, and were settled in the usual primitive way—by recourse to the bow and arrow. It is not improbable that even the socialist ideal of the common ownership of the means of production was realised, and that the hoes with which they tilled the ground were owned, more or less, in common. Pagan tribes certainly smelt their own iron, and amongst the most primitive all the men of the community join in this industry each year before the farming season, and probably turn out jointly the number of hoes required. If to lead the simple life is to be happy, these simple pagans must have been ideally so. There were, however, certain drawbacks in this Utopian existence. They were everlastingly at war with one another, and never safe from slave-raids when they left the security of their village fastnesses to go to their fields. The husbandman worked with his bow over his shoulder and a watchful eye on the bush all round him, lest he should be suddenly seized and carried off into perpetual slavery. The advent of the British, notwithstanding their prohibition of slave-raiding, was in no sense welcome at first to the ignorant pagan. His motto was, "Noli me tangere"—Forbear to interfere with me. If the White Man, he thought, did not want slaves, he wanted tribute. The idea that the new Power stood for security to life and property never dawned on the pagan, for such things were unknown to him: to appreciate individual liberty, one must first experience it. For a long time the pagans fiercely resented being prohibited from making war on their neighbours, raiding cattle, and attacking traders, though they clamoured for protection from attacks by others on themselves. It takes time for primitive savages to learn that if they desire freedom to enjoy their own rights, they must respect the liberty and rights of their neighbours.

Next to these primitive pagans—many of whom were cannibals and wore no clothing whatever—were communities, also pagan, who possessed a definite tribal organisation under recognised Chiefs. Many of these owned allegiance to the Mahomedan states, and paid an annual tax or tribute, sometimes in produce, sometimes in the form of currency most widely in use—cowrie shells. They possessed few social distinctions and practically no arts or crafts: each man was an agriculturist, and the coarse cotton with which they clothed themselves was woven, as a rule, by the man who wore it. The village was the unit, though large towns often had one or more subordinate villages which generally paid a small tax to the Chief. These more advanced pagan tribes were the ones which suffered most from the slave-raiding of the Mahomedan Emirs, though they occasionally purchased immunity for a time by paying a fixed annual contribution of slaves. They had as a rule no markets: goods were exchanged by friendly barter. In many of the towns which lay on or near the large caravan routes, however, Hausa colonies had settled and had built a regular Hausa quarter, with mosque and market. These Hausas considered themselves infinitely superior to the pagans, held themselves aloof, and paid no tax. As for the pagans' tax, if it was paid to a Mahomedan Emir it was assessed arbitrarily by the latter's representatives at the largest sum they thought they could raise, and was collected by the Chief in the form of a general levy on the whole of his subjects: if in slaves, households were called on in turn to provide them, and the balance was made up of men and women of the tribe condemned by the community to slavery for witchcraft or crime.

Finally, there were the highly organised Mahomedan communities, with an elaborate system of administration and taxation, based on the Koran and the Islamic books of jurisprudence. They differed slightly in details, but the general principles were the same, and to describe the organisation of one Mahomedan Emirate is to describe with a fair degree of accuracy the whole number.

The Emir received his appointment at the hands of the Sultan of Sokoto, after being nominated from amongst the members of one of the "royal" families, *i.e.* descendants of the original flag-bearers, by the principal officials of the Emirate. As Emir he was practically an autocrat, though he was much influenced by the advice and opinions of the various State officials, some of whom in many states constituted a council under his leadership. These officials held various titles, and were composed partly of relations of the Emir or members of another "royal" house, partly of Hausa notables, and partly of slaves or ex-slaves, who had risen to favour or eminence by their own qualities or abilities. The titles were not, as a rule, hereditary: they were in the Emir's gift, and when a vacancy occurred he filled it by appointing any one he thought fit. Each title had some special duty or duties attached to it, some of a purely military nature, others connected with the household or administration.

Emirs occasionally created new titles, to bestow on relations or favourites, and these were generally sinecures. To each title one or more towns, or possibly pagan districts, were attached. These paid their tribute through the holder of the title, who was thus a kind of feudal overlord, and he retained a share, handing over the remainder to the Emir. The title-holder, or overlord, was also permitted to exact supplies from his towns, and to call for labour and material to repair his residence in the capital, and possessed various other privileges. He himself resided in the capital, and accompanied the Emir to war; he rarely visited his towns, which were dotted about in different quarters of the Emirate, but he kept a large staff of messengers, who were despatched to the towns at the tax-collecting season, to give instructions regarding the tax, with orders to remain till it was collected. When the collection had been completed by the village headman, they accompanied him or his deputy with the tax to the capital, where it was first handed over to the title-holder and then taken to the Emir, to be divided up in the proper proportions amongst Emir, overlord, messengers, and village headmen. Thus the entire Emirate was divided up amongst title-holders, who numbered in a large Emirate anything from fifty to one hundred. If labour were required for some public work, such as the repair of the walls of the capital, the Emir would summon the overlords, and apportion the work amongst them; they would then divide their share amongst their various villages, and send out their messengers to call in the required number. In this way an excellent and highly efficient organisation was maintained.

As regards the taxes, the system was somewhat complicated and elaborate, but extraordinarily complete and well organised. The Mahomedan tithe of corn was paid by all followers of Islam; and although this should, by Koranic law, have been used only for charity, it was regarded as an integral part of the revenue. In every Hausa state, except Sokoto,[1]

[1] The Sultan of Sokoto derived a large and sufficient income from the annual contributions—chiefly of slaves—paid by the various Emirates.

there was, in addition, a tax called the "land-tax," paid by all the agriculturists; it was assessed on each "farm," or "plot," or "hoe," and varied from village to village. It was, however, constant throughout any one village, though liable to annual revision. It amounted in effect to a poll-tax, since practically every tax-paying individual owned and worked a farm; its name, however, shows plainly that it was looked upon as a rent for the use of land. It was collected annually by the headman of each village on the arrival of the messengers from the capital; it often took some months to collect, during which time the messengers remained in the village at the expense of the villagers. There were also taxes on certain special crops—sugar-cane, tobacco, onions, etc.—which required a special soil; and taxes on butchers, brokers, dyers, weavers, hunters, and many others. These were not collected by the village headman, but each had a special staff, whose head was appointed by the Emir, and who wandered over the entire Emirate, collecting from each village; as a rule the tax was farmed, and the Emir received a fixed amount. They formed, in reality, a system of licence duties, and were quite distinct from the land-tax, which was a rent.

The system, excellent though it was in many ways, possessed many grave disadvantages. It employed an enormous number of officials, and opened the door to an almost unlimited amount of corruption and oppression. Its worst feature, however, was that the educated and ruling classes were dissociated almost entirely from the towns and districts entrusted to their charge, since they delegated their powers to a host of minor officials, many of whom were unscrupulous rascals, without either principles or education. Probably it arose, to a great extent, from the fact that the Emir and his officials spent at least half of their time at war—generally slave-raiding. Each year a large war-camp was formed on the borders of the pagan districts, from which raids were conducted. This camp attracted all the riff-raff and adventurers of the countryside, and the neighbourhood was drained of supplies. Taxation in the Hausa States was never really heavy or onerous, for the simple reason that the main source of revenue was slave-raiding: slaves were currency, slaves were wealth. A few bags of cowries or a few bundles of corn, more or less, did not greatly matter to the Emir and his officials.

Each village was a unit, having its headman, who was nominated by the villagers, and received his appointment at the hands of the Emir through the medium of the title-holder. On appointment he was obliged, by custom, to make a large present to the Emir and the overlord; the office was not hereditary, although in practice it frequently remained in the same family for many generations. It was sought after primarily because of its prestige, but partly also because there were many small perquisites; the headman, for instance, did not himself pay any tax; he was allowed the use of certain land, which was attached permanently to the office; applicants for minor ranks in the village gave him presents, and so forth.

The headman was responsible for law and order in the village, settled disputes, inflicted small punishments —usually by fine—arranged for the accommodation of strangers and visitors, and could grant or withhold the right for an immigrant to settle. In all these matters he acted as the deputy of the Emir, to whom an appeal could always be made. If a crime were committed in or near the village, it was his duty to report it at once to the capital, and arrest the culprit. If a highway robbery occurred within the village boundaries, he at once proclaimed a hue and cry and turned out the inhabitants to track down the perpetrators. In each Emirate there were one or more Alkalis (the Hausa corruption of the Arabic *El Kadi*, the judge), who held a Court and dispensed justice according to Islamic law. There were also minor Alkalis in many of the principal towns. As a rule they legislated only in civil cases. Serious criminal cases were usually dealt with by executive officers, and by the Emir, assisted if necessary by the Alkali, to whom points of law could always be referred. Repeated theft was punished by cutting off the hand; murder by decapitation; adultery by stoning to death. These punishments took place publicly, in the market-place, and were in accordance with Koranic law. There was also a gaol at the capital, where prisoners were confined for various offences, being shackled with native-made leg-irons. They were not employed on any kind of work, and were often herded together under indescribably insanitary conditions.

A market was held daily in the capital city, and on certain fixed days in the smaller towns. Cowries were the medium of exchange, and prices were regulated by an official, appointed as head of the market. Stalls were set apart for the various kinds of goods —cloth here, foodstuffs there, live-stock in one corner, firewood in another, and so on.

Each town of any importance had its school, where the children were taught verses of the Koran, which they shouted aloud, parrot-like. Some of these children when they grew up became "mallams"—that is to say, priests or learned men, for education and religion are one amongst Mahomedans. These made a living by the writing of letters or charms; in some cases they learned needlework as well, and wove beautiful embroideries on Hausa gowns.

Amongst the wealthiest of the traders were the butchers, for though the staple food of the native is guinea corn, he is very fond of meat; and oxen, sheep, or goats are killed almost daily in most towns of any size. The meat is cut up and roasted, and sold in immense quantities in the markets. The tax on butchers was therefore farmed out for a considerable sum.

Such was the general organisation of a Hausa state. On the whole, it was an extraordinarily well-managed institution. The Hausa is a merry individual who enjoys life, is singularly well behaved and peaceable, and is a born trader. He has a peculiar affection for titles and the status of officialdom, and each village has its sets of officials, and each official another set, subordinate to him. He therefore readily understands organisation and discipline, and is amenable and law-abiding. He is a great contrast to the independent pagan. The latter values his liberty and independence above everything else in the world, and is so exclusive that he rarely leaves the immediate neighbourhood of the village in which he was born, and in which he will some day die. The Hausa, on the contrary, cares little what stranger comes and usurps the throne, so long as he himself is allowed to cultivate his farm, and to go on chaffering in the market on his leisure days, and journeying up and down the country with a caravan in the dry season.

We are now in a position to appreciate the problem of direct taxation which presented itself to the Administration as soon as the northern Emirates had been included in the Protectorate. Apart altogether from the question of revenue, it was of the utmost importance to preserve and secure to the ruling Chiefs the legitimate dues which they had been in the habit of receiving from their subjects. To allow these to lapse even temporarily, would have been to produce a state of anarchy and lawlessness which would have been both culpable and dangerous. Moreover, it was due to the rulers themselves to see that they did not suffer more loss than was necessary, since the prohibition of slave-raiding and slave-trading had already deprived them of the greater part of their incomes. The High Commissioner therefore issued instructions to the Residents to see that all customary dues were paid by the inhabitants to their Chiefs, as before, and to render all necessary assistance in collecting them. Further, those pagan districts which had suffered from slave-raiding, or had purchased a certain immunity by an annual contribution of slaves whilst retaining their independence, were to be taken under the direct protection of Government, in return for which a small annual tax in money was to be paid by each village or community, the amount being assessed by the Resident after frank discussion with the inhabitants themselves. The wilder districts were to be approached gradually, and brought under control as opportunity offered; our policy of protection was to be explained to the tribesmen who inhabited them, and a small tribute imposed, at first nominal, as an acknowledgment of our supremacy and in return for the protection afforded, and later, on the basis of population and wealth.

These instructions were put in force during the year 1903, and at the same time searching inquiries were being prosecuted by Residents as to the methods of taxation already in existence in their several provinces, for up to this time nothing definite was known on the subject. Early in 1904 a Proclamation was issued giving legal effect to a system by which Government would share in the taxes, the important Emirs paying into revenue a quarter of the gross amount of the income received by them. This was a temporary measure, intended to give time for the High Commissioner to obtain information through the detailed reports of the Residents, and his own observation during a rapid tour which he made through the Protectorate, before framing legislation which would satisfy more completely the existing conditions and necessities. The mass of information received has already been outlined and summarised in the description of the organisation of an Emirate. The merits and the faults of the prevailing system were clearly seen and could now be justly appreciated. The policy of the High Commissioner was directed to conserving the former and eliminating the latter; and he aimed further at promoting, as far as possible, a general uniformity in matters in which it was essential that a common policy should prevail throughout the Protectorate, whilst giving as great a latitude as possible to the varying conditions of each Emirate. Drastic changes were, he realised, injudicious in Africa, especially amongst a people so conservative of tradition as were the inhabitants of Northern Nigeria; yet the inauguration of British rule was the right moment for introducing such changes as were necessary, for at no later time would it be so easy or suitable to do so.

The first essential was, that the innumerable petty taxes should be amalgamated into one or more, to which legal sanction should be given by an Ordinance of the Government. This involved, as the High Commissioner wrote, "a truly colossal task," for it meant that each Resident should visit every town and village in his province, and by the help of the native authorities should assess its tax-paying capacity. The magnitude of the task will be realised when it is remembered that each province was in extent about the size of Ireland, and for the most part unexplored and unmapped.

The next important step to the simplifying of the taxes was the improvement of the method of collection. To the extortion which the prevailing method engendered was added the frittering away of a large part of the taxes paid by the peasantry amongst a host of collectors and their agents and followings, with the result that the net amount which ultimately reached the Emir was small, and bore an insignificant proportion to the total amount collected. A reduction in the number of petty taxes would lessen the number of collectors, and now that the ruling classes would no longer be engaged in warfare, they could assume their proper function of supervision of the minor officials in the towns and districts entrusted to their charge. Here a difficulty intervened. The towns allotted to each title were scattered more or less at random over the Emirate. If the holders were to supervise them effectively, a regrouping must take place, so that the towns pertaining to any one title should not be separated, but should lie within the boundaries of a single geographical area. As it would be the duty of the title-holder to maintain order in his district as well as supervise the collection of the taxes, it was essential that he should reside there, and not in the capital.

These reforms were communicated by the High Commissioner to provincial Residents, with instructions to discuss them fully with the Emirs and officials, and listen to any representations that might be made. The Emirs were at first distrustful of proposals which threatened their own authority by setting up a number of sub-districts administered on the spot by subordinates, who, they thought, would quickly arrogate to themselves independent powers. In this, however, they were reassured by Residents, who promised readily to support the central authority and to put down at once any attempt to disregard it. One further difficulty was disclosed as the proposals began to take shape. It appeared that in nearly every district there existed towns founded by immigrants from some distant parent city, and in many towns and villages themselves a portion of the inhabitants originated from some other town: in both cases these immigrants claimed to pay their tax to the town from which they had emigrated, and declined to acknowledge the authority of the local headman. This was obviously a relic of a patriarchal system, in which the unit was not territorial but tribal—not an area, but a group of individuals or a class. For this and other reasons it was found best to introduce the changes gradually, and not to hasten them unduly. Patience and sympathetic handling of the situation brought their own reward, and the Emirs, who had at first received the proposals with suspicion and distrust, ended by welcoming them as a solution to the problems that arose, and threw themselves heartily into the task of carrying them into execution.

In 1906 a Proclamation, superseding that of 1904, gave legal effect to a complete system of taxation, maintaining the original native organisation, but in an improved form. It was called the "Native Revenue Proclamation," and authorised the levying and collecting, in accordance with certain detailed provisions, of such sums as the Resident of each province, with the approval of the High Commissioner, should fix and assess. The basis of assessment was to be the annual value of the lands and produce, of the profits from trade and manufactures, of the flocks and herds of nomad shepherds, and of certain other existing sources of revenue. The Resident was authorised to divide his province into districts and to appoint chiefs as district and village headmen for the purpose of supervising and assisting in the collection of taxes under the Proclamation. The duties of these district and village headmen were laid down, and the share of the tax which they were to receive as remuneration: also the penalties that might be inflicted for offences detailed in the Proclamation—mainly extortion by collectors, the giving of wilfully false information, collection of unauthorised taxes or of taxes by unauthorised persons, etc. Proceedings to enforce payment of taxes were to be taken before a Provincial Court, and penalties were provided for refusals or persistent neglect to pay.

Instructions to Residents and explanations as to the working of the Proclamation were further elaborated in a series of Memoranda drawn up by the High Commissioner, in which full details were given as to the mode of assessing the taxes, bringing receipts to account, preparing their books for audit, and so forth. Counterfoil receipt-books, statistical, abstract, and other forms, were printed in the Government Printing Offices, and sent out to the Provinces.

The system thus introduced was based on the sum of existing taxation, modified and adjusted by the Resident after careful investigation, and for this reason introduced no drastic changes to vex and confuse the mind of the African native. It was, as the High Commissioner wrote, "neither a mere consolidation of existing taxes—increased or decreased, as the case might require—nor was it (except in hitherto untaxed districts) an arbitrary assessment, *de novo*, by the Resident. Its merit, in my view, was that it partook of both characters. So far as it was based on tradition and custom, it ensured ready acceptance among a conservative people, and its collection presented no novel difficulties, while so far as it was modified by the Resident and consolidated and fixed alternatively at a money value, payable only once in the year, it inaugurated the beginnings of principles recognised in more advanced communities, and enabled the collection to be made in a manner in which the proceeds could best be utilised by the Administration, and accounted for in accordance with financial instructions, while it ensured a more just incidence and greater uniformity."

At the beginning of this chapter the inhabitants of the Protectorate were described as subject to classification into three more or less distinct stages of civilisation. It is now possible briefly to relate how each of these was affected by the native revenue legislation.

First, as the unsettled districts inhabited by wild pagan tribes who had never paid a tax of any sort were brought under control, a very small sum was levied on the tribe as a whole, payable through the recognised head, who was left to distribute its incidence amongst his fellow tribesmen by mutual agreement. The sum was fixed arbitrarily by the Resident, who made a rough guess at the population and its general wealth, and assessed the tax at first at figures so low that there could be no difficulty in collecting it each year without having recourse to force to compel payment. In this way the pagans learnt the principle of making an annual payment for benefits received by the community, and grew to understand that they were not being robbed by a conquering power, but that the tax was a fixed sum, and that once paid, they were free of any further demands till the following year. As a revenue-producing asset, it was almost negligible. But as a principle it was of immense value, and laid the foundations of a fair and equitable system of taxation in later years, when commerce had spread and the "untutored savages" had developed into civilised communities.

With more advanced pagans the assessment was made on a population basis. A census was taken, and a rate fixed for each adult male, dependent on the wealth of the village or community, its proximity to markets or caravan roads, fertility of soil, and so on. This rate, multiplied by the number of adult males, with a small allowance made for casualties, was assessed as the tax on the village, to be collected by the Chief or headman and paid to the Resident. It was practically a poll or capitation tax, but as every member of these communities was an agriculturist, tilling his own farm, it may be said equally to have been a land rent, and to have approximated very closely to the "single tax" of Henry George and his followers. Its great merit consisted in the fact that every individual knew precisely the amount that he would be called upon to pay each year, and was thus not liable to any extortion on the part of his Chief.

Finally, in the Mahomedan Emirates, all the old taxes were conserved, and the peasant paid what he had always been accustomed to pay. He was, however, relieved from the crowd of greedy tax-collectors who had harassed and oppressed him in the past. He now paid all his taxes direct to his own village headman, and in case of oppression or extortion he could lay his complaint at once before the district headman—the old title-holder—who, however, resided on the spot instead of being far away in the capital.

Simple as this system may appear, the amount of labour which was entailed in putting it into working order was incredible. The task was, as Sir Frederick Lugard had truly said, "a colossal one." The country, as I have already pointed out, had to be explored and mapped. Every town, village, and hamlet had to be visited, inscribed on the map, its approximate population and total tax ascertained, history recorded, and information checked. All these details must then be entered in books and records at provincial headquarters, the towns grouped in districts, and districts in divisions, and an alphabetical index compiled. Then when taxes began to come in, receipts had to be made out, payments recorded, deficiencies noted and remedied, lists sent to administrative headquarters, and all accounts rendered monthly to the Treasury in such a way that they could be efficiently checked by the Auditor. With a political staff of about six in each province (two of whom would be on leave and one or more probably down with fever), and each province about the size of Ireland, there were not many hours of leisure during the twenty-four, nor of days during the year. The work, however, was done with a fair measure of success and a vast amount of enthusiasm. No one could complain that it was not interesting.

The first Revenue Proclamation had been enacted in June 1904, but the tabulating of villages and preliminary assessments had been begun a few months previously. The High Commissioner had estimated the local revenue of the Protectorate for the year ending March 31, 1905, as £54,445. When the accounts were made up it was found to have reached the sum of £94,026, a considerable increase over the previous year, when the total had been only £53,726. It was satisfactory to realise that the revenue had been obtained, not by imposing new or additional taxes on the people (for the amounts from newly taxed pagans were negligible), but by preventing leakage and waste amongst a horde of idle collectors and hangers-on.

CHAPTER IX

RISING IN SOKOTO IN 1906—RESIGNATION OF SIR F. LUGARD

THE narrative has been interrupted since the death of the ex-Sultan of Sokoto at Burmi in July 1903, and a long digression made on the subject of taxation and the reorganisation of the Mahomedan states, because the months that followed the fall of Kano and Sokoto were mainly taken up with these important reforms.

As soon as the inhabitants realised that no interference with their religion or customs was intended, and that the position of their rulers and officials was to be maintained under conditions promising more security to life and property, and less corruption and oppression, the country settled down with marvellous rapidity. Both rulers and subjects of the Mahomedan states entered into hearty co-operation with the Residents, and commerce increased by leaps and bounds. Fresh land was taken into cultivation, the defences of the walled towns began to crumble into ruins, and the inhabitants spread far and wide into the bush, cleared fresh tracts and built little hamlets and shelters on their farms, since they no longer feared the devastation of war or raids. Residents travelled unescorted through the length and breadth of the Emirates, and were everywhere welcomed by the inhabitants. Only in the pagan zones was hostility encountered. These ignorant and exclusive people, who had for centuries lived in terror of the slave-raiding invader, could not understand that any conquering power would come amongst them for any purpose but to harm them, and they were quick to resent with bow and arrow any attempt to enter their districts or prohibit them from raiding caravans or making war on their neighbours. In December 1903 the Resident of Bassa, a pagan province to the south of the Benue, while proceeding with an escort of soldiers and police to install a Chief, was set upon by a savage tribe in thick jungle and killed, together with the police officer who was accompanying him. An expedition was despatched from Lokoja to recover the bodies and exact reparation. In the following year several minor expeditions against pagan tribes were necessitated in the provinces of Kabba, Kontagora, Yola, and Bauchi, owing to raids on caravans and other acts of lawlessness. The West African Frontier Force had been increased early in 1903 by the addition of a regiment of mounted infantry, for service on the northern frontier, where raids from across the border by detachments of nomad tribes were prevalent. The force of civil police had also been increased and turned into constabulary, with the object, amongst others, of protecting Residents when touring through pagan districts where attacks might be expected. Provinces were now being divided into administrative divisions, each with a junior Resident, responsible to the Resident in charge of the Province, and small detachments of police or constabulary were needed at all these out-stations to guard treasure, convey prisoners to the provincial gaol, and act as escort to the political officer on his tours.

Thus the years 1904 and 1905 were taken up mainly with internal reforms, and efforts were directed to opening up the country to trade and commerce by peaceful means, bringing the backward peoples into touch with civilisation, safeguarding the more advanced communities from the oppression of their rulers, and training the latter to a right appreciation of the laws of justice and equity. Every Department was working at full pressure to keep pace with the rapid extension of the Administration. The Secretariat, the Treasury, the Public Works and the Postal Departments all had fresh burdens thrown upon them. More steamers were placed on the river to meet the increased demands for transport: tributary rivers were explored to test their navigability. A much-needed Transport Department was organised, and efforts were made throughout the Northern Provinces, away from the tsetse belts, to replace human porterage by animal transport. A cart road from Zungeru to Zaria and Kano was surveyed and construction begun, and it was hoped by building masonry bridges and culverts to enable cart convoys to carry stores to the interior along this route throughout the year. The delimitation of the northern frontier—a line nearly 1000 miles in length—by an Anglo-French Boundary Commission was completed, as was the delimitation of the eastern boundary from Yola to Lake Tchad by an Anglo-German Commission. Minor expeditions against pagan tribes in Bornu and elsewhere were undertaken, but they partook more of the nature of police patrols than of military operations.

The peace, however, was not destined indefinitely to remain unbroken. In January 1906 a quarrel broke out between some Hausa traders and local natives at a town on the Benue river, where the Niger Company had a store under a native agent. Beginning as a petty market squabble, it soon developed into a sanguinary contest. The local natives called in their allies, the warlike Munshi tribe, who came in large numbers, and practically annihilated the Hausas, of whom some 70 or 80 were killed, while others were lost in the river or carried into slavery; the victors then sacked and looted the Company's store, after which they set fire to it, and burnt it to the ground. This outrage demanded instant attention, the more so as members of the same tribe had a few months previously fired on the Resident's canoe, and it was necessary at all costs to safeguard navigation on the Benue, since it is an international highway, used by the Germans as well as the British. A large expedition was therefore prepared and despatched to the scene, troops being withdrawn for the purpose from headquarters, since the Munshis are a large tribe and inhabit a country which is most difficult for military operations.

At the moment when a large portion of the military forces was thus engaged in the extreme south of the Protectorate, an event occurred with startling suddenness in the far-distant north-west corner of so serious a nature as to cause for a brief period a situation of the gravest danger and anxiety.

It appears that a certain "Marabout" or itinerant priest, an outlaw from French territory, had come to a village not many miles from Sokoto, and, stirring up the religious fanaticism of the Moslem population, had begun to preach a *jehad* or Holy War, and the extermination of "unbelievers." This is by no means an uncommon occurrence in Mahomedan countries, and such men usually procure a small following amongst the more ignorant section of the population. The advent of the outlaw reached the ears of the Sultan, who immediately reported it to the Resident. The latter determined to proceed at once to the spot, arrest the leader, and bring him to trial. To support him he took with him the company of mounted infantry which formed the garrison, and he was accompanied also by his assistant and by the medical officer. Arriving in the vicinity of the village he decided to ride forward with his assistant and endeavour to effect his object without having to call upon the military to use force. He therefore left the troops and cantered forward, calling out to the assembled crowd that he had come in peace and wished to talk with them. He had hardly spoken when the mass of people, who were armed with swords and spears, charged down upon him, shouting, gesticulating, and brandishing their weapons. Meanwhile the officer in command of the mounted infantry detachment, seeing the distance that separated him from the Resident, and growing anxious for the latter's safety, had given the order to his men to mount and move forward in square formation. In the act of executing this manœuvre, whilst some of the men were mounted and others dismounted, the armed mob bore down upon them. Many of the horses took fright, and in the general *mêlée* that ensued, the Resident, his assistant, and the military officer were cut down, twenty-five of the soldiers killed, and the sole remaining European, the doctor, escaped with a spear thrust through his arm, helped on to a spare horse by a native soldier, whose gallantry was subsequently fittingly rewarded. The remainder of the detachment made their way back to the small fort at Sokoto.

At this time the telegraph line was in course of construction to Sokoto, and had reached to within 80 miles of the town. Runners were at once despatched to line-head, bearing a message from the doctor detailing the news and asking for reinforcements. A message was, at the same time, sent to a detachment of infantry quartered at a town some 100 miles distant, on receipt of which it marched at once to Sokoto. On the night of February 15, the day after the disaster, the telegram from line-head reached the High Commissioner at Zungeru. In view of the absence of a large portion of the troops on the Munshi expedition, the situation was one of grave anxiety. Those who have any knowledge of the outbreaks of Mahomedan fanaticism which have from time to time taken place in Egypt, the Indian Frontier, and elsewhere, and who realise the impetus given to such fanaticism by a disaster to British troops, will understand the danger which threatened the Protectorate owing to the likelihood of the unrest spreading throughout the whole of the Mahomedan states on the northern border unless immediate steps were taken to deal with the local rising. It was fortunate that the High Commissioner had, during the six years that the Protectorate had been in existence, pushed forward the construction of telegraphic communication with unremitting energy, even obtaining special grants for the purpose from the Imperial Exchequer. The wisdom and foresight of this policy were now demonstrated. It enabled him to receive news of the disaster within a few hours of its occurrence and to summon the military force necessary to meet the situation. The troops were at once recalled from the Munshi expedition; 75 rank and file—all that were available—

left Zungeru for Sokoto, to be reinforced *en route* by the garrison from Kontagora; 100 men were despatched from Lokoja, and two companies of mounted infantry were ordered by telegram to march with all speed from Kano to Sokoto. The news of the disaster was flashed in code to every provincial headquarters, and Residents were warned to take every precaution and to report any sign of unrest.

Fortunately the insurgents had contented themselves after their success with raiding some of the neighbouring villages, and had made no attempt to attack the remnant of the Sokoto garrison or to rouse the country. The Sultan of Sokoto and his officials identified themselves entirely with the British, and several Chiefs came in with offers of assistance. The arrival of the first reinforcements at Sokoto relieved the anxiety as to the garrison, and reports of a reassuring nature began to come in from the Provinces. It was evident that the rising was purely local, and affected neither the bulk of the people nor their rulers. By March 10, less than a month after the disaster, a sufficient force had been collected at Sokoto to deal with the insurgents, and marched out against them. The latter, encouraged by their previous success and hoping to repeat it, charged down on the advancing troops with fanatical courage, but were mown down by heavy rifle-fire and dispersed. Their leader was captured and brought to Sokoto, where he was tried in the Native Court and executed; the village where the rising had originated was razed to the ground, and the Sultan pronounced a curse on any one who should rebuild it or till its fields.

Although the important Emirates of Kano, Katsina, and Zaria had, as has been seen, proved perfectly loyal during this anxious time, there was one smaller Emirate, that of Hadeija, lying to the east of Kano, which adopted a very different attitude. The Emir had never willingly accepted the British régime, but had acquiesced in it with sullenness. The High Commissioner, during his tour throughout the Protectorate in 1904, had used every endeavour in a personal interview with this Emir to establish friendly relations between him and the Government, and trusted that patience would in time bring about a willing co-operation. The Emir, however, had proved obdurate, and his actions had been consistently marked with obstruction and hostility, culminating in the murder of a soldier, apparently by his orders and in his presence. When the news of the Sokoto disaster reached Hadeija there was public rejoicing in the city, and the Emir ceased to send his messenger to the Resident. Peaceful measures having been tried for a period of three years, and having failed, it was necessary after the rising at Sokoto had been dealt with, to resort to stronger measures, and in April 1906 a force was despatched to Hadeija with the High Commissioner's ultimatum. A defiant answer having been received, the town was entered, resistance overcome and the Emir's walled citadel captured, he himself being killed in the fighting. The remainder of the populace submitted, and, as at Kano three years previously, the town in a few days resumed its normal aspect, the market was well attended, and the people resumed their normal avocations. The heir was installed as Emir under the usual conditions, and was given a letter of appointment, after which the expedition returned to headquarters.

In one other Mahomedan province only was there

trouble during this critical period. Early in the year a few fanatical preachers had endeavoured to create unrest in the east of the Bauchi provinces, and to rouse the inhabitants to unite in a *jehad*. The Emir of Bauchi and the leading officials had, however, actively co-operated with the Resident in suppressing these dangerous fanatics, and the leader was arrested, and, after trial in the Native Court, executed. The effect of this prompt action was to allay the unrest and put a stop to any further seditious fanaticism. The rise of these "Mahdis" in different parts of the Protectorate, and the initial unprecedented success of one of them, could not be otherwise than exceedingly disquieting to the Administration. It is true that little serious damage need be expected from an undisciplined mob armed with spears and swords, when opposed by a well-drilled force armed with modern rifles and officered by Europeans. It must, however, be remembered that there are no European soldiers in Nigeria, and that of the natives composing the locally raised forces a very large percentage is Moslem. The so-called Mahdi, at any rate the fanatical and seditious preacher, is a feature common to all Mahomedan countries comprising semi-civilised peoples. It is idle to expect in Northern Nigeria that he will not frequently appear on the scene, and in many cases obtain a hearing and a following. He is not the outcome merely of alien or non-Mahomedan domination of a Mahomedan country, for he appears again and again, and in many cases raises the standard of revolt "in the name of the Prophet" when the rulers are of his own faith. The Fulanis were obliged to deal with many such before the British ever set foot in Nigeria—witness the ex-Mahdi, Mallam Jibrella, whose history has already been related. They constitute one of the dangers that must be expected in the future as in the present, and against which the Administration must be unceasingly on the watch.

Accepting then the fact, what are the means best calculated to guard against a seditious upstart developing into a real menace to the State?

I would suggest three, which seem to me the most important and most efficacious. First, the complete identification of the interests of the inhabitants with those of the Administration, so that there is ready and willing co-operation in the maintenance of law and order. Second, the delegation of power and responsibility to officials on the spot, so that they may deal promptly with any emergency that arises, and not be obliged to wait till it has assumed formidable proportions. Third, the improvement of communications, so that news can be instantly conveyed from one point to another, and troops despatched with all speed to any threatened quarter. The first is a matter of policy, dictated by the Secretary of State as representing the Government of which he is a member, and carried out by the officials responsible to him; the second is a matter of administration; the third is mainly a matter of finance. For all three the ultimate responsibility rests on the nation at large.

It may have been noticed that both in the case of Sokoto and of Bauchi, the offender was tried in the Native Court, that is to say, by the duly appointed Alkali and his assistants; in each case the Emir also attended, and was present throughout the proceedings. By this means the fact was accentuated that the rising had been directed, not against the British, but against those responsible for law and order, both native and

British. Cordial co-operation between the Emir, his officials, the peasantry, and the Resident, is the key-note of the policy of Northern Nigeria, and the ideal aimed at. If it fails, all fails. For there neither are, nor ever can be, any British troops permanently quartered in West Africa[1] to enforce British supremacy on a hostile or discontented people.

By the month of June the whole Protectorate had settled down once more into its normal aspect of peace and tranquillity, and the High Commissioner was able to proceed home on his well-earned leave. His health, however, had suffered severely from the climate and from the strain and anxiety of the past seven years since he had first assumed the duties and responsibilities of his arduous post. A period of rest and recuperation had become imperative, and in September of 1906 he reluctantly laid down the burden of office. Seven years previously he had taken over the administration of vast territories in which slave-raiding and war were rife, where every man's hand was against his neighbour, and security of life and property hardly known. He left to his successor a country well organised, divided into Provinces, each with its separate staff, with garrisons occupying central positions, communication established, taxation placed on a sound basis, and the native rulers cordially co-operating with the British Administration in the task of government. He left also the impress of his own personality—indomitable courage, unswerving devotion to duty, and untiring energy. Of him it might well be said that to have served under him was a liberal education.

The results achieved under him are best described

[1] I do not include the harbour of Sierra Leone, where there is a battery of garrison artillery in charge of the fortifications.

in the words of his immediate successor, Sir Percy Girouard, who wrote as follows in his first Annual Report: "Very few countries have witnessed such great changes for the better in such a short space of time as has been the case in Northern Nigeria. In 1900 some 30,000 square miles out of a total of 250,000 were under some form of organised control. The whole of the remainder was controlled and ruled under conditions giving no guarantee of liberty or even life. Slave-raiding with all its attendant horrors was being carried on by the northern Mahomedans upon the southern pagans, and the latter, divided into a vast number of small tribes, were constantly engaged in inter-tribal warfare. Extortionate taxation was exacted in most directions in the north, and in Bornu the country was being devastated and the population exterminated by Zubehr's cruel lieutenant, Rabeh. In the south, cannibalism, slave-dealing, witchcraft, and trial by ordeal were rife. In no direction were native traders, even when travelling within their own provinces, safe from the murderous attack of organised robber bands and their chiefs. No European trader had, for purely trade purposes, established a single post 50 miles from the Niger or Benue river. By 1903 the whole condition of the country had entirely changed. Sixteen provinces, comprising the entire Protectorate, had been organised by the never-ceasing efforts of Residents acting upon the policy previously described. The character of the work and its difficulties are only too clearly witnessed by the list of political officers who have laid down their lives in its accomplishment, and the lasting effects left upon the constitutions of many of those who remain to carry on the Administration, lightened though it may be of many of its previous personal discomforts and pioneer work. . . . The northern Mahomedan states have been purged of many radical defects and purified in their executive, administrative, and judicial functions. The confidence of the southern pagans has been gradually won as often by patience, diplomacy, and tact, as by resort to arms. The result is that, to-day, the unadministered area of the Protectorate does not exceed the administered in 1900."

CHAPTER X

EVENTS IN 1907—APPOINTMENT OF SIR PERCY GIROUARD AS HIGH COMMISSIONER—CONSTRUCTION OF RAILWAY TO THE INTERIOR

DURING the time that Sir Frederick Lugard was at home, and until a successor was appointed, the administration of the Protectorate was in the hands of the Deputy High Commissioner, Mr. (shortly afterwards Sir) William Wallace. On him devolved the duty of personally investing the Sultan of Sokoto at his capital with the Order of St. Michael and St. George, of which he had been created an Honorary Companion by His Majesty, in recognition of his loyalty and services during the disturbances of the previous year.

The year 1906 was devoted mainly to completing the arrangements for the collection of the tribute-tax,[1] and so much progress was made in this, that the Acting High Commissioner was able, at the end of the year, to recommend to the Secretary of State the abolition of the caravan tolls and canoe licences. Sanction having been received, Proclamations repealing them were enacted early in 1907, and Residents gained thereby more freedom to devote to touring their provinces and setting up the machinery of

[1] *i.e.* the tax collected under the Native Revenue Proclamation of 1906.

provincial organisation. The loss to revenue, however, was serious, for these two taxes had brought in between them upwards of £40,000 per annum. It was hoped that the loss would be compensated by a corresponding increase in the native revenue tax, owing to the closer assessment which Residents would now have time to effect.

Early in January 1907 the announcement was made of the appointment of Sir Percy Girouard, K.C.M.G., D.S.O., to succeed Sir Frederick Lugard as High Commissioner. The rising in Sokoto the previous year had directed attention to a matter which Sir Frederick Lugard had brought forward as early as his first Annual Report, and which he had mentioned on frequent occasions since, namely, the pressing necessity of a railway into the interior. Various schemes had been suggested, the Government of Lagos advocating the extension to Northern Nigeria of the railway already constructed from the port of Lagos to a considerable distance inland, while the High Commissioner of Southern Nigeria had suggested the construction of a railway from the port of Calabar towards Lake Tchad. Sir Frederick Lugard in his Report for 1900 had urged that a railway policy should be settled as soon as possible. So far as Northern Nigeria itself was concerned, the immediate necessity was, as he pointed out, for a railway from the Niger banks to Kano, and not for connection with Lagos, which could be left till later. "Every yard of a railway from the Niger to Kano would," he wrote, "by superseding the present caravan transport, tend greatly to promote the development of trade." The waterway of the river would, in this case, be used to convey to the coast the produce brought down by the railway from the interior. "Nor," he continued, "was it only a question of trade. Communication was needed to facilitate internal administration, and for the rapid concentration of troops and supplies."

Urgent as the matter was in 1900, it became still more so in 1903, when the northern provinces were taken under control. In his Report for 1902, the High Commissioner once more called attention to the immediate need for a railway, to supersede the costly and unsatisfactory human porterage which formed the sole means of communication with the interior. Alternative routes, he said, had been surveyed from Zungeru to Zaria by the Director of Public Works, and a feasible track for a surface-line found. A port on the Niger has also been discovered, whence a light surface-line could be constructed through Bida to Zungeru, thus saving the long ten days' journey round by water. In November 1903 an engineer with two assistants was sent out from England to make a survey for a line from the Niger to Zaria, and this was completed by June 1904, a route giving easy gradients throughout being found. The question of expense, however, was an almost insurmountable obstacle. The Protectorate was already receiving a considerable Grant-in-aid from the Imperial Exchequer, and the large additional cost of a railway could not be provided for. The High Commissioner was therefore obliged for the present to content himself with constructing a cart road from Zungeru to Zaria out of Protectorate funds, and with introducing a system of cart transport, until such time as money could be found for the more costly railway. In January 1905 the first cart convoy arrived at Zaria from Zungeru, and the difficulties due to having to rely solely on human porterage were temporarily obviated, though the carts were not able to continue running when once the rainy season set in. Every effort was made to organise an efficient system during the dry season of 1905-1906. Artificers and drivers had even been imported from India, and proved of the greatest use; depôts were established for supplies of fodder along the road; a veterinary surgeon was attached to the Department. In spite of all these efforts, however, the cart transport proved little less expensive than carriers.

It was known that Sir Percy Girouard, whose experience in railway matters was unrivalled, had received special instructions to investigate the question of a railway policy, and submit a report at the earliest opportunity. Shortly after his arrival in the Protectorate in April 1907, he made a rapid tour to Zaria and Kano, following the cart road, and returning by another route; he had also caused soundings to be taken along the course of the Niger in order to ascertain its practicability as a waterway. In May he was able to send home to the Secretary of State a despatch dealing exhaustively with the whole subject, and indicating the policy which he considered best fitted to meet the existing conditions. The decision of the Secretary of State was not long delayed, and in August 1907 telegraphic instructions were sent out from home authorising the construction of a line from Baro on the Niger to Kano, a distance of some 350 miles. The cost was estimated at one and a quarter millions, the gauge to be that of the Lagos railway (3 ft. 6 in.), and the line to be of a pioneer description. The difficulty regarding funds was obviated by an arrangement whereby the capital expenditure was to be provided by the Protectorate of Southern Nigeria (which had been amalgamated with Lagos), and the interest to be met by the revenue hitherto derived from the annual contribution from the Southern to the Northern Protectorate on account of Customs dues. At the same time the Governor of Southern Nigeria was authorised to push forward the Lagos railway till it eventually effected a junction with the northern railway not far from Zungeru. In this way, through railway communication would be established between Kano and the coast port of Lagos, with an alternative route by way of Baro and the Niger. The construction of the northern railway was to be undertaken by the Public Works Department of Northern Nigeria, the staff of which was to be increased by the inclusion of additional engineers, surveyors, and other expert officials; while a detachment of Royal Engineers was to be lent by the Imperial Government, their salaries being charged against the railway vote.

The moment sanction was received, the work was put in hand, all concerned displaying the utmost enthusiasm. Orders for the necessary material were made out and despatched to England, surveys were undertaken, and earthworks begun. The political staff was called on to provide local labour through the Chiefs and native officials, and scales of pay were laid down. All Departments were drawn on to render assistance, and the High Commissioner himself set the example by personally superintending the preliminary operations. In June 1908, only six months after work had been begun, 140 miles of location survey had been completed, and 170 additional miles of reconnaissance survey had been carried out, with the assistance of officers from the West African Frontier Force and other Departments; earthworks were proceeding over a distance of 100 miles; and arrangements had been made for the reception at Baro of 25,000 tons of material. The native Emirs took the greatest possible interest in the works, visiting them, and rendering every assistance in arranging for an ample supply of local labour.

At the same time, efforts were being made to improve the channel of the Niger from the coast up to Baro. A survey of the various bars and sandbanks between these points had revealed the fact that the obstructions caused by them extended over not more than three or four miles in a total distance of 400 miles. A suction dredger of special type had therefore been ordered, by means of which it was hoped to secure a four-foot channel throughout the year, which would suffice for the passage of the largest stern-wheelers in use. On the success of this experiment depended the use to which the Niger could be put in transporting goods to or from the interior. To facilitate the transport of materials, a fleet of three powerful stern-wheel tugs and fourteen lighters was placed on order at the latter end of 1907, and these were delivered the following year.

The improvement of the communications from the coast to the interior of Northern Nigeria owed its origin not only to strategical necessities, but to the hope that the Protectorate might thereby be developed into a great cotton-exporting country. Zaria, the centre of the cotton-growing industry, is 600 miles from the coast, and 300 miles from the nearest port on the navigable Niger. The tin-mining industry also demanded transport facilities, both to export the ore and to import machinery. The mining area is situated on a rocky plateau in the west of the Bauchi Province.

To reach it from the coast, the river Niger is ascended by steamer as far as Lokoja, a distance of 340 miles; thence by steamer or canoe to a port, Loko, 110 miles up the Benue; from Loko a march of nearly 200 miles intervenes to the mining area. In the absence of transport facilities, all goods had to be carried by porters over this distance, and every load was limited to a weight of 65 lbs., the maximum burden for a carrier. If a railway were constructed from the navigable Niger to Kano, it would be easy to connect it by a branch line with the mine fields 100 miles to the east, and thus afford a cheap and easy outlet to the coast.

It is difficult to over-estimate the importance to the Protectorate of this much-needed railway. It provided the natives with the means whereby they might place their produce on the world's market, and receive in exchange the manufactured and other commodities of foreign countries. As a civilising agent a railway connecting the interior of Africa with the coast, plays an important part, and lays the foundations of future prosperity. The very construction of a railway in a new region of tropical Africa has civilising results of a far-reaching character. Natives are brought together from distant parts, and learn the system of daily and weekly wages, and the use of money. To realise the influence which labour on earthwork construction possesses over the mind and character of the primitive pagan, and to understand something of the change which takes place in his ideas, one must first know him in his secluded village, and then watch him after a few weeks of work in a railway camp. His intelligence is awakened, his exclusiveness vanishes, his fears subside, and he becomes alert and self-respecting. The system by which the earthworks of each section of the line are constructed by natives employed temporarily from amongst the neighbouring districts, who return to their farms as soon as the work is completed, is one which is of direct benefit to the country, owing to its educative influence. The native is in no way de-nationalised, or taken permanently from his familiar avocations or environment. He mixes on friendly terms with members of other tribes, whom he has hitherto met only on the battlefield, if at all. He learns to trade, and to satisfy his growing wants, by means of the wages which he earns. "It is self-help which makes the man," said Gladstone characteristically, "and man-making is the aim which the Almighty has everywhere impressed upon creation." It is certainly the aim to be kept before administrators in tropical Africa, and railway construction, when conducted on sympathetic and understanding lines, is undoubtedly one of its most valuable aids.

That the railway to Kano will supersede the costly caravan traffic across the desert to the Mediterranean cannot be doubted. Arab merchants have for centuries been established in Kano, and have traded with Tripoli and Morocco by means of camel caravans plying backwards and forwards across the Sahara. Already they are using the route to the West Coast to import the articles which formerly reached them from the north, and a great impetus has been given to trade by the cheapening of communications with Europe. Kano is destined to become more than ever the emporium for Central Africa, and the railway will attract commerce from the French possessions of the Soudan. Earthworks have already been completed, and the line will be opened for traffic by 1912, if not before. Slave-raiding and tribal warfare are at an end, and their place will be taken by commerce. A new era is opened for the inhabitants of Northern Nigeria, and it remains for them to work out their own destiny.

Besides the organisation of the railway staff and the various details connected with construction of the line, there were other matters which demanded and received the immediate attention of the new High Commissioner. Before arriving in Northern Nigeria, Sir Percy Girouard had made a close study of the conditions of land tenure and assessment in India and other countries, and he now instituted inquiries into conditions obtaining in the Protectorate which he was called upon to administer. The Native Revenue Proclamation of 1906 had based the assessment on the value of the lands and their produce. The next step was to ascertain clearly the tenure on which the peasant held his land, and the relationship between himself and his Chief or overlord. With this end in view the High Commissioner drew up and circulated amongst Residents a lengthy memorandum dealing with the subject, and requesting information on various points connected therewith. The replies were collected and tabulated, and in 1908 Sir Percy Girouard submitted to the Secretary of State a despatch containing his own views and the observations of the Residents, recommending that expert advice should be sought on "a subject of such vital importance to the present and future welfare of the inhabitants of the Protectorate." "The condition of tenure obtaining in Northern Nigeria," he wrote in his Annual Report for 1907, "discloses a situation apparently allowing of a policy which would promise lasting benefits and protection to the native population." The Secretary of State concurred in the recommendation, and in June 1908 appointed a Committee in London to consider the whole question of Land Tenure and Assessment in Northern Nigeria. The conclusions at which it arrived will form the subject of a later chapter.

Besides these various problems there were many other questions to which the new High Commissioner gave his careful consideration, and in doing so displayed an energy and zeal as whole-hearted as that of his predecessor. The relations between civil and military officers in the various operations and patrols necessitated by the conditions of the country were put on a sound and definite basis after discussion by a representative Committee convened by the High Commissioner. The constabulary were reorganised and reconstituted as a police force, the dual control which had formerly existed being abolished; by withdrawing the police from the Mahomedan Emirates and substituting small bodies of prison-warders, a saving of £16,000 per annum on the Estimates was effected. The Political Secretariat, which had hitherto existed as a small Department directly under the High Commissioner, was incorporated in the Administrative Secretariat, and a few political officers were introduced temporarily into the latter with a view to bringing the provinces into closer connection with the central Administration. A beginning was also made in the all-important matter of education, and early in 1909 a Director of Education was appointed from amongst the political staff, and entrusted with the task of inaugurating a system on lines of which the general principles were contained in a Memorandum drafted by the High Commissioner. A small saving was effected in the military Estimates by a reduction in the mounted infantry force, though a corresponding increase was made to the rank and file of each infantry battalion, rendered necessary by the withdrawal of constabulary from the Mahomedan Emirates. The High Commissioner also introduced a system of weekly telegraphic "conversations" with provincial Residents, by which he succeeded in gaining an intimate personal knowledge of local affairs, enabling Residents at the same time to feel that they were not altogether cut off from headquarters and its immediate concerns.

Sir Percy Girouard proceeded home on leave early in 1908, returning in June, and at the close of the year made an extended tour through the Hausa States, being met by the various Emirs, to whom he explained the policy and intentions of the Government, demonstrating that the continuity of the policy introduced by his predecessor would in no way be interfered with.

In April 1909 the High Commissioner, whose title had now been changed to that of Governor and Commander-in-Chief, returned once more to England on leave, handing over the administration as usual to Sir William Wallace, to act for him during his absence. In July of the same year, news was received that Sir Percy Girouard had been appointed Governor of East Africa, and would not return to Northern Nigeria. The great ability which he had brought to bear on the many problems in which the Protectorate was involved, and his sympathetic understanding of them, had rendered his two years of administration conspicuous for the high level of progress which had been maintained, and his loss was keenly felt by those who had served under him. Sir William Wallace continued to administer the Protectorate till the arrival in December 1909 of the newly appointed governor,

Sir Henry Hesketh Bell, K.C.M.G. Thus within the short space of little over three years, Northern Nigeria has been administered by no less than four successive governors, a state of affairs which renders continuity of policy, not indeed impossible, but certainly extremely difficult.[1]

The appointment of Sir Henry Hesketh Bell brings the narrative up to 1910, and beyond this point I do not propose to follow it. The few remaining chapters will be devoted to the consideration of some of the problems which are either in process of solution in Northern Nigeria or which remain to be solved in the immediate future. Though apparently distinct they are in reality closely connected with one another, and it is almost impossible to deal administratively with one without affecting all the others as well. Their importance lies in the fact that it is on the manner in which they are dealt with that the future of the country depends.

[1] "Continuity of administration is one of the most necessary factors for the good government of African races." I quote this from the High Commissioner's Report for 1907.

CHAPTER XI

SLAVERY

"The radical vice of the Sudan, the disease which, until cured, must arrest all intellectual and material progress, is the general, constant, and intense prevalence of slave-raiding. . . . This can only be eradicated by the same vigorous means which we employ in Europe for the prevention of crime and violence."—Sir GEORGE GOLDIE, Preface to *Campaigning on the Upper Nile and Niger*, Seymour Vandeleur.

"This is the great debt which the European owes to the African, that after having caused, or at least increased, this nefarious system on his first bringing the natives of these regions into contact with his state of civilisation, which has had scarcely any but a demoralising effect, he ought now also to make them acquainted with the beneficial effects of that state of society."—BARTH, *Travels in Central Africa*, vol. ii. p. 133.

"God has ordained that your brothers should be your slaves: therefore him whom God hath ordained to be the slave of his brother, his brother must give him of the food which he eateth himself, and not order him to do anything beyond his power, and if he doth order such a work, he must himself assist him in doing it. He who beateth his slave without fault, or slappeth him in the face, his atonement for this is freeing him."—*The Table Talk of Mahomed.*

THE problem which stands out most prominently of all those which confront the European when he is called upon to administer a country—especially a Mahomedan country—in tropical Africa, is that of slavery. It meets him at every turn, its ramifications extend into every region of the social organisation of the country. Yet there is no problem which requires so steady a judgment. There are earnest humanitarians who look upon the state of slavery with such horror that they demand the instant manumission of every slave, no matter what injury may thereby result to the social organism of which he is a member. There are, on the other hand, equally earnest men who hold that the negro is, by his very nature, peculiarly adapted to the state of servitude, and that, at an early stage of his civilisation, he thrives better and is happier as a slave than as a free man.

The passion for personal liberty and freedom of action is so deep-seated amongst civilised nations in the twentieth century that it is difficult for them to approach the subject of slavery with an unbiassed mind. Yet it is of the utmost importance to realise that in Africa the idea that a human being may be or may become the absolute property of another human being appears as natural as the possession of an ox or a horse. From the dawn of history until comparatively recent times "Nubian slaves from Ethiopia" were bought and sold in European and Asiatic markets, and the condition of slavery in tropical Africa has, up till the present day, been looked upon as a natural state of affairs, a necessary and inevitable appanage to any complicated social organism. Amongst primitive pagan tribes, the institution did not, as a rule, exist; that is to say, they did not themselves own slaves. Their organisation was simple, there were no social distinctions between individuals, and there was no room for the employment of slave labour; but the idea of slavery was perfectly familiar to them, and they were, as a community, always ready to sell as slaves either individuals of their own tribe for particular reasons, or members of other tribes captured in war or by other means. With more civilised communities, particularly with those which had embraced Islam, slavery formed the very basis on which their social organisation rested. All labour not performed by individuals themselves was effected by slave labour; wealth and property consisted almost entirely in slaves ; strict rules existed regarding the treatment of slaves and their disposition ; bargains were conducted in terms of slaves, which formed a kind of currency. Such a thing as free or voluntary labour was practically unknown, and where a man required work done which he was unable to do himself, he possessed no alternative, even had he so desired, than to use slave labour.

So far as the actual condition of slavery was concerned, there is much to be said for it. The slave was relieved of all anxiety both for the present and for the future by the fact that his master was legally obliged to provide him with food and lodging, to look after him in sickness, and to allow him certain days on which he could work for himself. Slaves often rose to positions of great importance, and amassed considerable wealth. Many purchased their freedom, and became slave-owners themselves. It is true, a slave might be torn from his wife or children, or might be sold to some new master in a far-off land, but cases such as these were probably not very frequent, for besides the fact that in a Mahomedan community a master can, by Islamic law, be prosecuted for ill-treatment of his slave, there was a moral obligation amongst slave-owners which forbade cruel or inhuman treatment of their slaves except in cases of sloth or misbehaviour.

The real evil of slavery consisted in the method of enslavement. Those born in slavery had, as a rule, little to complain of, but they formed only a small proportion of the total number, and they were seldom exposed in the open slave market. It was war which furnished the victims for the latter, and it was the constant need of procuring fresh slaves which was ultimately the main cause of the endless bloodshed and misery in which the country was habitually plunged. Tribe waged ceaseless war upon tribe to procure captives to sell to the slave ships which visited the coast of West Africa in the seventeenth and eighteenth centuries to purchase slaves for the West Indian and American plantations. Yet the number of natives enslaved for this export trade probably bears but a small proportion to those dealt with in the internal traffic in the interior. The Mahomedan states were constantly raiding the pagan tribes on their borders, nominally either on religious grounds or to punish them for attacks on traders and others, but really in order to secure captives for the slave market or as part of their annual tribute. It was these virtual slave-raids and the miseries suffered by the captives both on their journeys to distant slave markets and their subsequent exposure there, which makes slavery so unspeakably cruel, and it is the description of such events by explorers, travellers, and missionaries which has aroused in Europe such a violent and genuine horror of African slavery.[1]

It is well, however, to insist upon the material difference between slave-raiding—using the term to cover the violent enslavement of human beings—and the mere condition of slavery. The latter, though absolutely incompatible with modern ideas, has, as has been shown, much to be said for it. The former is barbarously and inhumanly cruel, and has no justification whatever, except that it is a primitive and

[1] Barth, for instance, was informed by the vizier of Bornu that in the course of his pilgrimage to Mecca, forty of his slaves died in one night from cold and exposure. Denham records finding, round wells in the desert, hundreds of skeletons of slaves who perished when being driven across in caravans for sale in Tripoli.

extraordinarily cruel form of war. It admits, however, of a simple remedy, namely, the prevention of inter-tribal warfare and the imposition of peace. Without this, the horrors of slave-raiding can never be put an end to. It is hardly necessary for European Powers to remind themselves of the part they played in the past in instigating and promoting these inter-tribal wars to serve their own ends. The fact that they can now put a stop to iniquities which they once furthered not only justifies, but demands, the occupation and administration by them of the uncivilised portions of the African Continent. It is incumbent on them to atone so far as may be for the past wrongs inflicted by them on the natives of West Africa by setting up strong and efficient Administrations to impose peace, and make it impossible for any natives to be carried off into slavery.

The abolition of slave-raiding and inter-tribal warfare was therefore the first duty that devolved on the new Administration. But this meant nothing more nor less than a military occupation of the entire country, for it was idle to suppose that peace could be achieved from a distance by a mere decree without a force on the spot strong enough to impose it. Nothing but fierce opposition to a policy which prohibited slave-raiding could be expected from the Mahomedan states, whose entire social organisation depended on a sufficient supply of slaves, and whose so-called wars provided them with their main source of income. "Can a cat give up mousing?" was the reply of the slave-raiding Emir of Kontagora, when informed that under the British régime slave-raiding must cease. "When I die, it will be with a slave in my mouth."

The pagan tribes might be expected to welcome a

Power which promised them their immunity from the slave-raids which had devastated their countries for centuries, but they formed only a portion of the area to be administered. As events turned out, moreover, these pagan tribes proved even more troublesome than the Mahomedan states, for their suspicions of the new conquering Power were difficult to remove, and for reasons which will presently be given, they did not appreciate the new anti-slavery policy as warmly as might have been expected.

Before taking any action, however, it was essential to formulate a definite policy as regards slavery. It would clearly have been an act of gross and arbitrary injustice to declare the immediate emancipation of all slaves without compensation to the owners. In native eyes, as has already been remarked, the ownership of a slave was no crime, but was as natural as the ownership of cattle or any other form of personal property. Many a native had invested all his capital in slaves, and to have declared these free would have been equivalent to an act of confiscation with no shadow of justification. The Royal Niger Company, when by right of their Charter they were administering the country, had recognised this, and, on their defeat of the Emir of Bida in 1897, had met the difficulty by an Ordinance abolishing the legal status of slavery throughout the regions over which they held direct control. It is interesting to note that the action of the Company received the enthusiastic approval of the British and Foreign Anti-Slavery Society, which complimented it on its "admirably terse and pronounced decree," and heartily commended the wording of the document as "an example of brevity and force."

From the date of the assumption by the British

Government of the Niger Company's territories till the 1st April 1901, this decree was the only legislation in the Protectorate regarding slavery. On the date mentioned, a Proclamation was enacted which confirmed this policy, declaring the legal status of slavery abolished throughout the entire Protectorate, and stating that all children born after the date of the Proclamation would be free. The inclusion of the northern Emirates, and the extension of British administration over the entire Protectorate in 1903, enabled a further step to be taken, and in 1904 a new Proclamation was enacted, which, after repeating that of 1901, reaffirmed the abolition of the status of slavery, and in addition declared slave-trading an offence. This was repeated in 1907 by a final Proclamation, which forms the present law.

The main clauses of this Proclamation are as follows: The legal status of slavery is, and remains, abolished throughout the Protectorate; all children born since March 31, 1901, are free; transactions in slaves,[1] by non-natives, are illegal; slave dealing is declared unlawful and is prohibited; the offence is defined, and penalties laid down; finally, a clause declares that "no compensation from Government to persons claiming to be owners shall be recognised in respect of slaves who may acquire their freedom by virtue of this Proclamation."

We are now in a position to understand the effect which these various laws exercised over the state of slavery which existed prior to the British occupation of the country, when it was recognised by custom and by strict Mahomedan law. First, it rendered the enslaving of any free man impossible, whether by force,

[1] Including assistance in the surrender of a fugitive slave to his master.

purchase, or other means. Second, property in persons, as slaves, was in the eye of the law no longer recognised; a slave was henceforth accounted to be legally responsible for his acts, and competent to give evidence in court. Third, a slave had the right to assert his freedom if he wished to do so, and any attempt on the part of his master or other person to detain him in a state of servitude was illegal and punishable by law. Fourth, the transfer of the slave from one master to another, either by gift, purchase, or other means, was prohibited and constituted an offence. Fifth, no compensation could be claimed by an owner from the Government for the loss of a slave who obtained his freedom under the Proclamation.

This was obviously satisfactory from the point of view of the slave. How did it affect the master, who had acquired slaves before the advent of the British, when the purchase or ownership of a slave was no offence either by his laws, or his religion, or his customs? How was such a policy to be justified unless compensation were paid for the loss of slaves so acquired? Further, was there not a danger of upsetting the entire social organisation of the country, and producing a state of anarchy?

The subject was discussed in a series of memoranda written by Sir Frederick Lugard and circulated among Residents. The law was to be explained fully to Chiefs and people, and the co-operation of the former sought by means of frank discussion from all points of view. The situation was admittedly difficult: but it was by no means hopeless. The mere ownership of slaves was not illegal, provided the latter made no effort or had no wish to procure their freedom, and in a large number of cases they did not. By Mahomedan law, a slave was at all times entitled to purchase his freedom in court, and could claim freedom before a Mahomedan judge under certain circumstances ordained by law, such as cruelty at the hands of his master. Here, then, was a means by which any slave who desired his freedom could obtain it without any injustice being done to his master. The British occupation entailed a great demand for labour, both on the part of Government and of the natives: a large amount of money was being put in circulation. There was no difficulty in obtaining wages in return for labour, and it was easy for a slave to put by out of his earnings sufficient money to purchase in a short time his emancipation from his master through the native courts. Again, since there were no waste lands, and the rights over every area were vested in the hands of Government acting on behalf of the native rulers, a slave could be denied the right to settle on and cultivate land until he had contracted to purchase his freedom from his former owner. This was a necessary proviso in order to prevent vagabondage and the occupation of land by a horde of masterless runaway slaves, who sought to profit by the Government policy towards slavery by living a life of idleness and lawlessness impossible under native law and custom.

It will be observed that the task of Residents was no easy one, and the difficulty of acting with justice both to owners and slaves was very great. The best course open to them, after full discussion with the Emirs and Alkalis, was to leave the matter as far as possible to the native courts, and to treat each case which could not be so dealt with, on its merits. The success of the policy adopted by the Government depended mainly on the manner and spirit in which it was carried out. In a very large number of cases, difficulties between masters and slaves were settled in an informal manner by the political officer summoning both parties and inviting them to discuss their points of difference frankly before him. If any cruelty were proved, the matter could be dealt with either in the provincial or native courts. On the other hand, slaves were plainly informed that Government would not permit them to become vagabonds, but that arrangements would be made whereby they might earn a livelihood, and pay from their wages, by a system of instalments, the sum of money necessary to purchase their freedom through the native courts.

It is not to be denied that many slave-owners suffered considerable losses through no fault of their own, and the bitterness engendered thereby was not rendered less dangerous by the fact that such slave-owners belonged for the most part to the more intelligent and influential class of native. A great number of slaves, many of whom had recently been captured in war, seized the opportunity to return to their country. Many deserted their masters and took service under the Government, either as soldiers, police, transport carriers, or labourers in the Public Works Department.[1] On the whole, however, the policy justified itself by its results, and the transition stage from slavery to free contract has been marked by singularly little active discontent or disorganisation. The native rulers were quick to see that their interests lay, not in setting up a futile opposition to the known policy of the Government, but in co-operating with

[1] Where this was known, and a master complained of the desertion of his slave, an arrangement was usually effected by the Resident, whereby the ex-slave agreed to pay a sum out of his earnings to purchase his freedom, and was given a certificate of freedom by the native court.

Residents, and seeing that the change was effected with as little disturbance to existing conditions as possible.

It has been said that the pagan tribes did not appreciate the policy with regard to slavery as warmly as might have been expected. The reason for this attitude, which in some cases amounted to positive resentment, is curious. In the past, these communities had treated crime in their midst by the simple expedient of selling their criminals into slavery to a passing caravan; more important still, they had got rid in the same way of any member of their community suspected of witchcraft and exercising the power of the "evil eye," a superstition in which all pagans most profoundly believe. Long-standing debts were also commonly recovered by selling into slavery the debtor, or one of his family—for amongst pagans, families always recognise the responsibility in financial affairs of any of their members. Hence, when a Proclamation was issued forbidding the selling of any person into slavery, and making it a crime punishable with several years' imprisonment, the pagans found themselves unable either to get rid of their bad characters or witches, or to recover their debts. The first effect of the anti-slavery legislation in many cases was to cause these "witches" to be taken out secretly into the thick bush and killed, since they could no longer be sold into slavery. This, however, was a temporary difficulty, and was soon overcome; civilising influences gained a gradual hold over the minds of the primitive pagans, and caused them to abandon by degrees many of the superstitions and fears due to ignorance.

The policy pursued in Northern Nigeria with

regard to slavery has been assailed from several sides, extremists urging that it was not drastic enough, and that slavery should not be allowed to exist in any form, for a single day, under the British flag, even if compensation had to be paid to every slave-owner to effect this. Some competent critics, on the other hand, urged that the slave-owner had been unjustly treated by the refusal of the Administration to recognise in every case his rights in the ownership of his slaves. As regards the former view, it is sufficient to reply that a wholesale emancipation of slaves, even if compensation had been paid to owners, would have upset the whole social organism, and would have produced for the time being social anarchy; a policy by which slaves gradually regained their freedom was the only just and practical one, taking all this into consideration and acting for the welfare of the newly-acquired country as a whole. Those others who urge that the policy has inflicted some injustice on individuals, stand on much firmer ground; indeed, except for the fact that a precedent had already been created by the action of the Royal Niger Company, it might have been practicable to recognise the relationship between masters and slaves which existed when the Government took over the administration of the country, merely stipulating and declaring by proclamation that all children born after that date would be considered free, and that no free person could henceforth be enslaved on any pretext whatever. By this means, slavery would have died a natural death in one generation, and no injustice could well have been urged on behalf of slave-owners, whose possession of their slaves would have been legalised. The great objection to this policy is that it would have obliged the Government either themselves to pursue, arrest, and punish runaway slaves, or to permit the native authorities to do so. It is most improbable that any British Government would have sanctioned such a measure.

It will be seen, therefore, that though slavery still exists, it is moribund, and must of necessity die out in a single generation if the policy now in force be adhered to. The transition stage has been a difficult one, as must necessarily be the case in any great political change, but the main obstacles have been overcome, and the road to complete individual liberty lies open. Free labour and slave labour can never exist alongside of one another, and every year that passes will witness more free labour, which is already offering itself in considerable quantities now that commerce is spreading throughout the Protectorate. The great problem of tropical Africa—slavery—is, in short, in a fair way of being solved.

CHAPTER XII

COMMERCE AND TRADE

"It was a proverb at home that Africa was always producing something new, and this may hold good for a long while yet to come, not only in science and sensation, but in trade."—WINWOOD READE, *African Sketch Book*, vol. ii. 1862.

"There remains the interchange of products between the tropics and the temperate regions, an immense sphere of commercial activity, in which the great natural principle that lies at the base of the free trade theory must remain always operative on a vast scale. If present indications are not entirely misleading, we are about to witness an international rivalry for the control of the trade of the tropics on a far vaster scale than any which has hitherto been imagined."—BENJAMIN KIDD, *The Control of the Tropics*, 1895.

"The principal commerce of Kano consists in native produce, namely, the cotton cloth woven and dyed here or in the neighbouring towns. The great advantage of Kano is that commerce and manufactures go hand in hand, and that almost every family has its share in them. There is really something grand in this kind of industry, which spreads to the north as far as Tripoli; to the west, not only to Timbuktu, but as far as the shores of the Atlantic; to the east, all over Bornu; to the south, to Igbira."—BARTH, *Travels in Central Africa*, 1855.

NORTHERN NIGERIA, with upwards of ten millions of inhabitants, offers a fine market for the sale of European manufactures. The naked pagan of Central Africa may be tempted by a few beads or cheap-looking glasses, but it will be some time before he develops a taste for Manchester cottons or Sheffield cutlery in any quantity. With the Hausa and Fulani of the Mahomedan states of Northern Nigeria it is very different. His taste, not only for fine clothes and expensive luxuries, but for a thousand useful commodities, is highly developed already, and he needs no temptation to come forward as a purchaser. The question which the European asks is, What have the natives of Northern Nigeria with which to purchase these things?

The Protectorate is deficient in the palm oil which forms the chief export of Southern Nigeria, but it contains raw materials of considerable value, suited for export, of which the principal at the present time are cotton, tin, and hides.

Cotton has been cultivated in Northern Nigeria for many centuries, Kano in particular, as Denham reported nearly a hundred years ago, being famed all over Central Africa for its dyed cloth, which is to be found in markets so far afield as Timbuktu.[1] At present it is used entirely in local manufacture. That woven by the natives on their primitive hand-looms is strong, and lasts well, and for this reason is preferred to the flimsy samples sent out from home.

Manchester merchants long ago turned their attention to the possibilities of Northern Nigeria as a cotton-producing centre, and a deputation in 1906 waited on the Prime Minister to urge the need of a railway. The British Cotton Growing Association has for some years past devoted especial attention to Northern Nigeria, sending experts to report on the quality of the indigenous cotton and the suitability of the country for growing the plant on a large scale, and these reports have been very favourable. Ginning machines have also been sent out and erected by the Association, and buying stations established. The Government of Northern Nigeria rendered every assistance, and consignments of

[1] See Barth, vol. ii. p. 126. Writing about the year 1852 he estimates the annual export of cotton cloth from Kano to Timbuktu alone as 300 camel loads, say 100 tons.

American and other cotton seeds were forwarded to Residents to distribute amongst the people. Indeed cotton was confidently expected to become the great staple of the Protectorate as soon as cheap and ready communication could be established with the coast. Progress must, however, be slow at first, especially as the large amount of labour required for railway construction has prevented the planting of more cotton, and this will be the case for some years if a line to the Bauchi tin mines be undertaken. On the whole, it may be said that the prospects of the cotton industry are promising, now that railway communication with the interior has been established. The comparative scarcity of population renders for the present any great increase in the amount of cotton now grown unlikely, for the province of Zaria contains little more than ten inhabitants to the square mile, and although parts of Kano have a fairly large population, it is by no means great in proportion to its extent of country.

As regards tin, native reports had disclosed its presence in the Bauchi highlands as early as 1885, and the Niger Company had from time to time purchased small quantities from Hausa traders on the Benue. When Bauchi was occupied by our troops in 1902, a prospecting party from the Niger Company visited the tin-bearing district under the protection of an escort. The report of this party was most encouraging, and samples were brought home; alluvial tin was found in considerable quantities and of an excellent quality. As a result, several prospecting licences were taken out, and the Niger Company proceeded with the thorough investigation of the tin deposits in the area covered by their own licences. Early in 1906 a mining licence was granted to the firm, and they at once set to work smelting.

Notwithstanding the impossibility of transporting to the mining area any plant or machinery except such as could be carried by porters, a considerable amount of tin was washed and exported, and it was anticipated by the Company that an output of a ton a day of black tin could be realised. Not only, however, was the transport over 200 miles of bush track very heavy, but carriers were exceedingly scarce and difficult to obtain. The industry was assured, but the necessity of providing some means of transport to the navigable rivers other than porterage was obvious. The output of black tin during the year 1906 reached 130 tons. In the absence of facilities for transport the tin was simply washed from the gravel, dressed and dried, and put up in bags 65 lb. in weight—the maximum load for a carrier—and in this state conveyed to Loko, whence it was taken by river to the coast, and shipped home.

The construction of a railway to Kano, with a branch line to the Bauchi tin fields, will solve the difficulty of transport, and the industry may be expected to make rapid progress. It is necessary to point out, however, that native labour is not likely to be, at any rate for the present, plentiful. The mines are situated in a district occupied by pagan tribes of a very independent nature, to whom at present the prospect of a money wage in return for labour makes little or no appeal. The tin industry has up to now depended for labour upon Hausas, who have come in considerable numbers from the provinces of Zaria, Kano, and Sokoto, attracted by the prospect of good wages, for sixpence a day is a good wage to a native, who has few expenses, and whose daily food costs him perhaps a third of this sum. But the population of the Hausa States is by no means large,[1] and the vast bulk of the people are agriculturists. The price of food has gone up considerably since the British occupation, and an impetus has thereby been given to farming. It would, moreover, be of questionable benefit to the country if large numbers of the inhabitants left the cultivation of the soil in order to go and work in the mines. These considerations point to the necessity of labour-saving appliances and machinery being utilised to the greatest possible extent in the tin-mining industry, and water power made use of to generate electrical power and distribute it over the mining area. As soon as a branch line has been built by Government from the main Niger–Kano railway to the mines, there should be no difficulty in Mining Companies carrying out these arrangements.

Tanning is carried on to a considerable extent in all the northern provinces, and leather has been exported across the desert for many centuries. The hides of sheep and goats are tanned, and usually dyed with juice extracted from the stalks of the holcus, which gives them a rich red colour. Skins so dyed are in great request amongst bookbinding firms in England, where they are known commercially as "Niger leather." These skins can be bought in Kano and Zaria at prices varying from 6d. to 9d., and as bookbinders are prepared to give as much as 6s., or even more, for a good specimen, there is room for considerable profit.

[1]

Sokoto province, males . . .	270,569
Kano ,, ,, . . .	1,165,000
Zaria ,, ,, . . .	98,000

Kano leather is also in demand for the bootmaking trade, but in this case undyed skins are preferred, and attempts are being made in the Protectorate to encourage the natives to tan the hides without dyeing them.

Amongst the most important natural products of the Protectorate is the shea-butter tree (*Butyrospermum Parkii*), which grows in great abundance. The railway to Kano runs through forests of these trees, and there should be a considerable export of the valuable nuts in consequence. They form an important ingredient in the manufacture of soap.

Rubber, chiefly landolphia, is found in considerable quantities in many parts of the Protectorate, mainly in the forests on either bank of the Benue. Great difficulty has been experienced in trying to prevent the natives from digging up the roots of the vine when collecting it, and thus destroying the plant, and attempts at legislation have been made, but without much effect. The province which contains most rubber—Bassa, on the south bank of the Benue—is inhabited by pagan tribes in a very low state of civilisation, and these have only recently been brought under control. When this district is opened up to trade, a large quantity of rubber will be brought into the market by the natives. Ground-nuts are grown in large quantities all over the Protectorate, especially in the north, and they are in large demand in European markets on account of the oil which they contain. In Bornu there are numerous acacia trees, and the gum from these is already purchased in considerable quantities by the Niger Company store which has been established at Nafada, whence it is shipped to the coast by way of the Gongola, Benue, and Niger rivers.

Here also, as well as at Kano, ostrich feathers are to be bought, though they are not at present of very good quality.

Other products of the country are benni-seed, copaiba, peppers, cassava, indigo, tobacco, onions, tomatoes, and fibres of many kinds. In the forests near the Benue is some valuable timber, notably mahogany, ebony, and oroko. Beeswax is plentiful, and well-made candles of pure beeswax are sold in Kano for fivepence per lb., and the raw wax for a penny per lb.

The country supports a very large number of cattle, sheep, and goats, and immense herds of these are pastured on the wide tracts of open prairie land in the north. The Fulanis are essentially a pastoral race, just as the Hausas have the trading and industrial instincts, and the pagans are keen agriculturists. Every kind of human activity is thus represented and distributed throughout the Protectorate, and it needs only peace and a settled government to aid them to develop. The Administration has never failed to recognise its duty in this respect, and it has left no stone unturned to assist the natives of the Protectorate in utilising its natural resources, and placing their goods on the European markets. Sir Frederick Lugard, in compiling Estimates for the new Protectorate before its formation, recommended the appointment of an expert in economic products, mineralogical, botanical, etc., who could collect existing knowledge of minerals and products, examine applications for concessions, advise on the development of new products, and make suggestions as to general matters of commercial importance. It was found impossible at the time to provide funds for such an appointment, but a few years later,[1] the formation of a small Forestry Department was sanctioned, which constituted the first serious attempt at developing the economic resources of the Protectorate. A great number of samples, both vegetable and mineral, were sent home to the Imperial Institute, where they were examined and reported on, and their commercial value estimated. The following year the Secretary of State sanctioned the appointment of a mineral survey, consisting of two expert geologists, to explore the mineral resources of the country during the six months of its dry season, and return to England for the other six months to analyse and examine at the Imperial Institute the samples which they brought back. Thus every endeavour was made to bring expert knowledge to bear on the resources of the Protectorate, both vegetable and mineral, and by this means demonstrate to the inhabitants what articles the country possessed which could be exchanged for European products.

The policy of the Administration is opposed to any system of concessions to Europeans for directly developing the resources of the country. It is felt that natives are better left to grow their own products and raise their own stock, receiving advice as to what is required, and as to the best means of improving existing conditions. The whole effort of the Administration has been directed from the first to preserving the initiative of the native, and not turning him into a mere hewer of wood and drawer of water. Such a policy must needs be content with gradual results, for the African native is intensely conservative, and dislikes above all things to be hurried and hustled. Infinite patience is required, and never-failing sympathy

[1] In 1902.

with the native's ideas and limitations. The ideal to be pursued is cordial co-operation between the European and native, and not the subordination of the latter to the former. This is no mere matter of sentiment. It is a matter of practical policy which affects the British nation very closely; for I must once more point out that Nigeria is held alone by prestige, and by a force recruited entirely from amongst the inhabitants themselves. Herr Dernberg, till recently Imperial Colonial Secretary of the German Empire, made some observations on this subject, speaking in England not long ago, which are worthy of quotation. Referring to the attitude of European Powers toward their possessions in tropical Africa he asked: "What do we seek? We seek commercial advantage; we seek open markets; we seek to gather in our raw material. What have we got to give? We give the peace of our flag; we give care for the black man, even in his relations to the white man; we give them the science we have acquired in sanitation; we give them the chance of raising themselves and advancing in the ways of civilisation, while recognising that for them the path is longer than for us." It would perhaps not be out of place to add that we give them the means of transporting their sylvan and agricultural produce to European markets, and the knowledge of the commercial value of products previously considered valueless by them.

The theory that the African native is by nature idle and must therefore be forced to work has long ago been exploded. No one who has lived amongst the natives and watched them, year in year out, at their daily tasks, will say that the African is by nature more idle than the European. Work for work's sake is possibly a notion which is foreign to him: it is not universal in Europe, and where it exists it is probably the outcome of a habit of industry engrained by generations of bitter struggle for existence. Amongst primitive races needs are few, and there is no incentive to drive members of the community to incessant labour. But every man and woman rises at early dawn and goes about his or her business, and in the farming season the men frequently work the whole day on their farms, not returning till sunset. In more civilised communities the wealthy members surround themselves with a crowd of idle sycophants who lie about in the sun outside their patron's gate, and give the traveller the idea that all natives are lazy. But these idlers form an infinitesimal portion of the population. The vast majority of natives are at work practically the whole day. They perform their tasks in what appears to the European a desultory fashion, but that is their method of working. They may take ten hours over a task which could easily be performed in three, but they work the ten hours, and do not sit with idle hands, as so many Europeans imagine. The whole question of industry and idleness depends almost on incentive. When the African native is given an incentive to work he will work in a way that is sometimes almost astonishing. To put him to work which is of no interest to him, and to pay him a fixed salary irrespective of the work accomplished, is to tempt him to be idle and careless, as it would be in the case of any semi-civilised human being. When railway construction was in progress in Northern Nigeria, the work achieved by natives in a few instances when they were put on piece-work and paid in accordance with the task completed, was extraordinary. They were told they would receive a certain sum for every cubic yard of earthworks, and they were left to themselves to do as much or as little as they chose. I have seen natives under such circumstances go out to work with their spades over their shoulders in the faint starlight of dawn, and not return to their camp till after sunset. The native works far better when he is shown what is wanted and how to do it, and then left to carry out the task in his own way and in his own time. Carriers on the march will travel enormous distances with heavy loads on their heads if they are allowed to start when they choose and halt when they like; if they are obliged to conform to stated hours, they cover nothing like the same distance.

It is time the fallacy as regards the laziness of the African native were definitely abandoned. Give him an interest in his task, encourage his initiative by making him think for himself, thrust responsibility on him, demand results and not the mere mechanical performance of labour, and he will be found surprisingly industrious.

I do not think the best results will be obtained from Nigeria by forming large cotton plantations on European lines, with natives working at a fixed wage under the direct orders of the European. Small experimental plantations where the native is taught the best method of growing the plant, preventing pest and blight, picking, etc. etc., are the means I should advocate for developing the industry. Then let the native apply the lessons he has learnt in his own fields, and bring the cotton in to the buying station, where it can be sorted and valued according to its quality, ginned and baled, and shipped home.

The same principle can be applied to stock-raising,

and to every other form of industry. When the native realises that his personal gains depend on the intelligence which he uses, and not on the mere amount of mechanical labour which he performs, he will be an infinitely more valuable asset than if his brains are allowed to atrophy, and he is allowed to develop into a mere machine.

CHAPTER XIII

BRITISH AND NATIVE ADMINISTRATION

"It is certain that even an imperfect and tyrannical native African Administration, if its extreme excesses were controlled by European supervision, would be, in the early stages, productive of far less discomfort to its subjects than well-intentioned but ill-directed efforts of European magistrates, often young and headstrong, and not invariably gifted with sympathy and introspective powers. If the welfare of the native races is to be considered, and if dangerous revolts are to be obviated, the general policy of ruling on African principles through native rulers must be followed for the present."—Sir GEORGE GOLDIE, Preface to *Campaigning on the Upper Nile and Niger*, by Seymour Vandeleur.

IN formulating a policy for the administration of its newly-acquired possessions in tropical Africa, England had the benefit of nearly two centuries of rule in India, which, in a sense, has always been a vast Protectorate. But the conditions, in some respects similar, are in others wholly dissimilar. A great portion of India, as is well known, consists of independent States, ruled by their own sovereigns, collecting their own revenues, controlling even their own armies. To such states a Resident is accredited by the Governor of India, and this official acts as an adviser to the reigning sovereign, but has no power whatever to interfere with the internal affairs of the state. Outside the limits of these independent or semi-independent states, the country is directly administered by the Government of India through the Civil Service officials, practically all the senior and responsible posts being held by

Europeans. The entire revenue of the districts so governed is paid into the Government Treasury, and the officials, whether European or native, are salaried officials of the Government.

When the Administration of Northern Nigeria was assumed by the Crown, even before the large Mahomedan states on the northern border had been occupied by armed forces, the policy of ruling indirectly through the existing Chiefs was at once adopted. Indeed, no other policy was at the outset possible, nor, had it been possible, would there have been any justice in sweeping away the Chiefs and rulers, and setting up an alien rule in their place. A European staff large enough to administer the country and collect all the taxes would have been so costly as to be out of the question, nor, with the country unmapped, unexplored, and practically unknown, would such a staff have had at their disposal sufficient local knowledge to enable them to do so. Clearly the only possible method was to adopt the native machinery already in use and retain the Chiefs, appointing British officials to guide and advise them and to see that administration was carried out in such a way that its broad principles did not transgress modern notions of justice and clemency. The position of these officials, however, was of necessity much more than that of a mere adviser; they were the representatives and mouth-pieces of the High Commissioner, and the latter ruled the country directly as the representative of the King. Apart from any other reason, the attitude of the Administration towards slavery made it impossible to leave the governing power in the hands of the Chiefs, since non-recognition of slavery affected every question—labour, taxation, land tenure, criminal and civil law, estates, probate, currency, and so forth. Besides this, the financial question rendered it imperative to place the Chiefs in a position subordinate to the British officials attached to their Emirates.

These considerations were, however, from the native standpoint, at the outset mainly academical. The view taken by every native, from the Emir down to the humblest peasant, was, that the white man had conquered the country and intended to rule it, and that henceforth his word was law. There was no need to define the relations between the Emir and the Resident. The latter gave orders, the former obeyed them—or disobeyed them only in secret, and at his peril. No doubt it was galling to the pride of former autocrats to be thus placed in sight of all their subjects in a subordinate position, but in point of fact they were shorn of little of their actual power or prestige. To begin with, it was many years before the natives realised that the European had come to stay, and did not intend, after a brief temporary occupation, to vacate the country and leave it to relapse or collapse into the precise state in which he found it. The reasons for this firmly-held belief are many, but it would serve no useful purpose to give them; it is sufficient to relate the fact, and it is obvious that the peasantry were not under such circumstances disposed to offend the rulers whose autocratic power they believed to be only temporarily in abeyance. A further reason why the power and prestige of the Emir remained much as it had been before was that internal affairs continued in his hands, and he retained full power—subject to a veto which was practically never used—to make all appointments and promotions amongst the state officials.[1] Hence it was to the Emir that all looked for advancement. Finally, the Emir and his officials were a permanency, and had complete knowledge and practically complete control of all under-currents of their political and social world, whereas the British official changed frequently, and was, from his very position, unable to probe far beneath the surface. To offend the Emir and his officials was always dangerous, to curry favour with them usually profitable. So much was this the case that complaints of oppression or injustice against the native authorities were often not brought to the Resident, because the would-be complainant knew that, whatever the outcome, he was a marked man for the rest of his life. The situation was well summed up by a peasant who was asked by a friendly missionary, to whom he had confided a tale of petty oppression, why he had not taken his case to the white man. "The hand that strikes is so near," he said, "and the arm that saves is so far off."

As time went on, and the peasantry and people began to realise that the British Protectorate was a permanency, a very different state of affairs arose. It now became a question as to how best to maintain the prestige of the native rulers, for the peasantry began to bring their complaints direct to political officers and to ignore openly the authority of their immediate superiors. However great was the compliment paid thereby to the sympathy of the British officials, a proceeding of this nature struck at the very roots of the native administration, which such pains were being taken to uphold. The position was

[1] The Emir nominated, and the Resident appointed, subject to the approval of the High Commissioner.

indeed one of some difficulty. The functions of the Resident were political rather than administrative, in the true sense of the word. His instructions were to rule through the native Chiefs, and to educate them in the duties of rulers in accordance with a civilised standard, not to usurp their functions. Fortunately, the majority of the complaints brought to the Resident were such as could be adequately dealt with by referring them to the native courts, whose cases were reported monthly to the Resident, and which he was at any time at liberty to visit during their sittings. Other complaints could be referred to the Emir or Chief, and, if necessary, heard by him in the presence of the Resident, who could thus ensure that justice should be done. The best method, in short, of upholding the prestige and influence of the Chiefs was by letting the peasantry see that Government treated them as an integral part of the machinery of the Administration; that there were not two sets of rulers working separately, but a single Government, in which native and British were complementary to one another, and worked in co-operation. The machinery whereby orders might ultimately be enforced—the military and police—was, it is true, entirely in the hands of the British, but it was made clear that this machinery would be used if necessary to compel obedience to lawful orders by Chiefs which had the approval of the High Commissioner, conveyed through the Residents. The disbanding of the armed followings of the native Chiefs was not, in fact, to be permitted to result in their subjects throwing off their allegiance and resisting all control. Both rulers and peasantry were quickly reassured on this matter.

A further danger to the prestige of native Chiefs

was of a more subtle character. Official ceremony and etiquette are held in great regard by African Chiefs, and are strictly enforced among themselves. It is difficult for a busy British official, always impatient of such matters, to realise their importance in the native mind, and, moreover, it takes time and long knowledge of the country to learn their intricacies. The prestige of a Chief might frequently suffer, and a feeling of soreness and humiliation be engendered by a thoughtless and quite unintentional act. To meet this difficulty the High Commissioner drew up and circulated a Memorandum, in which he described the rules which should be observed by Residents in their relations towards native Chiefs, and he also indicated generally the main points of etiquette and ceremonial which should be adopted. Difficulties in these respects tended to disappear as Residents grew better acquainted with the country, and with its people, their language and their customs.

In order to provide a legal instrument for enforcing legitimate orders of native authorities and at the same time dealing with illegal or unjust orders, an important Proclamation was enacted in 1907, called the "Enforcement of Native Authority Proclamation." By its provisions provincial courts were authorised to enforce orders or judgments given either by native courts or by recognised native authorities, and to inflict punishment on any person who might have disregarded or disobeyed such orders; similarly, in cases where orders given by native courts or recognised native authorities were, in the opinion of a provincial court, improper, illegal, or unjust, it was entitled to set aside such orders, and to take such action with respect to the native authorities as, in its discretion, appeared best suited to meet the circumstances of the case.

It was clear that Residents, acting as the representatives of the High Commissioner, held paramount power over the Chiefs and all minor officials in their provinces. In extreme cases, where an Emir or Chief maintained an attitude of hostility towards the Government, or persisted in acting oppressively or unjustly towards the people under his charge, the Resident was instructed to make a full report of the circumstances to the High Commissioner, who, if he considered necessary, might depose the Chief, and install in his place a suitable successor.

Cordial co-operation between British and Native Administration was the ideal aimed at. To what extent it was secured depended in the main on the character and personality of the Resident and the Chief concerned in each case. The relations between the two were of so peculiar and unusual a character that there was room for much difference in the conception of their precise nature. In some cases a Resident, placing little or no faith in the character of an Emir or Chief, would give him clear and precise orders on every subject, and look upon him rather as a puppet than as a constitutional ruler. In other cases, a Resident would conceive his duty to be merely that of an adviser, the Chief being a semi-independent ruler, who was to be interfered with only to prevent absolute oppression and injustice. And between these two extremes there were innumerable shades of opinion. The actions of the Resident were of course dependent to a very large extent on the character and intelligence of the man with whom he was dealing. The difference between an enlightened Mahomedan like the Sultan of Sokoto and the ignorant Chief of some primitive pagan tribe, was immense, and here again between these two extremes, Chiefs of every degree of intelligence existed. The administration of pagan communities was necessarily of a far more direct kind than that of the northern Mahomedan states. Taking the latter alone into consideration, however, the question was, to what extent was indirect rule to be carried? Were the Emirs constitutional sovereigns ruling by hereditary right, or were they merely deputies appointed at will by the British Administration to carry out certain functions? In so far as they collected the taxes of the inhabitants they would seem to be semi-independent hereditary rulers, and the portion of the tax which they handed over to Government might be considered an annual tribute in return for protection and benefits conferred. In so far, on the other hand, as the whole of their executive and administrative actions were subject to the control of the Resident, they appeared to be officials acting under his orders and supervision, and it might be argued that they collected the taxes in the capacity of officials of the British Administration, and were allowed to retain a portion in return for the service rendered. The question of the actual status of the Emirs became more acute when the matter of land tenure began to be discussed. In 1907 an Emir claimed to levy a land-tax on some pagans who lived in a range of hills in a neighbouring province, and who paid their tax direct to Government through the Resident of that province, but who had, since the arrival of the British, cleared the bush and were cultivating some farms on previously unoccupied land, admittedly within the boundaries of the Emir's territory. If the British Government intended to recognise the Emir as a hereditary semi-independent sovereign, it followed that the pagans must either cease to use the land, or must come and live on it and give their allegiance to the Emir, and pay their tax to him. If, on the other hand, the Emir was considered to be merely an official appointed by the High Commissioner to perform certain functions, it was evident that the latter could, if he wished, simply alter the boundary so as to include the previously unoccupied land in that apportioned to the pagan community for its use. The Emir, on being pressed, admitted that before the British occupation the ultimate right in the land was vested in the Sultan of Sokoto; hence, since the British Government had now formally acquired from the Sultan the rights in the land which his predecessors had possessed, the ultimate rights in the land in question were vested in the Government, which was accordingly clearly entitled to readjust the boundaries if it saw fit. A temporary compromise was arranged till such time as the matter should be definitely settled. Meanwhile the precise status of Emirs and their exact relation to the British Administration remains in doubt. Generally speaking, it is of little immediate practical importance: but it must be settled before long. At present in the important Mahomedan Emirates the native Administration receives half the tax collected under the Native Revenue Proclamation; this includes the shares of all native officials and all expenses connected, not only with the collection of the tax but with the administrative functions of every kind, apart, of course, from those borne directly by Government. As it forms practically the sole source of income of the Emirs and officials, there is no distinction between their private and official funds. This introduces another point, with which I will deal presently. With the advent of the railway and the rapid development of the country, the total value of the tax, based as it is on the value of land and of its produce, will increase very rapidly and very largely; and as the increase will be mainly due to Government expenditure and effort, it is manifestly absurd to allow the incomes of the Chiefs and officials to rise proportionately, as they must do automatically under the present system. One obvious solution is to maintain the sum which they are at present receiving and turn it into a fixed salary, allowing all increase in taxation to accrue to the public revenue. But if the Emirs are thus placed on a fixed salary, they become mere officials of the Government, and their prestige as semi-independent rulers vanishes. Would this be to the good of the country?

An alternative suggestion is to form in each Emirate a Public Treasury, an institution well known in Mahomedan countries under the Arabic name of Beit-el-Mal. Into this the native share of all moneys received from taxes and other public sources should be paid: salaries and all necessary administrative expenses could then be paid out of it by the Emir, and the balance be used for public purposes—namely, education, sanitation, public works, such as the buildings of mosques and roads, etc.—under the guidance and supervision of the Resident. The important step at present is undoubtedly the separation of the public moneys from private, *i.e.* household and other expenses, To allow these to continue intermixed and indistinguishable is impossible. No financial regularity can be expected while such a system obtains. An increased revenue would simply mean unchecked extravagance and waste on useless luxuries, and, so far from being any benefit to the country, would tend to the ruin of the enlightened classes. The problem is one of extreme difficulty, and its early solution is of the utmost importance.

These remarks apply mainly to the Mahomedan states. Pagan communities, whose organisation is far more primitive, stand at present on a very different footing. Their administration by the British officials must necessarily be of a far more direct nature, and the establishment of native treasuries would in their case be premature. The household expenses of the Chiefs and officials are almost negligible, and there is no costly state to keep up. By the Native Revenue Proclamation, the proportion of tax paid into Government by these pagan communities varies, according to their status, from 75 to 95 per cent. Time may be allowed to elapse and development to take place before the question of dealing with their revenues is taken seriously in hand. *Festina lente* must be the motto throughout the Protectorate in every case where circumstances do not actually clamour for a speedy solution to a native problem. The more knowledge that be gained of the people, of their language, their habits, their thoughts, and their ideals before introducing new methods the better will it be for the country.

CHAPTER XIV

BRITISH AND NATIVE COURTS OF JUSTICE

"When some European magistrate rules according to Western ideas, giving the people *British* justice, and consequently upsetting all precedents, there must of necessity be a feeling of discontent in the hearts of the natives."—DUDLEY KIDD, *Kafir Socialism.*

"The mind of the negro is not a *tabula rasa* on which the white man may write what he pleases; white law is not to the negro so superior that he is at once pleased with it; on the contrary, the law which seems to us so just and necessary is often to him the grossest injustice. Every native tribe is bound together by laws and customs resting originally on a religious basis, *i.e.* resting on certain ideas as to man's nature, his relations to his fellows, and to the other world. On the basis of these ideas different tribes have built up very complex systems of laws and observances, resting on, and bearing witness to, certain habits of mind."—W. L. GRANT, *Revue Economique Internationale*, March 1909.

THE dual authority exercised by the British and Native Administrations finds a close parallel in the system of Provincial and Native Courts, exercising their judicial functions side by side.

The law of the Protectorate is made by legislative "Proclamations" by the Governor, subject to any Order-in-Council by His Majesty. On the formation of the Protectorate on January 1, 1900, the common law of England which was in force in England on that date was introduced by proclamation as the "Fundamental Law," but its application was modified in 1902 by an important Proclamation directing that judges should, in causes affecting the natives of the Protectorate, have the right to enforce native law and custom in certain conditions. In 1904 a Proclamation was enacted which suspended English Criminal Law by a local criminal code.

In each province is a Provincial Court, the full jurisdiction of which is exercised by virtue of his office by the Resident in charge of the province. He can pass sentence of death or imprisonment for life, but no sentence of imprisonment exceeding six months can be carried into execution until confirmed by the Chief-Justice, to whom full minutes of such cases have to be sent, or of death until confirmed by the Governor. A Resident has no judicial powers outside his own province. All other political officers and police officers are Commissioners of the Provincial Court of the province to which they are appointed, and as such may hold courts simultaneously with the Resident's Court to the extent of the judicial powers vested in them. These powers are laid down by proclamation, and may be increased in any individual case by the Governor.

A monthly "Cause List," setting forth the details of every case tried in the Provincial Court during the month, is submitted to the Chief-Justice, and operates as an appeal on behalf of the convicted person.

It may seem startling that such large judicial powers should be entrusted to an official who, in many cases, has had no previous legal training. The fact is, that in the early stages of the Protectorate no other course was possible. Political officers could not be selected solely from the legal profession; and in such an immense and widely scattered country it was obviously impossible to bring every case for trial before the Chief-Justice or other legal officer. The records of ten years' actual practice are sufficient to show that the confidence reposed in these amateur judges has been justified. The majority of cases tried in the Provincial Courts were criminal cases of a very simple character, in which no deep legal knowledge was necessary—an impartial mind, and a robust common-sense being all that was required to deal fairly and justly with the evidence produced. Civil cases between natives could almost always be referred to the Native Courts, and were best dealt with by them. But the most effective safeguard against any miscarriage of justice was the provision by which the full minutes of every case of any importance had to be sent for confirmation to the Chief-Justice before the sentence became operative. They were thus subjected to close scrutiny by a trained legal official, and if any decision were found to have been based on evidence legally inadmissible, confirmation could be refused. As the Chief-Justice's comments on every case were transmitted to the Resident who had tried it, political officers received in this way a valuable training in legal procedure.

There are many advantages, in a country like Northern Nigeria, in combining judicial and executive functions in one official. It gives him a very necessary prestige amongst the natives for whose administration he is responsible: while the fact that he is in close touch with the people and with the political situation gives him an advantage in investigating cases which cannot be possessed by an official whose duties are solely judicial. On the other hand, the system possesses one very grave defect. It may happen that the official who deals judicially with a case is the very person to whom, in his executive capacity, the crime was first reported, and who arrested the accused, collected the evidence, and held the preliminary investigation. Under such circumstances, the position becomes one of great difficulty and demands a balanced judgment and self-restraint of the highest order. The appointment to each province of a police officer, who could undertake the preparation of cases for trial in the Provincial Court, was a great assistance in this respect.

In dealing judicially with semi-civilised races, an acquaintance with native character and modes of thought is often far more valuable than the most extensive legal knowledge. British and native conceptions of justice and ethics are by no means invariably identical. It is said that in South Africa, if a native injures himself with a borrowed knife, the responsibility rests, according to native ideas, on the man from whom it was borrowed. The instance will serve to show that a British judge dispensing the most unimpeachable British justice may possibly deliver what appears in native eyes a most unjust judgment. Again, the tendering of false evidence need not necessarily, according to native ideas, be immoral. It may, under certain circumstances, be a highly moral act, according to native code. In a Provincial Court, a Resident is of course obliged to conduct his proceedings according to the laws of the Protectorate, even if these conflict with the native code; but in certain ways he may often, by knowledge of native character, and by the exercise of imagination and sympathy, arrive at a far more correct decision than if he proceeded on strict legal principles. The native who takes his case before a European likes to be allowed to tell his story in his own way, to wander frequently from the point, to assume as facts mere conjectures and suspicions, and to record as events that have actually taken place information which he has received at second or third hand. A strict enforcement of rules as to the introduction of irrelevant matter often does more harm than good. The patient judge will let him say his say without interruption, and, picking out the salient points, will question him on them. Bearing in mind the fact that evidence can generally be obtained in practically unlimited quantities by litigants who have a long purse or influential friends, the judge will probably reach his conclusion as to the truth far more by the extent to which he has gained an insight into the workings of the native mind than by the sheer balance of evidence produced. Political officers who conduct their trials on these lines learn to arrive at a correct verdict by a sort of instinct rather than by any logical process of inductive reasoning. Natives, even when the verdict has gone against them, perhaps wrongly, leave the court without any feeling of bitterness or soreness against the judge when he has allowed them to state their case in their own way, and possibly call witnesses whose evidence has not been strictly relevant. "The judge did his best," they say: "he tried the case with absolute fairness, and it was only owing to A. bringing so many false witnesses that the case went against me." On the other hand, where they have been checked in their statement, and not allowed to call some witness on the ground that his evidence is irrelevant, they harbour a resentment in their hearts, and consider that the trial has been conducted unfairly, and undue favour shown to their opponent.

In some British Protectorates, and also in certain of the countries administered by France, Native Courts have been set up over which a European official presides, the intention being to combine, by this means, the minimum of interference with the maximum of supervision. In Northern Nigeria, Sir Frederick Lugard determined boldly to carry the principle of non-interference further, and to set up Native Courts whose members should consist of natives alone, and in the first year of the Protectorate a Proclamation was enacted, authorising Residents to set up such courts in their provinces. In 1906 this was superseded by another Proclamation of a more detailed description. By its provisions, courts of two descriptions are authorised — Alkalis' Courts and Judicial Councils. Speaking generally, the former are applicable to Mahomedan districts, the latter to pagan.

These courts are established by warrant, which is signed by the Governor, sealed with the Protectorate seal, and notified in the Government Gazette. The warrant is made out by the Resident, who inscribes the names of the judge and members, defines their powers, and details the area over which they hold jurisdiction. The scale of fees which the court is permitted to charge is also affixed.

The Resident has at all times access to a Native Court, and may transfer any case from it to the Provincial Court. There is no formal right of appeal from a Native Court, nor does a Resident formally confirm or approve their sentences, which, if within the powers assigned to the court, are absolute. He is given power, however, of his own motion to suspend, reduce, or otherwise modify a sentence, or to transfer a case at any stage of the proceedings to the Provincial Court. He has thus complete control and supervision over the Native Courts in his province, although he takes no active part in the proceedings, even if he himself is present in the court. In this way, a native judiciary was created throughout the Protectorate, working independently, but subjected to a supervision which effectually prevented any possibility of gross injustice or oppression. Its chief merit was that it introduced no alien innovation, but merely developed already existing institutions. In Mahomedan districts the previously existing Alkalis' Courts were regularised, and their powers sanctioned by law, and in addition they were obliged to keep and submit to the Resident at stated intervals a written record of their proceedings. The Judicial Councils in pagan districts gave formal and legal sanction to the arbitrary power previously exercised by the Chief, who became the President of the Court. But the arbitrary element was quietly abolished by the limitations imposed; by associating with the Chief a small council of his leading officials, and by the necessity of reporting the proceedings to the Resident.

The law to be administered by Native Courts was defined in the Proclamation as "the native law and custom prevailing in the territory over which a Native Court has jurisdiction," a proviso being added that no punishment involving mutilation or torture repugnant to natural justice and humanity, might be inflicted.

The difference between the two kinds of Native Courts was very great. An Alkali's Court consisted of one or more Mahomedan judges, trained in the written law of the Koran and the Mahomedan law books, dispensing justice in conformity with this orthodox code. They therefore constituted a native judiciary separate from, and independent of, the native executive authorities, namely the Emir and his administrative officials. Sir Frederick Lugard, in his instructions to

Residents, stated that he saw no reason why both an Alkali's Court and a Judicial Council should not be set up in the same city, with concurrent jurisdiction, and, if desirable, co-extensive powers. This, in fact, was done in Bida and Kano, which had both an Alkali's Court and a Judicial Council, of which the Emir was President. The reason for this is that in Mahomedan countries the Kadi usually dispenses common law, and deals chiefly with matters of divorce, inheritance, etc., whilst criminal cases are dealt with for the most part by executive officers. If the functions of the two courts had been kept quite separate in Northern Nigeria, all civil cases being taken before the Alkali, and all criminal cases before the Emir and his Judicial Council, the policy might have been in accordance with custom, but the two courts were given jurisdiction both in civil and criminal cases, and the result was not always satisfactory. The subject is too long and complicated to be discussed here, but it would seem on the whole best in Mahomedan districts to set up only Alkalis' Courts, which would deal with all cases, both civil and criminal; in other words, to keep judicial and administrative functions entirely separate, and to allow each to be dealt with by its own officials. This was done in other provinces, and although at first it gave rise in one or two cases to friction between the Emir and the Alkali, it appears in the end to have proved more satisfactory. All the minor Alkalis' Courts throughout the province were made subordinate to the Alkali's Court at the capital, and they submitted their returns to him, to be forwarded with his own to the Resident. His court was also appointed a court of appeal for them.

The Judicial Councils in pagan districts were of a

very different nature, for here there was no written code, and therefore no trained judge. The Chief sat as President, and dealt with all cases, civil and criminal, in accordance with tribal law and custom, which is mainly a matter of precedent. These Judicial Councils, in fact, merely legalised the old patriarchal system, under which the Chief is the fountain of justice, and his decisions are accepted by his people as law.

So far, all is clear and simple. We have Mahomedan districts in which a special judiciary, separated from the executive, deals with all cases, civil and criminal, in accordance with written Islamic law,[1] and pagan districts, in which the Chief, assisted by elders of the tribe, deals with all cases in accordance with tribal custom. The situation becomes complicated when we are confronted with pagan communities in Mahomedan districts, and Mahomedan communities in pagan districts. Various methods of dealing with it have been tried by different Residents. In some cases a Mahomedan official—probably the district Headman—has been appointed President of a Judicial Council, consisting of the Chief and leading elders of a pagan tribe. The difficulty here is that he is probably unacquainted with either Mahomedan law or pagan custom. In other cases, where a Mahomedan community exists in a pagan district, a mixed court has been set up, with the Chief as President, and representatives of both Mahomedans and pagans as members. This has proved unsatisfactory, because it has been found that, while his pagan subjects have gone as usual to the Chief for decisions in their cases, the Mahomedans have gone to those members of the

[1] The law administered by the Mahomedan courts in Northern Nigeria is that of the Maliki school.

court who belong to their faith, and these have dealt with the case by themselves, ignoring the pagan Chief. It would seem best, where a Mahomedan community exists in a district governed by a pagan Chief whose independence has been recognised by Government, to insist that they should obey the laws of the tribe as interpreted by the Chief and elders sitting as a recognised Judicial Council. If they wish to bring a civil action against another native in the district, whether he be a pagan or one of their own faith, they can either take their case before the pagan Council and abide by its decision, or, in the last resort, they are always at liberty to refer to the Resident, who can, if he think fit, deal with the case in his Provincial Court.

In some cases, where a pagan tribe is subject to a Mahomedan ruler, a Judicial Council has been set up with a right of appeal from it to the Mahomedan Alkali's Court at the capital. In such a case a pagan committing a crime may be tried under three distinct codes, namely, his own tribal law, Koranic law, and the Protectorate code. Such a state of affairs can hardly be considered satisfactory. In any case, a native is always amenable to at least two courts of justice, administering two different kinds of law—his own Native Court, and the Provincial Court. It is difficult to see how this can be avoided. The remedy, so far as pagan districts are concerned, seems to me gradually to teach the Chiefs and Judicial Councils the Protectorate criminal code, and persuade them to adopt it as the recognised native law and custom. Already a summary of the criminal code in a very simple form has been compiled and translated into Hausa by a Resident of the Protectorate, and copies have been printed and sent out to provinces. Since no pagan tribe has a written code, and their native law and custom is merely the outcome of precedent, and is practically Chief-made, it follows that, if a Chief accept the Protectorate code, it becomes *ipso facto* "native law and custom." All that is necessary is to move very slowly and cautiously, and to see that native ideas are not roughly upset. It ought not to be impossible in this matter, by acting very gradually, to conform to the golden rule never to introduce a reform until it has received the willing acceptance of the native Chiefs and leaders.

Mahomedan courts have their written code. How far this can be co-ordinated with the Protectorate code, or it with them, cannot be determined without a full knowledge of Mahomedan ideals, which few Europeans possess.

There remains the question of mixed Mahomedan and pagan communities. If the ruling Chief is pagan, and hence has been appointed President of a Judicial Council, I consider, as I have already said, that there is no hardship or injustice in insisting that Mahomedans who take up their residence in his district shall conform to the laws of the district. If these laws can eventually be brought into line with the Protectorate code, so much the better. In mixed communities, where the ruling Chief is Mahomedan, I confess the difficulty is great. The Mahomedan legal code is so bound up with the Mahomedan religion that to insist on pagans conforming to it is very nearly akin to giving the religion of Islam a Governmental recognition, which conflicts with our solemn promises with regard to religious doctrines. The only alternative seems to me to throw open the Provincial Courts freely to the pagans in Mahomedan districts, making full use of pagan Chiefs and elders as assessors. It is unfortunate that Provincial Courts have to be used more than is absolutely necessary in cases which concern natives alone, but in this instance it can hardly be avoided. As time goes on, and Native Courts become more and more efficient, it is to be hoped that Provincial Courts will deal almost exclusively with cases to which non-natives are parties, and which cannot ever be left to Native Courts. Provincial Courts will then be of the nature of Consular Courts, the Native Courts taking all purely native cases. Already the higher courts have very large powers. Those in the chief Mahomedan capitals, such as Sokoto, Kano, and Zaria, have power to try criminal cases in which the death penalty is awardable, and have practically unlimited power in civil cases. The machinery for dealing with every class of offence, and every kind of civil action, is therefore in existence, and only requires developing and perfecting. One important matter still needs attention. The penalties which may be inflicted by Native Courts are fines, flogging, stocks, imprisonment, and death. Fining is, in general, I consider, the worst form of punishment, because it opens the door to extortion and corruption.[1] We are left, therefore, with imprisonment, flogging, and stocks as the usual form of punishment: this necessitates a gaol or lock-up in every town where there is a Native Court. The arrest of the criminal and his custody while undergoing detention should be left to the executive authorities, namely, the Chiefs,

[1] I have been informed by an intelligent Alkali that fines are not recognised as a punishment in Mahomedan law, but I do not know if this is the case. Monetary compensation for injury and loss is, of course, a different matter altogether, and the principle is well recognised.

R

the district and the village headman; the Alkalis' and Native Courts being concerned only with hearing and deciding on cases brought before them and passing sentence. Hitherto the fines and fees of court have been paid to the President and members of the Native Courts, and the latter have in some cases been charged with maintaining the prisoners, and with other duties and expenses. When native public Treasuries are introduced, all these matters can be satisfactorily dealt with. All fees and fines will then be paid into the native Treasuries, and members of Native Courts can be paid fixed salaries from the same sources. The building and maintaining of gaols, and the establishment of native gaolers, will be undertaken by the Emir and his administrative officials—district and village headmen—and all expense connected therewith will be defrayed from the native Treasury. District headmen will be responsible for the reporting and detection of crime, and for seeing that sentences awarded by Native Courts are carried out. The organisation of all this most necessary machinery in each province is the work of the immediate future. The training of the native judiciary is one of the most interesting and most important tasks which lie before Residents, and it will be by no means an easy one. Meanwhile, the Native Courts of the Protectorate are even now achieving results of which the value can hardly be over-estimated.[1] Not only are they training the native Chiefs and officials in the duties of sifting evidence and administering justice, but the records furnished by them give an invaluable insight into the manners and customs of the natives, the classes of crime most prevalent, and the methods of dealing with

[1] They tried 10,000 civil and criminal cases in Kano province in 1910.

it. Finally, they are a tangible proof that the new Administration does not desire to deprive the natives of their rights, responsibilities, and powers, but to guide and assist them in self-government, which has always been their much-prized privilege.

CHAPTER XV

LAND TENURE

"All lands in the country are in the keeping of the Chiefs for the members of the tribe to whom the land belongs. There is not a foot of land that is not claimed or possessed by some tribe or other, and the members of each tribe can apply to their respective chiefs for a grant of land to be used and cultivated for farming and other purposes. Any land so granted becomes the property of the grantee for life, and for his heirs after him in perpetuity, with all that grows on it and all that lies underneath it. But such land must be made use of; *i.e.* it must be cultivated or used beneficially; if not, the grantee is liable to lose it, and it may then be given to another who will make use of it."—*A Yoruba Native.*

WHEN Government took over from the Royal Niger Company the government of the territories, henceforth to be known as Northern Nigeria, it obtained sole and absolute title to certain lands which were stated by the Company to have been privately acquired and held by them in their private right as a commercial concern, outside their functions of administration as a Chartered Company. These lands were extensive, and included amongst others a mile inland from either bank of the Niger, from the frontier of Southern Nigeria to Lokoja. By presumption these lands became the absolute property of the Government, though, as a matter of fact, native towns were situated on them. In addition to the lands thus theoretically acquired, certain other lands were taken up by the Government for public purposes, and became Crown Lands, such, for instance, as the sites of various provincial headquarters, and of Zungeru and Lokoja.

Apart from these Crown Lands, which might be described as the private property of Government, the ultimate title to certain other lands became vested in Government by right of conquest, notified by a Proclamation enacted in 1902, and these were called "Public Lands." The justification for this proceeding was that the Mahomedan rulers had assumed the ultimate title to all the land which they conquered, and when a Mahomedan Chief was himself conquered or deposed by Government, the title vested in him lapsed to the latter. When an Emir was installed, this ultimate title to the land was expressly reserved to Government in the Letter of Appointment which he received, and to the conditions of which he subscribed.

In course of time the whole Protectorate became Public Lands, for although no legal instrument was necessary in the case of pagan tribes, they well understood the consequences which resulted from the acceptance of British control, and no specific declaration that the right to the land became vested in Government was necessary.

By an important clause in the Proclamation of 1902, it was made illegal for any non-native[1] to acquire an interest in any Public Lands except with the consent of the High Commissioner; and it was further enacted that all rentals from lands acquired by non-natives should accrue to the public revenue. In this way natives of the Protectorate were safeguarded from the alienation of their land by private individuals or companies from outside.

This, then, was the position. The Government held certain lands as Crown Lands, which were, so to

[1] I use this term throughout this chapter to signify any person not a native of the Protectorate, *e.g.* a European, or a native of Southern Nigeria or Sierra Leone.

speak, its private property, and any person entering or building upon them without permission committed a trespass. The remainder of the Protectorate was "Public Lands," held administratively by the Government, which in no way interfered with private titles, transfers, or sales between individuals, but had the right at any time to take up land for public purposes, and could alone grant a title for any land to a non-native. If, then, a non-native wished to acquire a right in any land in the Protectorate, he must apply to the High Commissioner. If the area desired were a portion of Crown Lands, a lease could at once be granted; if of Public Lands, the Government might, if it thought fit, acquire the land, making all arrangements for paying compensation for any private rights or disturbance affected, and then lease it to the applicant.

Sir Frederick Lugard dealt with the subject at some length in a memorandum to Residents, which explained and elaborated the Crown Lands and Public Lands Proclamations, and also indicated the general terms on which leases would, as a rule, be granted, according to the extent and position of the land required. Building leases might be for twenty-one years or over, with option of renewal at a rate to be agreed upon; the present rent to vary, according to the position of the land, from about 10s. to £25 per acre. Separate terms were indicated for agricultural holdings. In the town of Lokoja (which was all "Crown Lands"), plots were set apart for natives and non-natives on two-year leases, with the obligation to build thereon a house worth £20. The rental was about £4 per annum for an area 20 by 150 yards, larger or smaller plots being leased proportionately;

compensation for buildings would be paid by Government if the lease were terminated within ten years. The issue of leases on easy terms was contemplated in case land were required for experimental farms, ranching, ostrich farming, etc., provisions being made that an adequate stock should be placed on the land, or cultivation be carried out, within a given period, the title lapsing if these conditions were not fulfilled. Mining rights were treated under a separate proclamation, and need not be here discussed; they were not included in any rights in land.

The question as to whether a native might sell or lease to a non-native private property within an area declared to be Public Lands was discussed in the memorandum, and an instance given of houses or lands in a native city, where individual rights were well established. Sir Frederick Lugard pointed out that the Proclamation stated in clear and precise terms that all rentals of Public Lands should form part of the public revenue, and he recorded his opinion that it would be inadvisable to ignore the principle, that Government alone could be the landlord of a non-native. He therefore suggested that the lease might be drawn so as to give compensation to the private individual, and that this compensation might include the bulk of the rental to be paid by the lessee, Government only retaining such a nominal sum as would safeguard its theoretical title.

Meanwhile, investigations into the system of taxation obtaining in the Hausa States had disclosed the existence of a tax called Kurdi-n-Kassa, which means, literally, "land money," *i.e.* ground rent. Sir Percy Girouard, on arriving in the Protectorate, instituted inquiries from Residents as to the system of land tenure in vogue amongst the natives, and as to the rights which agriculturists possessed in their farms. The replies received established the fact that the idea of private property in land was foreign to the country; that the entire land was held in trust by the Chiefs for the use of the people: in short, that the position throughout the Protectorate corresponded, more or less, with the statements made in the quotation which heads this chapter.

The question was of such supreme importance that Sir Percy Girouard referred it to the Secretary of State in a lengthy despatch, and in June 1908 a Committee, convened by the latter, met at the Colonial Office to investigate and report on the matter. The services of Sir Kenelm Digby were secured as Chairman, and with him were associated two members of the Indian Council, Mr. Josiah Wedgwood, M.P., two Colonial Office officials, and two Residents of the Protectorate who were at home on leave. The subjects of discussion were Land Tenure and Land Assessment in Northern Nigeria. Many witnesses were examined, and at the end of July a report was signed and submitted to the Secretary of State, by whom it was subsequently presented to both Houses of Parliament in the form of a Blue Book.

It was clearly established from the evidence before the Committee that the use of land by the inhabitants throughout the Protectorate could be, and was by custom, transferred and inherited, but that it was the use of the land, and not the land itself, which was thus dealt with. Clearly under such circumstances there was a very narrow dividing line between the right of use and the actual ownership—between the *jus utendi* and the *jus possidendi*. The actual difference lay in the power to revoke the original grant; and the evidence was overwhelming that this power always remained in the hands of the paramount Chief.

The Report of the Committee may be summarised as follows. They recommended that a Declaratory Proclamation should be passed to the effect that the whole of the land of the Protectorate is under the control and dominion of Government; that this control should be exercised with due regard to lawful customs existing; that the person or community entitled to the occupation and use of the land should have exclusive right thereto against all persons other than the Government; that the Government should be entitled for good cause to revoke the title of any occupier; that in the event of the land being required for public purposes, due compensation should be paid by Government to the occupier.

The expression "good cause" used above, they recommended should include non-payment of taxes; voluntary alienation without the consent of Government; and requirement of the land by Government for public purposes.

The Committee had also discussed the subject of land assessment, particularly with regard to the "Native Revenue Proclamation," which has been referred to in a previous chapter. Their recommendations under this head were, briefly: that, in order to prepare the way for the introduction of a land revenue based on survey, the present taxes should be divided into two distinct parts—rent payable to the State for the use of land, and taxes on crafts and trade; that, in assessing these taxes, certain procedure indicated in the body of the Report should be adopted; that the responsibility of distributing among individuals the demand assessed upon a village should be assigned to the village headman, assisted by the village council, and that taxation should for the present be liable to revision every year.

The Report of the Committee was accepted by the Secretary of State, who directed that legislation should be drafted to give effect to its recommendations. In 1910, therefore, a Proclamation was drawn up, termed the "Natives' Rights Proclamation," in which the whole of the lands of the Protectorate, whether occupied or unoccupied (except those already declared to be "Crown Lands"), were declared to be Native Lands, under the control of the Governor, who should hold and administer them for the benefit of the natives of the Protectorate, having regard to native law and custom. The Governor was authorised to grant rights of occupancy to natives and persons other than natives, and to demand a rental for the use of the land; nothing in the lease was to preclude him from revising the rent at intervals of not less than seven years; he was not empowered to revoke rights of occupancy except for good cause, which was defined; if the rent were raised or revised the occupier might surrender his rights, in which case he was entitled to compensation to the value of his unexhausted improvements; claims arising under the proclamation might be prosecuted before the Supreme Court; and in determining or revising the rental the Governor should take into consideration the rental obtainable for land in the immediate vicinity, but should not take into consideration any value due to capital expended on the land by the occupier.

We are now in a position to review briefly the

situation which has been reached in the Protectorate with regard to Land Tenure and Assessment.

The Governor, as His Majesty's representative, occupies the position formerly held by the various Chiefs and Emirs, and virtually becomes the landlord of every acre of land throughout the Protectorate, charged with the duty of dealing with it in certain prescribed ways for the benefit of the inhabitants. The inhabitants stand, in regard to the land, in the same position towards him as they formerly did towards their paramount Chiefs, namely as tenants at will; their rights are secured to them in perpetuity, and they cannot be dispossessed except for good cause, which is rigidly defined. In return for the right of occupancy the Governor is empowered to demand an annual rental, determined by the value of the land, and liable to revision at intervals of not less than seven years. No occupier may alienate his right of occupancy by sale, mortgage, or transfer, without first obtaining the consent of the Governor.

Precisely the same conditions apply to non-natives, to whom rights of occupancy may be granted. It is here that difficulties begin to be raised. Who, say the critics, will apply for rights of occupancy of a plot of land on which the expenditure of much capital may be contemplated, if the rental is liable to revision at intervals of not less than seven years? The reply is that the lessee is safeguarded in three ways. First, the Governor is prohibited, in any revision of rent, from taking into consideration any value due to capital expended upon the land by the occupier, or by any increase in the value of the land due to the employment of such capital. Second, should the rental be raised on revision, the occupier may surrender his rights, and thereby oblige the Governor to pay him compensation, to the value of his unexhausted improvements. Third, he may prosecute before the Supreme Court claims relating to the value of unexhausted improvements or the amount of compensation due for disturbance. It might have been advisable to set up a Court of Arbitration to deal with such cases instead of referring them to the Supreme Court. It is obvious that the decision as to whether an increase in value of land is due to the activities of the occupier, or to outside causes, must depend on evidence of so complicated a nature that it may become in practice largely a matter of opinion : and in such a case, a lessee who was not a Government official would probably feel more secure if one at least of the members of the tribunal charged with giving a decision had been nominated by himself. This is a matter, however, which hardly affects the principle of the policy we are discussing, and which has been adopted for Northern Nigeria. It remains to be seen how the policy justifies itself in the immediate and distant future.

With regard to the assessment and collection of rents from the natives, there are a vast number of problems whose solution will be extremely difficult, and which are at the present moment undecided. The one clear principle at the moment is, that the village remains still, as it always has been in the past, the unit. It is hoped in the far future that a cadastral survey may be made of the entire Protectorate, and land classified and valued, rentals being fixed accordingly. For the present all that can be done is to make a rough-and-ready assessment, and introduce no more change in native customs than is absolutely necessary. The recommendations of the Committee were that each Resident should fix and notify a rate for each unit in a village, the rate varying from village to village, according to richness of soil, proximity to markets, and so on. This rate, multiplied by the number of revenue-paying units, should constitute the aggregate demand of the village, and the village headman, assisted by a village council, should distribute the tax amongst individual units. The reason for the Committee using the general term unit was that it did not wish to prejudge the question, whether the revenue should be levied upon the hoe, or compound, or farm, and wished to give latitude in the matter, to suit the varying conditions of the several districts and provinces. The point as to whether the headman should be left complete power to decide the proportion which each individual should pay, or whether definite rules should be laid down for the assessment of each individual, is open to much argument. The Committee, however, quoted a statement made by the Government of India in 1898 when reviewing a tax upon the household or family which they found in existence in Upper Burma. In this, they "considered that the distribution of the tax as among the component families of a village was exceedingly equitable, far more so than any assessment which Government itself could frame, and infinitely more so than an all-round capitation tax. Their feeling was strongly in favour of leaving the people to manage their own affairs as far as possible, and not to be in haste to bring in a more rigid and mechanical system. So long as the favouritism which always accompanies an indigenous system is kept within bounds and the people do not complain, it may be safely concluded that they think it a cheap price to pay for the permission to make their own distribution."

These are words of wisdom which merit deep consideration by every official called upon to administer a semi-civilised people. In a civilised country the taxpayer wishes to know the exact sum which he will be called upon annually to contribute, so that it will be impossible for him to be obliged to pay a farthing more. The member of a semi-civilised community, on the other hand, detests a rigid, inflexible system. He likes to think that he may escape lightly if he can secure the goodwill of the tax-collector, and holds that it compensates him for the occasion when, owing probably to his own want of tact—as he considers it—he is mulcted of more than his due by a tax-collector whom he has offended. In other words, he prefers to bargain over his tax, much as a housewife does in the market, rather than pay a fixed, rigid sum. The one desideratum is that he should always have the opportunity of appeal to an authority who cannot be bribed or otherwise placated. This authority cannot, for the present, be any other in Northern Nigeria than the British political officers. In the readiness with which appeals can ultimately be made to them lies the question whether the inhabitants of the Protectorate are well or ill governed.

The railway which is now being constructed into the interior, and which will reach Kano this year, will cause a very large rise in value in the land in its vicinity. The "Natives' Rights Proclamation" secures the consequent increase in rentals for the benefit of the people concerned. One of the most complicated and difficult problems with which the present Administration has to deal is the securing for public revenue of the economic value of the land in towns and cities, a value which will shortly become very large, especially in those situated on or near the railway. Formerly agriculturists were taxed for their farms, and craftsmen paid licences, but there was no taxation of land on which houses were built or market stalls erected. The principle of land rent, in short, was not applied to urban sites. To extend it to these will not conflict with any native customs; on the contrary, it is the logical outcome of these, and there is no doubt that the native rulers and officials will readily perceive this, and give willing assistance in formulating a scheme to carry it out. Accurate measurements are not at present practicable or necessary. No doubt a simple classification of plots by size and possibly site value can be arranged, and a tabulation and assessment of urban sites on these lines carried out by natives themselves under the supervision of the political officers. The more that intelligent natives are encouraged to think for themselves instead of relying perpetually on advice and instructions from Residents, the better it will be for the country. They have been deprived of the excitement and occupation given by wars and the exercise of despotic power, and there is a real danger of their settling down into apathy and eventual discontent unless they are given an interest in things beyond the mere routine of official duties, and their sympathies engaged in our efforts for promoting the novel and material interests of the country at large. The future of the country depends solely on the extent to which Residents can gain the sympathy and cooperation of the native rulers and their officials.

CHAPTER XVI

RELIGION AND EDUCATION

"The great and momentous struggle between Islamism and Paganism is here continually going on, causing every day the most painful and affecting results. We find Mahomedan learning engrafted on the ignorance and simplicity of the black races, and the gaudy magnificence and strict ceremonial of large empires side by side with barbarous simplicity of naked and half-naked tribes."—BARTH, *Travels in Central Africa*, 1858.

"Lightly to undermine the native faith, and to endeavour, with the best intentions, to fill him with English ideas, is to give him at most a few superficial English observances, resting on no firm basis, and to leave his moral nature without any support to prevent it from relapsing into chaos, to produce that most evil creature, the native inhabitant of the coast town. Even to touch a native custom which seems to us objectionable, is to run the risk of pulling down a whole edifice, of destroying a whole system of morality, imperfect indeed, but infinitely better than the chaos which supersedes it."—W. L. GRANT, *Revue Economique Internationale*, March 1909.

ISLAM was introduced into Bornu in the eleventh century, and into Hausaland probably somewhat later. It is said that the unknown people who made themselves masters of Hausaland about A.D. 1000 were Mahomedan, but soon lapsed into the same practices as their subjects,[1] which appears to have been an enlightened paganism. According to the Kano Chronicle, a native record recently discovered, Islam was introduced into Hausaland from the West in the middle of the fourteenth century A.D., the then reigning King of Kano being converted to the faith. A mosque was built by him, and every town was ordered to observe the times of prayer. A century later, accord-

[1] Palmer, *Journal of the Royal Anthropological Institute*, June 1908.

ing to the Chronicle, the Fulani came to Hausaland, bringing with them books on divinity and etymology; for before this there was only the Koran, with the Books of the Law and the Traditions. The Fulani did not apparently stay, but passed on into Bornu. Mention is made in the following reign of a revival of Islamism, from which it seems that many of the inhabitants had relapsed into paganism, and it is impossible to study the Chronicle without coming to the conclusion that there was a perpetual strife continued through many centuries between the two religions. Nominally, no doubt, the rulers were followers of Islam, and maintained the religious observances of that faith, but it was probably much mixed with pagan beliefs and superstitions, while a great number of the peasantry held openly to their pagan doctrines. It was the return of the Fulani priest, Othman dan Fodio, from Mecca early in the nineteenth century which was the cause of the great religious upheaval which took place, and ended in the scattered and independent Hausa States becoming knit into one Mahomedan Empire, and the green flag of Islam being carried down to the banks of the Benue and across that river to the pagan states in Adamawa.

The events which followed Othman dan Fodio's declaration of a *jehad* have always been described as a Fulani conquest of Hausaland. There was every reason for this assumption. The rulers who established themselves on the thrones of the various Hausa States, and of the new Mahomedan states carved out of pagan districts, were in every case except one[1] Fulanis, who had received their "flags"—the emblems of authority—from Othman. They naturally proclaimed

[1] The exception was Bauchi, whose conqueror and flag-bearer was a Hausa.

it as a Fulani conquest, and travellers and historians assumed that it was so without question. The Kano Chronicle distinctly says that "in King Alwali's time the Fulani conquered the seven Hausa States on the plea of reviving the Mahomedan religion, and drove Alwali from Kano," and a Fulani succeeded him as king. The natives, therefore, looked upon it as a Fulani conquest, but it is difficult to see how a handful of Fulanis could have conquered the numerous inhabitants of the Hausa States unless they received help from a portion of the Hausas themselves. From the evidence which has come to my knowledge in the country itself, I have been led to believe that the so-called Fulani conquest was in reality a vast religious upheaval, of which the author, Othman dan Fodio, was a Fulani, but that his adherents were both Fulanis and Hausas, and that these combined to hurl from power the rulers who had, as they considered, defiled the true faith by engrafting on it pagan superstitions.

The question, however, need not be here discussed. The important point is that the whole of the Hausa States became converted to Islam, and that large pagan districts to the south came under the dominion of Mahomedan rulers. Islam, in short, received a tremendous impetus, and its doctrines were spread far and wide over what is now the Protectorate of Northern Nigeria. I have discussed in a previous chapter the effect of Islam on pagan tribes. It is undoubtedly a religion which appeals very strongly to the African native. Its simplicity is probably one of the chief causes of this. "There is one God, and Mahomed is his prophet," is a doctrine which is crystal clear, and can be grasped in an instant by the most ignorant pagan. The Koran, in a spirit of true benevolence, teaches that every professor of the religion, however abject in life his condition may be, is strictly on terms of equality with his neighbour. At the great Mahomedan festival, Emir and slave kneel side by side in the vast concourse which assembles in prayer outside the city walls; master and servant together turn their faces towards the east and prostrate themselves in the prescribed manner in one common act of devotion. It is an impressive sight which is not easily forgotten to watch the thousands of white-robed figures reverently prostrating themselves on the great plain sloping down to the river, with the rising sun shining full upon the sea of kneeling figures, united without distinction of rank in one act of religious devotion. To the pagan it makes the same appeal of common brotherhood as the Christian religion made to the slaves and outcasts in Rome eighteen hundred years ago. The religion of Islam, wherever it prevails, whether at the courts of Constantinople, Delhi, or Morocco, or in the less ostentatious governments of West Africa, is uniform, both in its practice and in its influences on the minds of men. The "dead hand of Islam" is sometimes spoken of, as if the religion were a blight which withered all progress amongst the nations who profess it, though the Arabs in Spain held aloft the torch of civilisation at a time when the rest of Europe was wrapped in darkness. But even if it be true that Islam lays a dead hand on a people who have reached a certain standard of civilisation, it is impossible to deny its quickening influence on African races in a backward state of evolution. Amongst the pagan tribes of Northern Nigeria it is making its converts every day, sweeping away drunkenness, cannibalism, and fetishism; mosques and markets spring into existence, and the pagan loses his exclusiveness, and learns to mingle with his fellow-men. To the negro Islam is not sterile or lifeless. The dead hand is not for him.

Not that the spread of Islam amongst pagan tribes is wholly beneficial. Its appeal to his sensual nature is not without its effect. The very civilisation which Islam brings, teaches its vices as well as its virtues. But when the balance is struck between Islamism and Paganism there can be but little doubt which of the scales weighs the heavier.

It is generally believed that Islam is a militant religion which is spread by the sword alone, and the events of last century in Hausaland afford a ready example of the fact that at times the faith is indeed carried far and wide in a tempest of war. But it is safe to say that the majority of converts were made by very different means. The author of a book on West Africa[1] gives an account related to him by Dr. Blyden of the conversion to Islam of a town in the hinterland of Sierra Leone. "On a certain day," he says, "the inhabitants of the town observed a man, black like themselves, but clad in a white garment, advancing down the main street. Suddenly the stranger prostrated himself and prayed to Allah. The natives stoned him and he departed. In a little while he returned and prostrated himself as before. This time he was not stoned, but the people gathered about him with mockery and reviling. The men spat upon him, and the women hurled insults and abuse. His prayer ended, the stranger went away in silence, grave and austere, seemingly oblivious to his unsympathetic surroundings. For a space he did not renew his visit,

[1] E. D. Morel, *Affairs of West Africa*.

and in the interval the people began to regret their rudeness. The demeanour of the stranger under trying circumstances had gained their respect. A third time he came, and with him two boys also clothed in white garments. Together they knelt and offered prayer. The natives watched and forbore to jeer. At the conclusion of the prayer a woman came timidly forward and pushed her young son toward the holy man, then as rapidly retreated. The Muslim rose, took the boy by the hand, and, followed by his acolytes, left the village in silence as before. When he came again, he was accompanied by three boys, two of them those who had been with him before, and the other the woman's son, clad like the rest. All four fell upon their knees, the holy man reciting the prayer in a voice that spoke of triumph and success. He never left the town again, for the people crowded round him, beseeching him to teach their children. In a short time the entire population of that town, which for three centuries had beaten back the assaults of would-be Muslim converters by the sword, had voluntarily embraced Islam!"

A number of Christian missionary societies have established stations in Northern Nigeria, but it has been deemed prudent by the authorities to restrict missionary enterprise in the northern Mahomedan states until railway communication has rendered the military situation more secure. The Church Missionary Society, however, secured permission, on the formation of the Protectorate, to establish a Mission station in a Hausa town some 40 miles south of Zaria, and in 1904 the Mission, with the Governor's sanction, moved to Zaria itself, and rented a compound in the middle of the town. Before granting permission for this move, the Governor instructed the Resident to inquire of the Emir if he had any objection to a Mission station being established in his capital, and to explain that the attitude of the Government was, in religious matters, entirely neutral. The Mission has done much valuable medical work in the town and neighbourhood, and is looked upon with much respect by the inhabitants.

In pagan districts several missionary societies have stations, in which both industrial and educational work are carried on. At Bida the Church Missionary Society has a school in which there is a special class for the instruction of the educated Mahomedans in reading and writing Hausa in Roman characters. Industrial missions in Muri, Zaria, and Bauchi provinces endeavour to teach the use of implements, farming, carpentering, and other industries, and at the same time give medical attendance to the natives, and have schools in which Hausa is taught. Much has been done by many of these Missions towards the study of the local languages, and useful vocabularies of some of the latter have been compiled. It is early yet to discuss results among the natives. The position frankly and most wisely taken up by many of the missionaries is that their first duty is to learn, before they can really make any successful attempt to teach. Meanwhile the natives have suggestive object-lessons before them in the unselfish lives the missionaries lead, in their industry, the cleanliness and neatness of their houses and compounds, their high standard of conduct, and the consideration which they show to all around them.

Missionary enterprise in a new country like Northern Nigeria demands the highest qualities from those responsible for its operations, and tact is no less necessary than zeal and self-denial. Sir Frederick Lugard, in his Report for 1906, touched on the subject of the preaching of equality of Europeans and natives, "which," he wrote, "however true from a doctrinal point of view, is apt to be misapplied by people in a low stage of development, and interpreted as an abolition of class distinction." It is difficult for Europeans to understand the danger of disintegrating a native social organism by upsetting ideas which are the result of centuries of evolution. In a primitive community, individualism is strictly subordinated to the duty of each member to the State, and the greatest crime is one which affects the community rather than the individual. This is shown most clearly in the attitude of the pagan towards witchcraft. Witchcraft is not looked upon as a supernatural power. It is rather a gift possessed by an individual of divining the powers of nature and of utilising his knowledge. If this supposed gift is used for the benefit of the community by foretelling rain, for example, or the issue of a trivial quarrel, or the detection of a criminal, the possessor is looked up to with the utmost reverence. If, on the other hand, the gift is used for personal and selfish ends, for the satisfaction, for instance, of a private wrong by the exercise of the power of the "evil eye" (a superstition profoundly believed by all natives), the individual concerned is considered guilty of a crime against the community, and subjected to universal execration. It is such individuals to whom the most rigorous punishments are meted out: he or she will be hurriedly sold as a slave to a passing caravan, that the community may be rid of a dangerous criminal, who by harming a member of the community weakens its strength.

Missionaries are naturally anxious to establish themselves in each newly opened up pagan district before Mahomedan emissaries have gained access to it, or not at least to be behind the latter. The subject is a very difficult one, and it is certainly fair to prevent the advent of proselytising Mahomedan missionaries into such districts if the establishment of Christian Missions is hindered by Government. That the latter should in certain cases be delayed until the district has been brought under control by a political officer is evident to any one who has had any experience in such matters. The first contact of Europeans with an African tribe is a matter of tremendous importance, for the nature of the early impressions made on the latter determines to a large extent the subsequent attitude and behaviour of the tribe. If the political officer to whose care the new district is entrusted prove tactless, he can immediately be replaced and transferred elsewhere. If, on the other hand, a Mission station is established, Government has no influence over a tactless or over-zealous individual, and can take no action unless it appears that an actual breach of the peace is likely to occur. Missionaries in Northern Nigeria have, I think, always shown themselves most anxious to avoid embarrassing the Government, and have loyally acquiesced in all decisions even when these have conflicted with their own opinions, and a frank discussion between Residents and missionaries has usually had satisfactory results.

The question of Education has never been lost sight of since the Protectorate was formed, but funds were not at first available for the purpose, and the Administration had its hands full in other directions. Sir Frederick Lugard in his Report for 1902 pointed out that, with the resources at his disposal, the utmost that could be done would be to endeavour to improve by very small grants the primary education given in the Mahomedan schools. He suggested that in some of these the Roman characters might by degrees be substituted for the Arabic. Hausa is spoken throughout the northern states, with the exception of Bornu, which has a different language, though Hausa is understood by most of the educated classes. It is not, properly speaking, a written language. Written communications are usually couched in Arabic, which is necessarily known by the educated Mahomedans through the medium of the Koran. Documents are, however, in existence written in the Hausa language in Arabic characters, the words being spelt phonetically. Since Hausa is the *lingua franca* of the Protectorate, and is the Court language of practically all the Emirates, it is obviously of importance for the future welfare of the country to endeavour to introduce the Roman character, and thus render the language legible to the civilised world, and not only to the Mahomedan nations. In this endeavour the Church Missionary Society concur, and have been followed by other Missions. In the Freed Slaves Home, founded by Sir Frederick Lugard for the reception of homeless children rescued from slave caravans, elementary education was given on these lines. Apprentices were taught in the various Government departments — workshops, printing, marine, transport, telegraph, and so on—and a small sum was expended in the purchase of school materials for Mission schools. The lack of funds, however, prevented any serious steps being taken to provide for a general scheme of education throughout the

Protectorate. At one or two of the provincial capitals attempts were made by Residents to establish schools for the sons of Chiefs and high officials, where instruction was given by the educated Coast clerks out of Government hours, a small fee being paid them through the Resident by the parents.

In the Mahomedan schools scattered throughout the Protectorate, instruction is limited to reading and writing in Arabic for the most advanced scholars, and for the others, to learning verses of the Koran.

The education mainly required in the immediate present and future falls under three heads. First, for intelligent natives of the "Mallam" class, who would be taught Roman characters for writing Hausa, colloquial English, and finally reading and writing English, arithmetic and geography, so that they may qualify for clerkships in Government and other offices, and gradually replace the native clerks who have of necessity been drawn hitherto from other West African colonies and possessions where schools are in existence. Second, for the sons of the ruling class, who would be brought up preferably as boarders in a school or college, and receive primary education without imbibing ideas of European dress and habits unsuited to their environment, or necessarily forgoing their own religion. Third, general elementary schools for children on a secular basis, with industrial teaching in addition.

In 1906 the Church Missionary Society offered to open a boarding-school in some central position such as Zaria or Kano, to which the ruling Emirs should send their sons: the teaching to be secular, and no interference to be made with the exercise of their religious observances by Mahomedans, provided that the Mission should be free to exercise its influence with its pupils out of school hours. The Mahomedan Emirs, however, were naturally averse to allowing their sons to be taken away from home influences, and brought up in a Christian school. With Mahomedans education and religion are almost synonymous terms, and for this reason in matters of education it is most difficult not to arouse suspicions as to religious tendencies. All the Emirs and leading Mahomedan officials were found to be genuinely desirous of obtaining secular education for their children, but they displayed considerable anxiety lest an anti-Mahomedan influence should be at the same time brought to bear on the latter.

Sir Percy Girouard, on his arrival in the Protectorate in 1907, took the matter up warmly, and in the following year one of the political officers was appointed Director of Education, with instructions to prepare a scheme for a regular system of education, much on the lines adopted by Lord Cromer for the Egyptian Soudan. In order to examine the systems in force in other countries, the new Director visited the schools in Lagos, the Gold Coast, and in Egypt, including the Gordon Memorial College at Khartoum.

As a result, schools were started in Kano in September 1909, houses of native pattern being erected on a site two miles from the Residency and one mile from the city gates. The site has peculiar advantages, as it is within easy reach of the Residency, but is removed from the undesirable influence of soldiers, servants, carriers, and their followers who surround a European station. It is within close touch with the Emir and the best of native life, but being outside the town avoids too close contact with the temptations which a market and large city like Kano inevitably offer. One room in the Director's quarters is set aside for the library, which now possesses a useful collection of the best books dealing with the history and geography of West Africa in general, and Nigeria and the Western Soudan in particular.

Temporary huts were rapidly built for the Chiefs' Sons' School, which was transferred from its former quarters in the Residency compound, and for the Mallams destined to form the nucleus of the teaching staff. Larger buildings of a more permanent character were designed to house the pupils, Chiefs' sons, Mallamai, and apprentices who began to pour in from other districts and provinces.

The schools are of three kinds :—

(1) Chiefs' Sons' School.

(2) Mallamai School.

(3) Technical and Vernacular Schools.

All instruction is given in the Hausa language, which is written in the Roman character. Later on English will no doubt be needed by the more advanced pupils, but for the present the Hausa language is the best medium for popularising education and preserving and developing native character and abilities on their own lines.

The object of the first school is to give the sons and relatives of Emirs and Chiefs a good general education, to make them more fitted to hold responsible executive offices in the Administration. Their ages are approximately from eight to eighteen.

The second or Mallamai School is of equal importance with the first. It aims at training (*a*) teachers for all schools, (*b*) men to work as writers, agents, clerks, and surveyors, either under the native administration or directly under European officers. It is not desired to draw any hard and fast line between these two schools. Several of the older pupils in the Chiefs' Sons' School have already proved of valuable service as pupil teachers or clerical assistants in the native Treasury and Native Courts, and in land survey. Candidates for the Mallamai School must have had the ordinary education given in the native Koranic schools. Starting with a fair knowledge of the Arabic character, these pupils easily learn the Roman within a few weeks. Some again are already acquainted with the Arabic numerals, and these have little difficulty in learning the elements of arithmetic. Multiplication and division are seized on with avidity and practised almost as a source of amusement. Vulgar and decimal fractions are soon within their range.

Lastly, there are the Technical and Vernacular Schools. Apprentices working in the various Technical Schools unite for a few hours daily in the Vernacular School, where they are given instruction in the "three R's." Great importance is attached to the Technical Schools, since it is essential that education should not be divorced from the crafts and industry of the people. Pupils of the Chiefs' Sons' School were required from the outset to spend a short time every week at work in the garden. Limes, mangoes, oranges, kola, pineapples, arrowroot, cinnamon, and other useful plants and trees were obtained from the Government plantations in Southern Nigeria, besides vegetables and flowers, and various tropical shade-trees. Next year the boys will be encouraged to keep small gardens and plantations of their own. They will learn in this way not to regard manual labour as beneath their dignity, and will at the same time gain some knowledge of agriculture and the plant life of their native country, and the possibilities of developing and improving it.

The Technical Schools have a great future before them in teaching those manual and mechanical crafts in which the native has so much to gain from the European. Well-equipped workshops and trained instructors are required for this purpose, but for the time being a commencement has been made by engaging a carpenter from Southern Nigeria, and the best leatherworkers and blacksmiths who could be found in Northern Nigeria. In addition to their monthly wages, these men are paid so much to instruct and support a number of apprentices. Sets of carpenters' tools for instructor and apprentices, a forge and anvil and some smith's tools were imported from England. A certain amount of good timber was also obtained from England, but the bulk of that used is cut from a local species of acacia tree which the carpenter and his apprentices fell and use as required. The workshops proved of great practical use from the outset, by supplying the requirements of the school buildings. The carpenter's first task was to provide writing-desks. These are about two feet high, since the pupils naturally sit on the ground in native fashion. Doors, window-frames, iron hinges, nails, water-cans for the garden, etc., are all turned out by the workshops. The school buildings are constructed in quadrangles, some with closed class-rooms, others with open cloisters which can be conveniently divided between different classes.

In addition, it was found necessary to provide living quarters for the Chiefs' sons who came from other districts and provinces. Those belonging to

Kano Emirate live in their own homes in Kano town. Those who come from a distance are given temporary lodgings in the town and transferred to the school quarters as soon as these can be erected. The plan adopted is to build large compounds containing from six to a dozen round huts with quarters for a Mallam, who is placed in charge of each compound, and is responsible for the catering and care of the boys and the cleanliness of their huts and compounds. Each compound is appropriated to the pupils from a particular group, district, or province. Each Chief's son is expected to have a servant to cook his food, or, if old enough, a wife, and one boy or man-servant who looks after his master's horse if he possesses one. The boy-servants attend the Vernacular School with the apprentices from the workshops. A charge of 12s. per month is sufficient to feed each pupil and his servants, and allow the boy a small weekly pocket-money. Parents are encouraged to send their children presents of clothing from time to time, but not food.

From November 1, 1910, the following scale of fees was instituted :

Chief's son	2s.	per month.
Mallamai	1s.	"
Apprentices and Vernacular School .	6d.	"
Medical Fee	6d.	"

The subsistence allowance for the Mallamai is generally £1 per month, but sometimes less : fees and subsistence money from other districts and provinces are paid into the Residents' accounts and drawn from the sub-treasury at Kano.

By December 31, 1910, the number of pupils in the different schools and classes was over 200, and may easily exceed 400 in the course of the next twelve months.

Boys of all classes, Chief's sons, apprentices, and servants, join in the games, cricket, rounders, jumping or running races every evening, and show great keenness and enthusiasm.

With regard to funds, the Government Estimates for 1910-1911 allow little beyond the salary of the Director of Education and that of his assistant. The bulk of the cost of buildings, tools, stationery books, etc., has been defrayed from a grant of £1000 per annum set aside for education purposes by the Kano native Treasury. The Emir has a keen personal interest in the schools, and visits them constantly with the Resident or Director of Education. At his suggestion several of the boys' compounds have been built by prison labour from the native gaol. It is hoped that the Emirs of other provinces, whose sons and relatives are at the schools, will contribute either personally or from their native Treasuries another £500 per annum.

It is not intended that the Kano schools should take the place of provincial schools, but, on the contrary, that every province should eventually have its central school and a number of Vernacular Schools in every important town and district. To attain this ideal, a numerous and well-trained staff of teachers is necessary, and these cannot be obtained all at once. The idea is that the Chiefs' sons, at any rate from all the northern provinces, should continue to go mainly to the Kano schools, and the Mallamai School there should supply teachers for the provincial schools as soon as it is in a position to do so. This scheme will secure some uniformity of training, and bring all for a time at least under the influence of the Director of Education and European teachers. Only in this way will it be possible to ensure the right tone throughout the provincial schools.

All Mahomedan pupils, *i.e.* all the pupils at present in the Kano schools, regularly attend readings from the Koran by a qualified Mallam.

A point is made of permitting all boys to return to their homes for at least one month in every year, and it is found convenient that this holiday should coincide with the month of Ramadan, with the great Sala festival at its close.

Mallamai with a fair knowledge of arithmetic and able to write Roman characters legibly are always in demand for work in the Administration of the Emirates, and earn good salaries from their native Treasuries. The Director of Education, therefore, frequently finds himself divided between the desire on the one hand to keep all his capable men for a more thorough training as teachers, and on the other hand to popularise education by permitting them to get to work at once and earn good salaries in the task of administering the country.

The Director of Education has drawn up a scheme of simple rules for spelling the Hausa language, with the assistance of Hausa students amongst the missionaries and Government officials, and it is hoped thereby that a common spelling will be generally adopted. He has also drawn up a carefully graded curriculum of studies for the different schools and classes. From the outset great stress has been laid on the importance of making pupils use their own powers of observation and keeping free from the ruts of parrot learning by rote, which is the system followed in the native

Koranic schools. The Director of Education is preparing a set of Hausa School Books and Readers which will be printed shortly.

Until these are completed the task of supplying fresh material for their classes is no light one for the teachers.

By April 1, 1911, it is hoped that a European technical instructor will be available, and be able to commence work with larger and better-fitted workshops. Possibly there will be in addition a European teacher with a good knowledge of Hausa to take the higher classes of Mallamai.

CHAPTER XVII

CONCLUSION

"What is needed is a clear conception of what we, the higher races, are aiming at: what it is that we stand for."—ALSTON, *The White Man's Work in Asia and Africa.*

"Our rule over the [native] territories can only be justified if we can show that it adds to the happiness and prosperity of the people."—Mr. CHAMBERLAIN.

"The real issue is whether, and under what circumstances, it is justifiable for Western nations to use compulsory government for the control and education in the arts of industrial and political civilisation of tropical countries and other so-called lower races."—J. A. HOBSON, *Imperialism.*

IT is impossible to read the history of ten years' administration in Northern Nigeria without asking ourselves the question whether our occupation of this vast portion of tropical Africa has been for the benefit —present or ultimate—primarily of the inhabitants, secondly of the British Empire itself. Although the small opposition encountered in occupying and establishing British administration in the northern states tends to show that the event was acquiesced in not altogether unwillingly by at least a section of the populace, it may be assumed that the inhabitants of the Protectorate as a whole resented domination by a white race. They did not, in other words, consider it was for their immediate benefit. Will they ultimately take another view? The answer to this question seems to me to be that it depends entirely on the extent to which their customs and institutions are interfered with. There are many profound observers of human nature who maintain that a nation prefers submitting to the worst government by members of its own race than to the most perfect government that can be conceived by an alien race, even if the latter be archangels from heaven. The statement contains a large element of truth, but history proves that it requires qualification. Nations suffering under the intolerable tyranny of leaders of their own race have welcomed the domination of aliens who have come from outside and taken the place of their rulers. It is probably true that no people will submit permanently to be ruled by aliens if the aliens hold themselves permanently aloof as a separate race; but so long as the impression of the misrule of their former rulers lasts, the people will endure willingly the good government which has replaced it.

If we, as a nation, are called to account for our rule in Northern Nigeria, can we say that we have replaced misrule by good government? Surely the question can have but one answer. Judged by European standards, the country is immeasurably better governed than it was before. And, judged by native standards, we can say the same with some confidence, because the government is still carried on by native rulers, and hence the conditions are capable of accurate comparison. Changes have been made, but the foundations remain as before: the alterations are not structural. It is not as if machinery of an entirely different type had been set up, and we claimed that the output were of a better quality or greater quantity in consequence. The improvement in results has been effected notwithstanding that the original machinery has been retained.

The question that remains for the future is how

long the present peculiar relationship between British and native administration can continue. I do not know of any precedent in history which will serve as a guide. Hitherto an alien race assuming the administration of a conquered country has done one of two things: either it has undertaken the direct governing power, and has used the native machinery in a wholly subservient position under its own definite orders; or it has left the country to carry on its own government in its own way, and to collect its own taxes, maintaining an official merely to advise, who interferes only to prevent specific acts or policies, and exercises otherwise only a general supervision. In Northern Nigeria, it seems to me, an entirely new experiment is being tried. British and native officials rule side by side. The attempt is made to leave the native rulers to carry on their own government, but the Resident does far more than advise. He has power to arrest, try, and sentence natives in his own court, without referring in any way to the native rulers. With regard to taxation, he conveys precise orders from the Governor as to the amounts to be collected, mode of assessing and collecting, and so on; visits and assesses farms and villages in person; investigates complaints as to over-assessment or extortion; and generally carries out a direct interference in all the internal affairs of the State. In some provinces the tax is brought direct to him, and he hands over a portion to the native rulers and officials; in others, the latter receive the taxes themselves, and hand over a portion to the Resident. The difference between these two proceedings is surely of immense importance: clearly they represent two distinct policies. In one case, the Resident assumes the position of the direct ruler of the country, acting for the Governor, and the native Chief is a salaried official under his orders; in the other case, the Chief is in the position of a ruler collecting his taxes and paying over a portion to the Resident in return for protection afforded and expenses incurred thereby. Which policy is the correct one? What, in fact, is the true status of the ruling Chiefs in Northern Nigeria? Are they rulers under the protection of the British Government, or are they salaried officials of the latter, performing certain duties under direct orders? The whole position seems vague and undecided. It was right in the first instance to leave it so, for it was necessary to discover to what extent the existing native administrations were faulty or oppressive, and what were the characters and abilities of the ruling classes. But the time has come now when some clear and definite policy must be adopted, and the relationship between the British and native administrations defined. It is obvious that the greatest possible freedom to manage their own affairs must be left to the inhabitants of the Protectorate and their native rulers; but as a matter of practical policy, what is the greatest possible freedom? Unless some clear guiding principle is laid down, there is a danger that each local official will interpret his duties according to his own ideas. At present, the instructions are to rule through the Chief. But this, clear as it seems, in reality makes it possible for a local official who conceives all native rule to be necessarily corrupt, to use the native Chief and his subordinates as mere puppets to carry out orders.

The ideal for an alien official governing a people through their own rulers would appear to me to be to introduce no reform until it has first won the willing and genuine approval of the Chief and people. It would then be certain that the reform would be in accordance with the habits of thought of the people and would not upset their ideas of right and wrong, or of good government. This ideal, however, is unattainable in its entirety. For instance, if the British Government waited to prohibit slave-raiding till the policy had won the genuine approval of the rulers and people, it would probably have to wait many generations. However, if we eliminate slave-raiding and a few somewhat similar customs which are universally condemned by civilised races as repugnant to modern ideas of justice and humanity, the ideal would form a basis on which to form a definite policy. What seems to me necessary is to make up our minds what is the ultimate goal at which we are aiming. Once this is settled, the methods by which we intend to endeavour to reach it can be thought out step by step. To continue pressing on we know not whither, some Residents setting one goal before them, some another, is impossible. One thing is certain: whatever is the policy eventually adopted, it must fulfil this condition: it must be a policy which will ensure cordial and genuine co-operation between the rulers and ourselves. If the rulers are discontented, the discontent will be reflected throughout the entire country. The peasantry invariably look to their rulers for guidance. Secure the affection and respect of the rulers, and you secure that of the country. The co-operation of the rulers must not, however, be secured by allowing them altogether a free hand in their dealings with their subjects. There is always the danger in ruling through the Chiefs that the latter, if not carefully and ceaselessly watched and guided, will utilise the power given them by the British forces to bind on their subjects fetters far more galling than those they were able to forge in the days when an oppressed peasantry could in the last resort rise in revolt without the fear of having to face modern rifles and Maxim guns. This is the really difficult problem which faces the Western nations in the countries of tropical Africa which they have taken upon themselves to administer. There is need of a policy which, while securing the masses from oppression, will give to the ruling classes the utmost freedom to manage their own affairs on their own lines, so long as these lines are in accordance with the main Western ideas of humanity and justice. Ten years of administration in Northern Nigeria, so far from solving the problem, have only begun to make its outlines clearer. Indeed it is doubtful if many administrators are aware that the problem exists. It is a common belief that the establishment of the Pax Britannica and of law-courts where British justice is dispensed, necessarily secures the approbation of all right-thinking natives. It does nothing of the sort. What they want is good and efficient government under their own rulers. It ought not to be beyond the wit of Western statesmen and administrators to devise a system whereby this may be secured. But it has not yet been devised.

Has the occupation of Northern Nigeria been to the benefit of the British Empire? Measured in terms of human life, it has been no light undertaking. The death-roll has been large, and shattered constitutions many. But the taxpayer will experience a more immediate concern in the amount of public revenue expended on the undertaking. Without considering the funds expended by Government on exploration in the past, the actual sum contributed towards setting up an administration amounts to several millions of pounds, roughly speaking, four and a half millions.[1] The Protectorate is still a heavy charge on the Imperial Exchequer. What is there to show in return for the expenditure of these large sums?

The system by which Customs dues on all imports by sea into both Southern and Northern Nigeria are collected by the Government of the former country, makes it impossible to state precisely what the total value of such imports into the Northern Protectorate amounts to each year; but that a large and expanding market has been opened up is obvious.[2] Commercially speaking, the country is in its infancy. The nearly completed railway to Kano will revolutionise the commercial aspect, and a large proportion of the nine million inhabitants will in time become eager purchasers of European goods. It is not probable that five million pounds will prove to have been a bad investment for the British nation.

This is the economic aspect of the question. But although it was undoubtedly the primary cause of Great Britain's action in assuming administrative

[1] The actual figures are as follows:

Amount paid to Royal Niger Company on revocation of charter	£865,000
Imperial expenditure on W.A. Frontier Force, 1897 to 1901 .	611,190
Imperial grants-in-aid from January 1, 1900, to March 31, 1910	3,035,030
Total . .	£4,511,220

[2] The official figures in the last published Report give the value of imports as about £600,000 and of the exports as £275,000.

Of these, the principal were—

Tin ore . .	£70,000
Shea nuts . . .	70,000
Palm kernels . . .	47,000
Gums	9,000

Both imports and exports are greater than is shown by these figures, however, as a great proportion of the articles entering the Protectorate are consigned to Southern Nigeria, and distributed from there, and an overland export trade similarly exists. The total import and export trade might be estimated as about a million sterling.

responsibility for the territories, it was not the only one. There was a genuine desire to rescue the country from the miseries of slave-raiding and internecine war, and, in Mr. Chamberlain's words, to "add to the happiness and prosperity of the people." The former result has certainly been achieved. The latter is open to argument, and depends mainly on the policy to be pursued in the future. Supposing, however, that this be left out of the question for a moment, is the sum expended by the British Exchequer a large price to pay for the abolition of slave-raiding and the gradual extinction of slavery? The British Government has in the past paid large sums in other countries as compensation to slave-owners for the loss of their slaves; no compensation whatever has been paid directly to a single slave-owner in Nigeria. The policy adopted has already been described and discussed, and the indirect means indicated whereby the change from slave labour to free labour is being gradually introduced with a minimum of disturbance and injustice to owners. Did England owe Africa no debt for the past?

Discussion is futile as to whether there is any justification for Western nations exercising any interference at all in the affairs of tropical African countries. Economic reasons necessitate the development of the resources of tropical regions, and the native races are at present both unable and unwilling to do this unaided. Not less do humanitarian reasons compel the civilised races to act. An illustration of the conditions of the districts of tropical Africa before they are controlled by civilised nations is afforded by the description recently published of such a district in the uncontrolled hinterland of Liberia at the present moment. "All kinds of savage and barbarous customs," it runs, "take place in Pandeme. Life is held to be cheap there, as it often is in barbaric Africa, and human sacrifices are enacted. Large quantities of slaves are bought and sold. In fact, the object of most of the raids and the attacks of the Sofa warriors was the capture of slaves, and these forages extend over wide areas of country. . . . While in this town I saw seven slaves who were secured by the leg in wooden stocks. They had been in that position for some months. One of them told me that he had been kept thus for two years. . . . I noticed an empty grave, which it appeared had been used for the purpose of burying a man alive as a sacrifice; and I was informed in a most matter-of-fact way, and as if the occurrence was quite an ordinary one, that the unfortunate victim's body had been lately exhumed to obtain certain portions for the purpose of manufacturing fetish medicines."[1] This was in the summer of 1908. "To those who utter the single cry of warning, *laissez-faire*, hands off," says a writer who is an ardent opponent of Imperial expansion as a general principle, "it is a sufficient answer to point out the impossibility of maintaining such an attitude."[2] The same writer proceeds to suggest three conditions which might render interference by civilised nations with "lower races" legitimate. First, that such interference must be directed primarily to secure the safety and progress of the civilisation of the world, and not the special interest of the interfering nation. Second, that it be attended by an improvement and elevation of the character of the people who are brought under control. Lastly, that the determination of the two preceding conditions be not left to the arbitrary will

[1] "A Tour in the Liberian Hinterland," by Captain Wallis, late H.M.'s Consul-General for Liberia, *Geographical Journal*, March 1910.

[2] J. A. Hobson, *Imperialism*.

or judgment of the interfering nation, but that it proceed from some organised representation of civilised humanity.

Let us apply these tests to the British administration of Northern Nigeria. With regard to the first, by international agreement, the Niger and Benue rivers are kept open by Great Britain as international highways; her Free Trade policy gives to traders of all nationalities exactly the same rights as those enjoyed by her own; all revenues collected in the country are devoted solely to the benefit of the natives themselves. There does not appear here much room for the charge of the interference being directed to the special interest of the interfering nation.

With regard to the second, the whole policy of the Administration is directed towards improving and elevating the character of the people by inculcating modern ideas of justice and humanity, and by encouraging the ruling classes to develop their abilities and highest moral qualities in the government of those under their charge.

Lastly, though no actual tribunal of European nations has ever been convened to criticise the manner in which the various Governments carry out their moral obligations in tropical Africa, yet the Berlin Conference of 1885 distinctly recognised these obligations; and both the Press and the Parliaments of Europe constantly criticise the policy and actions of the various Governments in this respect. Is it, however, altogether beyond the range of practical politics to suggest that an agreement might be arrived at between the principal Powers of Europe whereby they should undertake to pursue a common policy in their dealings with the countries of tropical Africa of which they have assumed the responsibility? Slavery, equality of trading opportunities, neutrality of tropical African regions in case of European war, are questions which surely might be discussed, and possibly an international agreement reached. Already international agreements exist with regard to the importation of spirits and also the importation of firearms. The scramble for Africa is over, and the European nations find themselves entrusted by international agreement with the responsibility of millions of square miles of territory in tropical Africa, which they can never colonise, and which they admittedly only hold in trust for the inhabitants. Each nation maintains a handful of European officials, scattered over these wide territories, depending for their safety upon the goodwill of the people and on a few locally raised troops. The justification for the presence of the white races as administrators and virtual rulers in tropical Africa is, to use the words of the late Imperial Colonial Secretary for the German Empire, Herr Dernberg, "the acknowledged trusteeship by European nations over inferior nations." Surely it is both fitting and wise that the trustees should meet together and decide how their trust should be best carried out by some common policy adopted by mutual agreement? "In matters of science and humanity all nations ought to be united in one common interest, each contributing its own share in proportion to its own peculiar disposition and calling."[1]

Northern Nigeria forms but a small portion of the great African Continent. Its very name is probably unknown to many English men and women, and its problems undreamt of. The object of this book is to give some idea of what has been done so far, and

[1] Barth, Preface to vol. i., *Travels*.

what still remains to be done. Nigeria is held in trust by the British nation, and no citizen of the Empire can escape the responsibility which lies on the nation as a whole for the welfare of the inhabitants of these wide tropical regions. Administrative officials need the support and sympathy of their fellow-citizens both at home and in the Colonies, and well-informed criticism is a help, not a hindrance. If material is found in these pages to assist in the formation of a sound judgment on the many problems which confront those engaged in the government of our West African possessions, the book will have fulfilled its purpose.

APPENDIX I

TREATY

National African Company and Sokoto.
Transfer of Rights, etc., 1st June 1885.

Copy of English duplicate of Treaty between Umoru, King of the Mussulmans of the Soudan and Sultan of Sokoto, for himself and Chiefs, on the one part, and those Europeans trading on the Kworra and Benue, under the name of the "National African Company (Limited)," on the other part.

Art. I.—For the mutual advantage of ourselves and people, and those Europeans trading under the name of the "National African Company (Limited)," I, Umoru, King of the Mussulmans of the Soudan, with the consent and advice of my Council, grant and transfer to the above people, or other with whom they may arrange, my entire rights to the country on both sides of the River Benue and rivers flowing into it throughout my dominions for such distance from its and their banks as they may desire.

Art. II.—We further grant to the above-mentioned Company the sole right, among foreigners, to trade in our territories, and the sole right, also among foreigners, to possess or work places from which are extracted articles such as lead and antimony.

Art. III.—We further declare that no communication will be held with foreigners coming from the rivers except through the above-mentioned Company.

Art. IV.—These grants we make for ourselves, our heirs and successors for ever, and declare them to be irrevocable.

Art. V.—The Europeans above named, the National African Company (Limited), agree to make Umoru, Sultan of Sokoto, a yearly present of goods to the value of 3000 bags of cowries, in return for the above grants.

Signed and sealed at Wurnu, the 1st of June 1885.

(Signature of the Sultan in Arabic.)

(Great Seal of the Empire of Sokoto.)

For the National African Company (Limited).

Witnesses W. J. Seago.
D. Z. Viera.
T. Joseph.

[*An Arabic duplicate was at the same time executed by both parties.*]

TREATY

Royal Niger Company and Sokoto.
Jurisprudence over Foreigners, etc., 15th April 1890.

Literal translation of second Treaty, in Arabic, between Umoru, King of the Mussulmans of the Soudan, and Sultan of Sokoto, on the one part, and the Royal Niger Company (Chartered and Limited), on the other part.

Be it known that I, Umoru, King of the Mussulmans, am desirous of introducing European trade in all parts of my dominions, so as to increase the prosperity of my people, and knowing that this cannot be effected except by securing to foreigners the protection of European government, with power of exercising jurisdiction over foreigners, as is the custom with them; also with power of levying taxes upon foreigners as may be necessary for the exercise and support of this jurisdiction: I, Umoru, King of the Mussulmans of the Soudan, with the consent and advice of my Council, agree and grant to the Royal Niger Company (Chartered and Limited)—formerly known as the "National African Company (Limited)"—full and complete power and jurisdiction over all foreigners visiting or residing in any part of my dominions. I also grant you jurisdiction and full rights of protection over all foreigners; also power of raising taxes of any kind whatsoever from such foreigners.

No person shall exercise any jurisdiction over such foreigners, nor levy any tax whatsoever on such foreigners than the Royal Niger Company (Chartered and Limited).

These grants I make for myself, my heirs, and successors, and declare them to be unchangeable and irrevocable for ever.

I further confirm the Treaty made by me with the National African Company (Limited)—now known as the "Royal Niger Company (Chartered and Limited)"—in the month of June, according to European reckoning, 1885.

Dated at Wurnu this 15th day of April 1890.

APPENDIX II

CORRESPONDENCE WITH SULTAN OF SOKOTO

1. Proclamation

Be it known to all men, that by the order of Her Most Gracious Majesty the Queen of Great Britain and Ireland, Empress of India, the Administration of the Protectorate of Northern Nigeria, hitherto known as the Niger Territories, situated between the possessions of France to the West and North, and of Germany to the East, and bounded on the South by the Protectorates of Lagos and Southern Nigeria, will cease from this day to be vested in the Royal Niger Company Chartered and Limited and is hereby assumed by Her Majesty. And be it known further to all men that the treaties concluded by the Royal Niger Company by and with the sanction of Her Majesty and approved by Her Majesty's Secretary of State will be and remain operative and in force as between Her Majesty and the Kings, Emirs, Chiefs, Princes, or other signatories to the same, and all pledges and undertakings therein contained will remain mutually binding on both parties, and all rights, titles, and interests, of whatsoever nature, acquired by virtue of the aforesaid treaties will be vested in Her Majesty, and all obligations thereunder undertaken by the Royal Niger Company will henceforth be undertaken by Her Majesty. And be it known further to all men that Her Majesty has been pleased to appoint as High Commissioner for the said Protectorate, Colonel Frederick John Dealtry Lugard, Companion of the Most Honourable Order of the Bath, Companion of the Distinguished Service Order. And that the said Frederick John Dealtry Lugard has this day taken the requisite oath of Office and assumed the Administration of the said Protectorate. In virtue whereof he has made this Proclamation, whereto his signature and seal are appended, this first day of January one thousand nine hundred.

(Signed) F. D. Lugard.

1st January 1900.

2. Letter from High Commissioner to Sultan of Sokoto, *re* Kontagora

In the name of the Most Merciful God. Peace be to the Generous Prophet. Salutations, peace, and numberless honours.

To the Emir of Mussulmans in Sokoto, whose name is Abdul-Lahai the son of the late Emir of Mussulmans, whose name is Atiku.

I desire to inform you who are head of the Mohammedans and to whom the Fulani rulers in this country look for advice and guidance that the Emirs of Bida and Kontagora have during many years acted as oppressors of the people and shown themselves unfit to rule. More especially in these latter days they have raided the towns and villages in the districts close to their own cities, and have depopulated vast areas so that the fields are lying uncultivated and the people are destroyed or fled. Moreover they have gratuitously attacked my men when proceeding with mails or canoes, and have seized the mails, and stolen and destroyed goods in the canoes. I have therefore found it necessary to depose both these Emirs, and to place troops near their respective cities, to keep the peace and protect the people.

In the case of the Emir of Bida, I have made the Makum Emir instead of Abu-Bakri, which proves to you that I have no hostility to the Fulanis or to your religion, provided only that the Emir of a country rules justly and without oppression. In the case of Kontagora, many evil people tried to burn the town. It may have been the slaves who had been ill-treated by their masters or it may have been the carriers with my troops. But through all the night the Commander of the Force made the soldiers and carriers extinguish the flames, so that the town has not suffered.

I desire that the people shall return and live in peace under a just ruler, and I write to you to appoint a man who will rule justly, and if he does so I will support him and uphold his power; send him to me with a letter and I will install him as Emir of Kontagora with pomp and honour. But warn him that if he acts treacherously and with deceit, he will share the fate of Kontagora the Gwamachi.

With peace from your friend Governor Lugard.

(Signed) F. D. Lugard.

March 18th, 1901.

3. Letter from High Commissioner to the Sultan of Sokoto, *re* Bautshi

(Titles, Salutations from the Governor, etc.)

I have heard that you sent a letter to the Emir of Bautshi warning him to desist from oppressing his people, but he does not obey your instructions nor listen to your words of wisdom. I have, therefore, been compelled to send my troops to compel him to act properly. I do not know whether he will oppose them and fight. If he does so, he will probably lose his place. But I do not wish to drive out the Fulani and the Mohammedans, I only wish that they shall rule wisely and with humanity. If, therefore, the Emir is driven out because he himself attacks my troops I shall endeavour to find his proper successor and shall install him as King if he is a man who will rule well. So also in the matter of Kontagora, I hear that he and Abubekr will not listen to the words of your messenger or desist from raiding the towns of Zaria. So Zaria has appealed to me for help, and I have sent troops to support him and to drive out these marauders.

Peace be with those who seek peace and trouble on those who make trouble.

Since I wrote this letter I have news that Ibrahim of Kontagora and all his people and following have been captured by my troops. I am restoring all the people to their places, but Ibrahim and his chiefs will be sent to me to be judged.

(Signed) F. D. Lugard.

(L.S.)

About March 1902.

---

4. Translation of Arabic Letter from Sultan of Sokoto to the High Commissioner

(Seal undecipherable.)

From us to you. I do not consent that any one from you should ever dwell with us. I will never agree with you. I will have nothing ever to do with you. Between us and you there are no dealings except as between Mussulmans and Unbelievers ("Kafiri")—War, as God Almighty has enjoined on us. There is no power or strength save in God on high.

This with salutations.

(Received about May 1902.)

5. TRANSLATION OF ARABIC LETTER FROM SULTAN OF SOKOTO TO THE HIGH COMMISSIONER

(Seal of) Em r l'Muslimin.

In the name of God.

To Governor LUGARD.

I have to inform you that we do not invite your administration in the Province of Bautshi, and if you have interfered we do not want support from any one except from God. You have your religion, and we have ours. We seek help from God, the Best Supporter, and there is no power except in him, the Mighty and Exalted. Peace.

(Received about June 1902.)

---

6. LETTER FROM COLONEL T. L. N. MORLAND TO THE SULTAN OF SOKOTO

In the name of God. Blessing and peace on the Prophet the exalted.

From Colonel Morland the representative of the High Commissioner (Governor Lugard) salutations, peace, contentment and increasing honour to the Prince of the Believers Attahiru Emir El Muslimin. After salutations know that the cause of our fighting with Aliu is that Aliu received with honour Magaji, the murderer of a white man, when he came to Kano, and that he also sought war between us. For those two reasons we fought him, and are now sitting in his house.

We are coming to Sokoto, and from this time and for ever a white man and soldiers will sit down in the Sokoto country. We have prepared for war because Abdu Sarikin Muslimin said there was nothing between us but war. But we do not want war unless you yourself seek war. If you receive us in peace, we will not enter your house, we will not harm you or any of your people.

If you desire to become our friend you must not receive the Magaji. More, we desire you to seek him with your utmost endeavour and place him in our hands.

If you are loyal to us, you will remain in your position as Sarikin Muslimin, fear not.

If you desire to be loyal to us, it is advisable for you that you should send your big messenger to meet us at Kaura (or on whatever road we follow). Then he will return to you with all our words.

My present to you is five pieces of brocade.

(Signed) T. L. N. MORLAND.

February 1903.

---

7. TRANSLATION OF ARABIC LETTER FROM SULTAN OF SOKOTO TO COLONEL T. L. N. MORLAND

From us to Colonel Morland. All salutations to you. Know that I have seen your messenger with your letter, the purport of which I understand. I have sent to call in my councillors from every district, but now that I see they are taking some time to assemble, I am sending you back your messenger. When we have assembled and have agreed on our decision I will write to you what is enjoined on me by them for the settlement of this affair. Salutations.

APPENDIX III

FIRST ADDRESS BY THE HIGH COMMISSIONER TO THE WAZIRI AND HEADMEN OF SOKOTO, MARCH 20TH, 1903.

Present:—WAZIRI, GALADIMA, UMARU SARIKIN[1] GOBIRI, MARAFA or MAITURARE, SARIKIN BURMI, SARIKIN SANFARA, SARIKIN KEBBI.

"I am very glad to see you, very glad that you have come back. You made war on us; we beat you and drove you away; now the war is over and it is peace. It is not our custom to catch the people who fight us or kill them; therefore all those who have run away must come back to their houses.

"There will be no interference with your religion nor with the position of the Sarikin Muslimin as head of your religion. The English Government never interferes with religion; taxes, law and order, punishment of crime, these are matters for the Government, but not religion.

"I have come to you now that the fighting is over to settle your country so that all can settle down in peace. But that can't happen till there is a Sarikin Muslimin; therefore it is necessary at once either to find and reinstate Attahiru or to appoint a new Sarikin Muslimin. I want you to talk it over and let me know this evening what you think; whether Attahiru will come back or whether it is best to appoint some one else, and if so whom."

The Marafa then asked leave for the headmen to go out and discuss and settle the matter at once. Permission granted. After an interval a message was sent in to say that the whole council was of opinion that Umaru Sarikin Gobiri should be appointed Sarikin Muslimin, and that they were all ready to follow and obey him.[2]

On the Council's return the High Commissioner continued:—

"I have heard your answer. I see that Umaru is the eldest son of Alieu and apparently the rightful heir. I should like to think it

[1] Sarikin = king of.

[2] Later when Attahiru (the present Sultan, not the ex-Sultan of same name) came to salute me the elders reversed their choice and begged for him as Sultan. I would not agree until they had fully thought it over and discussed it. They retired again for the purpose and came back unanimous, and I therefore agreed.

over to-day and see you all in camp to-morrow morning. Then I will explain to you all matters connected with our rule and the conditions of appointment for the Sarikin. If things are all right, if you all agree to the conditions, the day after to-morrow I will install the Sarikin. I want you to send out to-day for all the remaining headmen and people, so that all men may hear my words and be present at the installation." (At this point there were complaints about the returning fugitives being looted on approaching Sokoto by soldiers and labourers, and complaints about the slaves, especially slave women and concubines, being harboured in camp. Reassurance and promise of protection were given in both cases.)

"You must send messengers to tell Attahiru to return. The Council has elected the Sarikin Gobiri to be Sarikin Muslimin, so Attahiru cannot return to the kingship. But he must go back to his town (Chimola), and there he may live in peace.

"But Dan Tanmusa, the Magaji of Keffi, must be caught. If Attahiru keeps him with him after this, or if he takes him back with him to his town, he will be arrested himself. From to-day any one who harbours or entertains the Magaji will be treated the same as the Magaji himself."

The Waziri here said that the Magaji's intended refuge was always Kano, not Sokoto. "He only came here in Alieu of Kano's suite. He is not likely to return here again."

The High Commissioner replied, "The Magaji will bring trouble on any man who harbours him, but there will be a reward of 50 bags of cowries for any one who catches him and gives him up."

N.B.—The above was taken down, as spoken in Hausa at the interview, by Major Burdon, Resident.

SECOND ADDRESS BY SIR F. LUGARD, HIGH COMMISSIONER, TO THE SULTAN, WAZIRI AND ELDERS OF SOKOTO, REGARDING THE CONDITIONS OF BRITISH RULE, REASONS FOR THE WAR, ETC., MARCH 21ST, 1903.

Translated to them by Kiari, and checked, word by word, by Major Burdon, Resident, Sokoto (Hausa Scholar), and others.

Present:—Sir F. LUGARD; Colonel MORLAND, D.S.O., Commandant; Major BURDON, Resident; Lieut.-Colonel McCLINTOCK, Commanding Battalion; Major CUBITT, R.A., Brigade Major; Captain ABADIE, Resident, Zaria, and others. Also the SULTAN elect, the WAZIRI, GALADIMA, MAITURARE, and other Elders of Sokoto.

"The Royal Niger Company made a Treaty with Sokoto many years ago. The Sultan promised friendship and alliance; the

Company promised to pay a subsidy, and did so. Three years ago the King of England sent his own officers to administer this country instead of the Company and appointed me as Governor. I at once sent my trusted messenger, Kiari, to take my salutations to the Sultan of Sokoto, and to say that I held to the promises made by the Company, and I looked to the Sultan to fulfil his pledges. I brought money to pay the subsidy when it should fall due. But take note of what happened. My messenger was treated with indignity. It is he who is now interpreting. Ask him what happened and he will remind you. No answer was sent to my letter, which was an insult to me and to my King. Owing to the treaty the Sultan had made with the British the French could not touch his country. But the Sultan of Sokoto sent no friendly message. The Treaty was made in the name of all the Mahommedan Emirates under Sokoto, but they took arms against the British—Nupe, and Illorin, and Yola, and Kontagora, and Kano. But I did not wish to denounce the Treaty, and I sent to the Sultan to ask him to nominate an Emir for Kontagora, when Ibrahim fought against us and was driven out. Again he sent no reply, till a year ago I received this letter declaring war (*original letter shown to the Elders for identification*).

"So the Treaty was killed by you yourselves and not by me. Then the Magaji of Keffi murdered the Resident—a lame man without arms to defend himself—and he ran to Kano and the Emir Alieu received him with honour. So we went to Kano and fought and drove out Alieu, and the Magaji ran to Sokoto and was treated with honour. Again I wished not to fight with the head of the Mussulmans and I sent a friendly letter, but I said that the Magaji must be given up, and that I wished to place a Resident and garrison at Sokoto. I came with troops, for though the Sultan had made a treaty of friendship it was well known that a white man could not come as a friend alone to Sokoto. My letter was put aside and the army of Sokoto came out to fight. We fought and your army was dispersed, and the Sultan fled and no one knows where he is gone. Now it is necessary for me to place a Resident and a garrison here, for this country is close to the country of the French and we are responsible for keeping peace and good order on our frontiers. The Resident is Major Burdon, who comes to you as an adviser and a friend. You will consult him on all matters and be guided by him.

"The old treaties are dead; you have killed them. Now these are the words which I, the High Commissioner, have to say for the future. The Fulani in old times under Dan Fodio conquered this country. They took the right to rule over it, to levy taxes, to depose kings and to create kings. They in turn have by defeat lost their rule, which has come into the hands of the British. All these things which I have said the Fulani by conquest took the right to do now pass to the British. Every Sultan and Emir and the principal officers of State will be appointed by the High Commissioner throughout all this country. The High Commissioner will be guided by the usual laws of succession and the wishes of the people and chiefs, but will set them aside if he desires for good cause to do so. The Emirs and Chiefs who are appointed will rule over the people as of old time and take such taxes as are approved by the High Commissioner, but they will obey the laws of the Governor and will act in accordance with the advice of the Resident. Buying and selling slaves and enslaving people are forbidden. It is forbidden to import firearms (except flint-locks), and there are other minor matters which the Resident will explain. The Alkalis and the Emirs will hold the law-courts as of old, but bribes are forbidden, and mutilation and confinement of men in inhuman prisons are not lawful. The powers of each Court will be contained in a warrant appointing it. Sentences of death will not be carried out without the consent of the Resident.

"The Government will, in future, hold the rights in land which the Fulani took by conquest from the people, and if Government requires land it will take it for any purpose. The Government hold the right of taxation, and will tell the Emirs and Chiefs what taxes they may levy, and what part of them must be paid to Government. The Government will have the right to all minerals, but the people may dig for iron and work in it subject to the approval of the High Commissioner, and may take salt and other minerals subject to any excise imposed by law. Traders will not be taxed by Chiefs, but only by Government. The coinage of the British will be accepted as legal tender, and a rate of exchange for cowries fixed, in consultation with Chiefs, and they will enforce it.

"When an Emirate, or an office of state, becomes vacant, it will only be filled with the consent of the High Commissioner, and the person chosen by the council of Chiefs and approved by the High Commissioner will hold his place only on condition that he obeys the laws of the Protectorate and the conditions of his appointment. Government will in no way interfere with the Mohammedan religion. All men are free to worship God as they please. Mosques and prayer places will be treated with respect by us. Every person, including slaves, has the right to appeal to the Resident, who will, however, endeavour to uphold the power of the native courts to deal with native cases according to the law and custom of the country. If slaves are ill-treated they will be set free as your Koran orders, otherwise Government does not desire to interfere with existing domestic relations. But slaves set free must be willing to work and not to remain idle or become thieves. The Resident may give permits to trustworthy men to bear firearms. Any person who harbours the Magaji of Keffi will be liable to be arrested and punished. It is his duty to catch him and bring him to the Resident.

"It is the earnest desire of the King of England that this country shall prosper and grow rich in peace and in contentment, that the population shall increase, and the ruined towns which abound everywhere shall be built up, and that war and trouble shall cease. Henceforth no Emir or Chief shall levy war or fight, but his case will be settled by law, and if force is necessary Government will employ it. I earnestly hope to give effect in these matters to the wishes of my King.

"In conclusion, I hope that you will find our rule sympathetic and that the country will prosper and be contented. You need have no fear regarding British rule; it is our wish to learn your customs and fashion, just as you must learn ours. I have little fear but that we shall agree, for you have always heard that British rule is just and fair, and people under our King are satisfied. You must not fear to tell the Resident everything and he will help and advise you."

(*This outline was, of course, amplified and fully explained in the verbal translation.*)

F. D. L.

LIST OF SOME OF THE AUTHORITIES CONSULTED

Travels and Discoveries in North and Central Africa. By Henry Barth. London, 1858. (5 vols.)

Campaigning on the Upper Nile and Niger. By Seymour Vandeleur. London, 1898.

Historical Researches into the Politics, Intercourse, and Trade of the Carthaginians, Ethiopians, and Egyptians. By A. L. Heeren. Translated from the German. Oxford, 1838. (2 vols.)

Journal of a Residence in Ashanti. By Joseph Dupuis. London, 1824.

The History and Description of Africa. By Leo Africanus. Done into English in the Year 1600 by John Pory. (3 vols.) London, 1896.

The African Sketch Book. By Winwood Reade. (2 vols.) London, 1873.

Affairs of West Africa. By E. D. Morel. London, 1902.

British Nigeria. By Lieut.-Col. Mockler Ferryman. London, 1902.

Ancient and Modern Imperialism. By the Earl of Cromer. London, 1910.

The Control of the Tropics. By Benjamin Kidd. London, 1898.

The White Man's Work in Asia and Africa. By Leonard Alston. London, 1907.

Imperialism: A Study. By J. A. Hobson. London, 1905.

The Travels of Mungo Park in the Interior Districts of Africa. London, 1816.

Kafir Socialism. By Dudley Kidd. London, 1908.

Travels and Discoveries in Northern and Central Africa in the Years 1822, 1823, and 1824. By Denham and Clapperton. (2 vols.) London, 1826.

The Niger and the West Sudan. By A. J. N. Tremearne. London, 1910.

A Tropical Dependency. By Lady Lugard. London, 1905.

Colonial Office List, 1910.

Northern Nigeria Annual Reports, 1900-1909.

West African Studies. By Mary Kingsley.

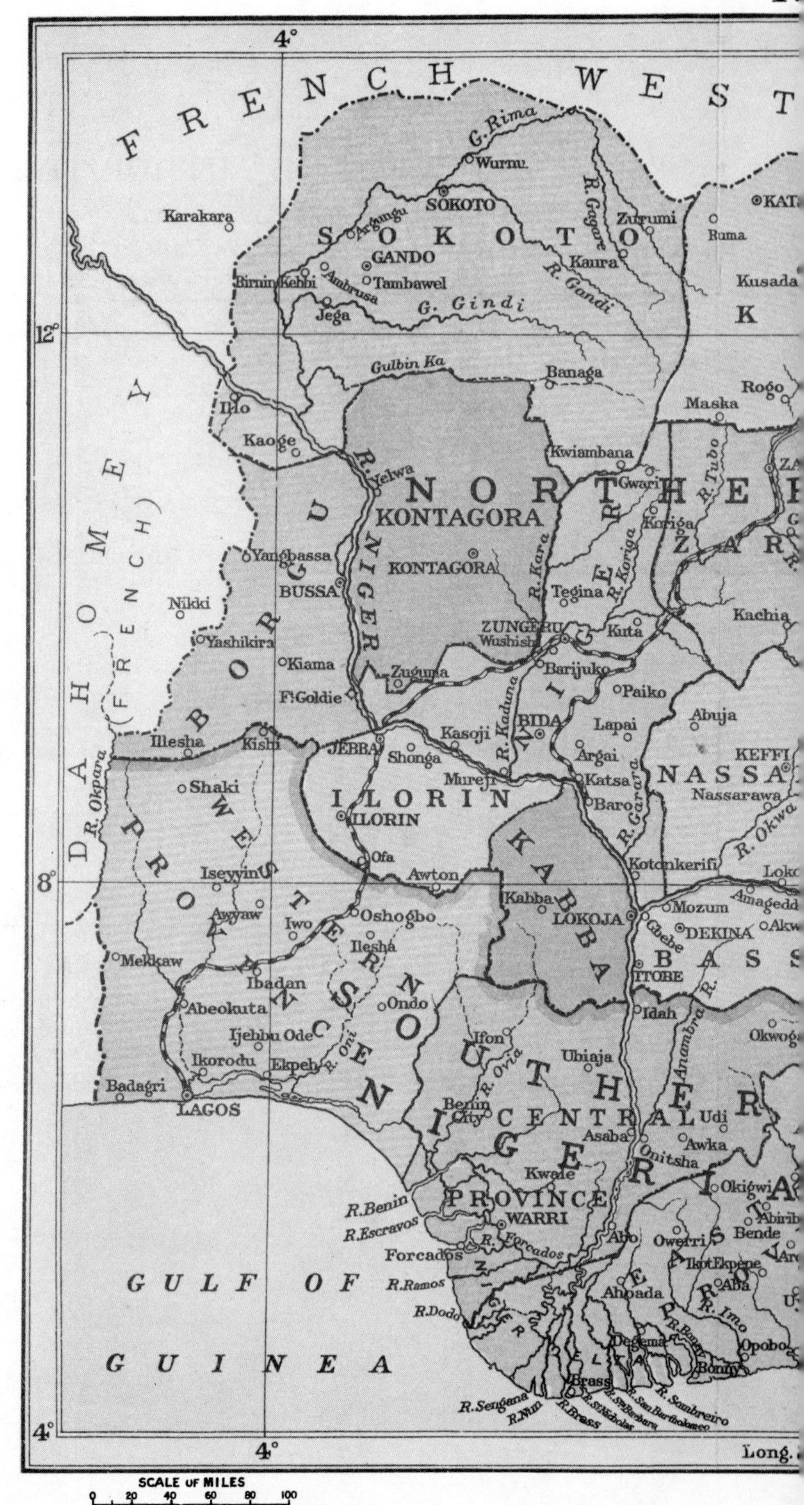

N
4°
FRENCH WEST
DAHOMEY (FRENCH)
SOKOTO
G. Rima
Wurmu
SOKOTO
R. Gagare
Zurumi
Karakara
Argungu
GANDO
Kaura
R. Gandi
Birnin Kebbi
Ambrusa
Tambawel
Jega
G. Gindi
12°
Gulbin Ka
Banaga
Illo
Kaoge
Kwiambana
Yelwa
NORTHERN
KONTAGORA
KONTAGORA
R. Kara
Gwari
R. Tubo
Koriga
R. Koriga
ZARIA
Yangbassa
BUSSA
R. NIGER
BORGU
Nikki
Yashikira
Kiama
Ft. Goldie
ZUNGERU
Wushishi
Kuta
Tegina
Kachia
Zuguma
Barijuko
Paiko
NIGER
R. Kaduna
BIDA
Abuja
Lapai
Kasoji
Illesha
Kishi
JEBBA
Shonga
Argai
KEFFI
Mureji
Katsa
NASSA
Nassarawa
Shaki
ILORIN
ILORIN
Baro
R. Garara
R. Okwa
R. Okpara
Ofa
KABBA
Kotonkerifi
8°
Iseyyin
Awton
Loko
Awyaw
Kabba
Mozum
Amagedd
Iwo
Oshogbo
LOKOJA
Gbebe
DEKINA
Ilesha
BASS
Mekkaw
Ibadan
ITOBE
WESTERN PROVINCE
Abeokuta
Ondo
Idah
Ijebbu Ode
Ifon
Okwoga
Ikorodu
Ekpeh
R. Oni
Ubiaja
Anambra R.
R. Ovia
Badagri
LAGOS
Benin City
SOUTHERN NIGERIA
CENTRAL
Udi
Asaba
Awka
Onitsha
Kwale
PROVINCE
Okigwi
R. Benin
R. Escravos
WARRI
Abiriba
Bende
Forcados
R. Forcados
Abo
Owerri
Ikot Ekpene
Aba
GULF OF GUINEA
R. Ramos
Ahoada
R. Imo
R. Dodo
Degema
Opobo
Bonny
Brass
R. Sengana
R. Nun
R. Brass
R. St. Nicholas
R. Sombreiro
4°
4°
Long.
SCALE OF MILES
0
20
40
60
80
100

A

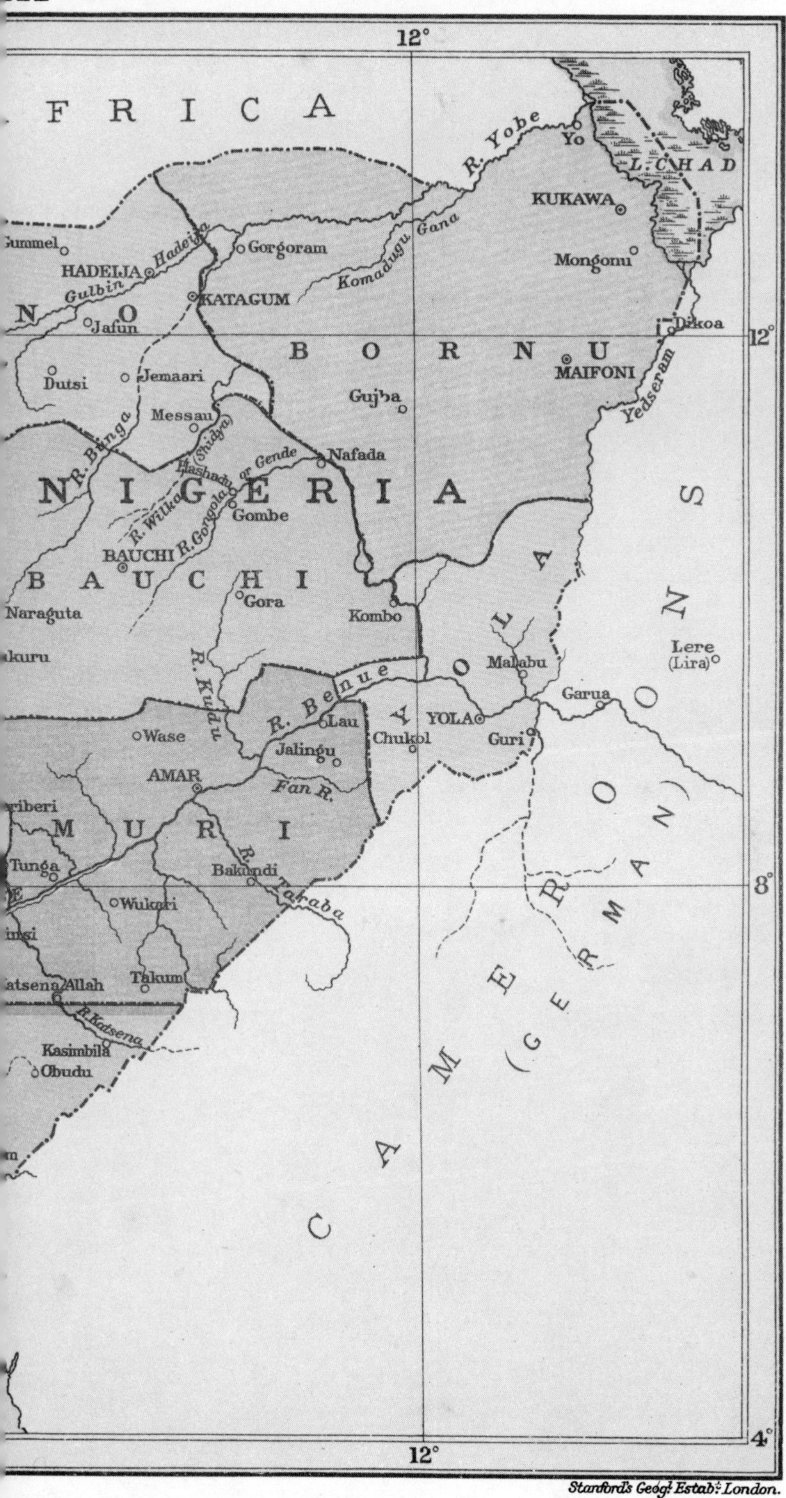

Stanford's Geog.l Estab.t London.

INDEX

THE END